Splatoon™

VOL. 13

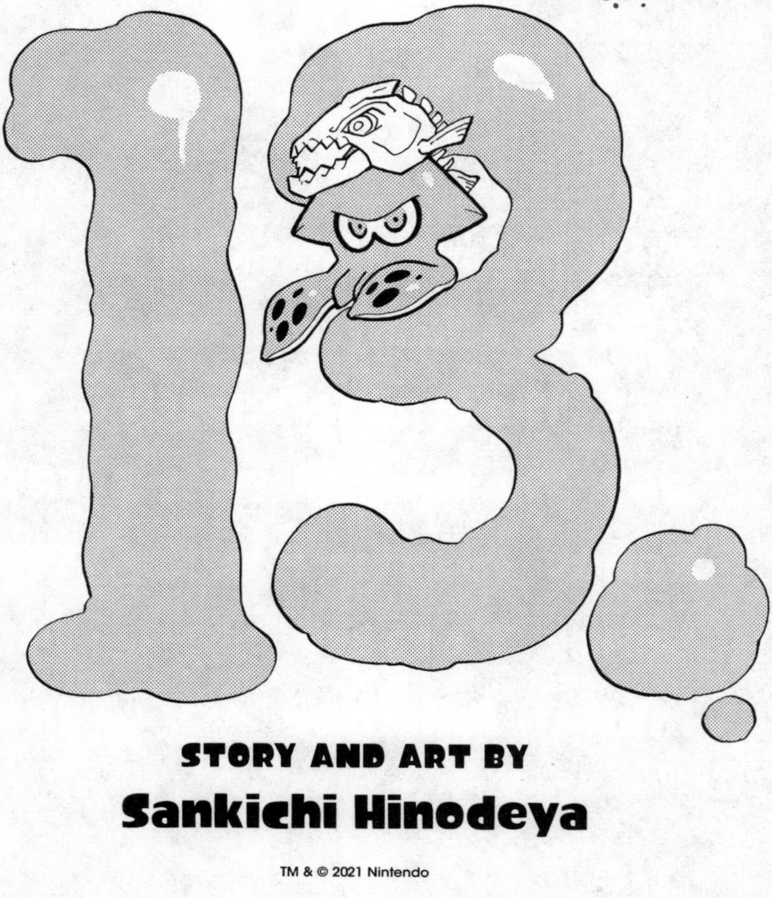

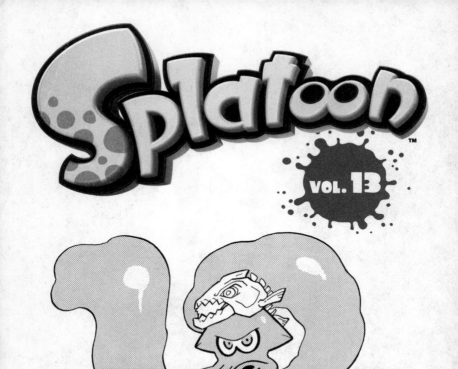

STORY AND ART BY

Sankichi Hinodeya

CONTENTS

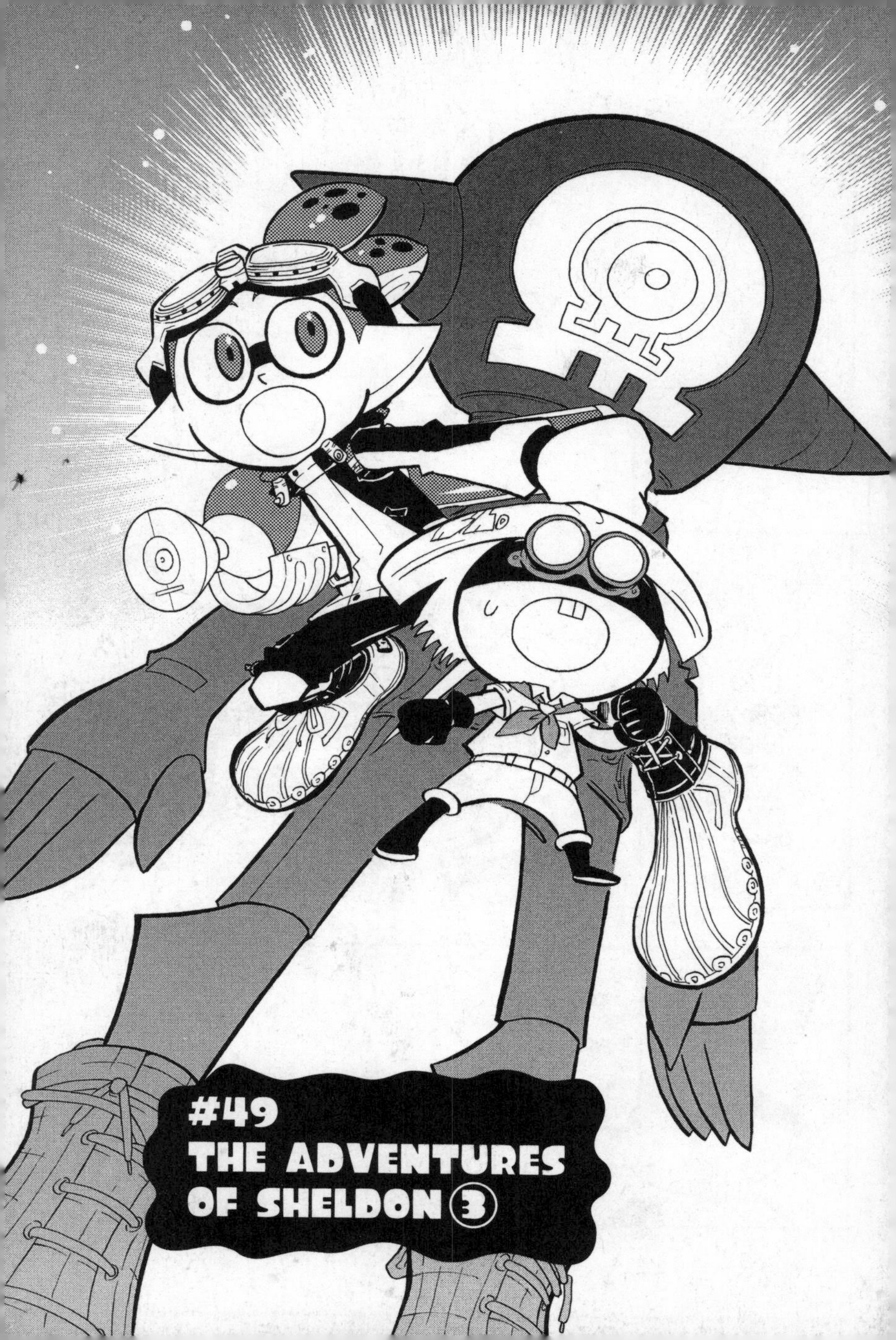
#49
THE ADVENTURES OF SHELDON ③

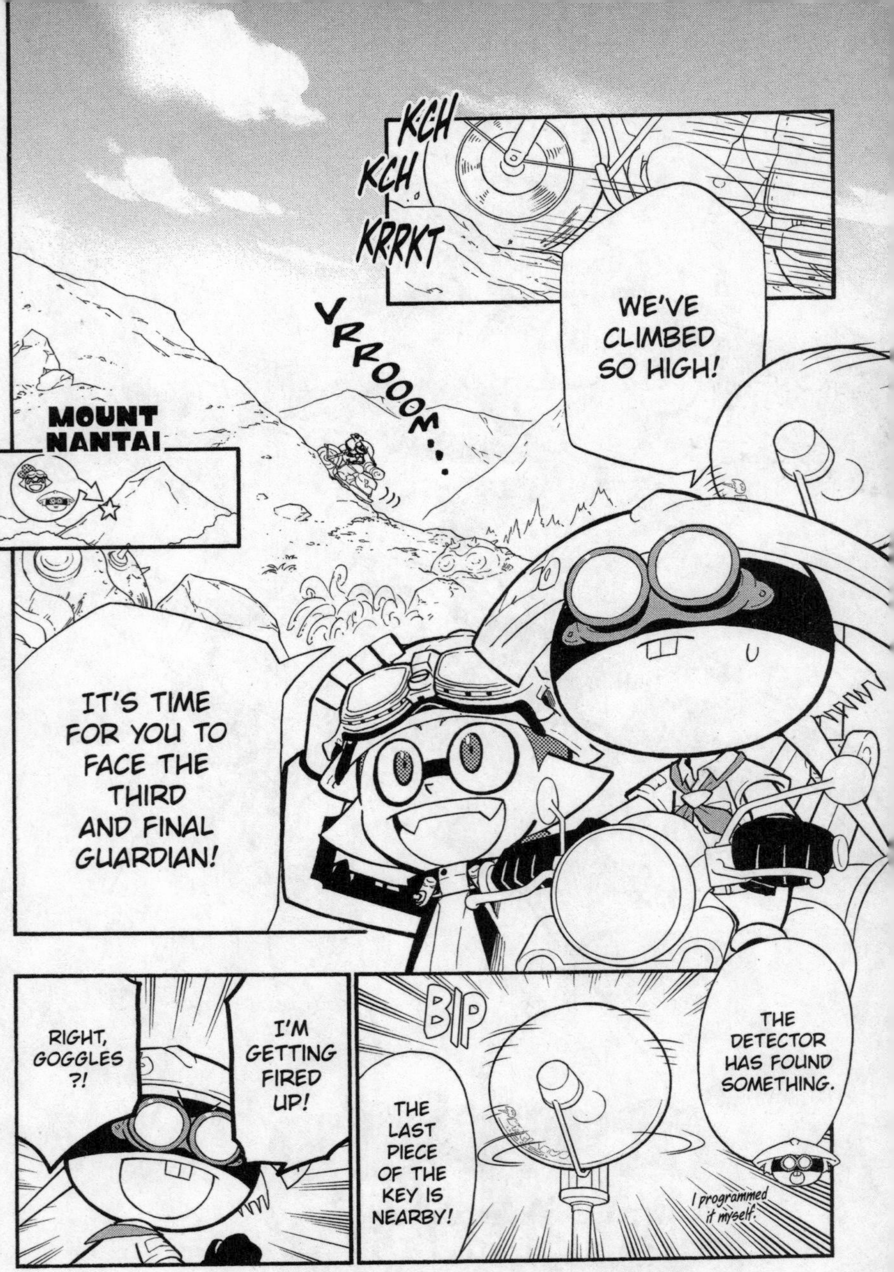
K-CH
KCH
KRRKT
VRROOOM...
WE'VE CLIMBED SO HIGH!
MOUNT NANTAI
IT'S TIME FOR YOU TO FACE THE THIRD AND FINAL GUARDIAN!
BIP
THE DETECTOR HAS FOUND SOMETHING.
I programmed it myself.
THE LAST PIECE OF THE KEY IS NEARBY!
I'M GETTING FIRED UP!
RIGHT, GOGGLES?!

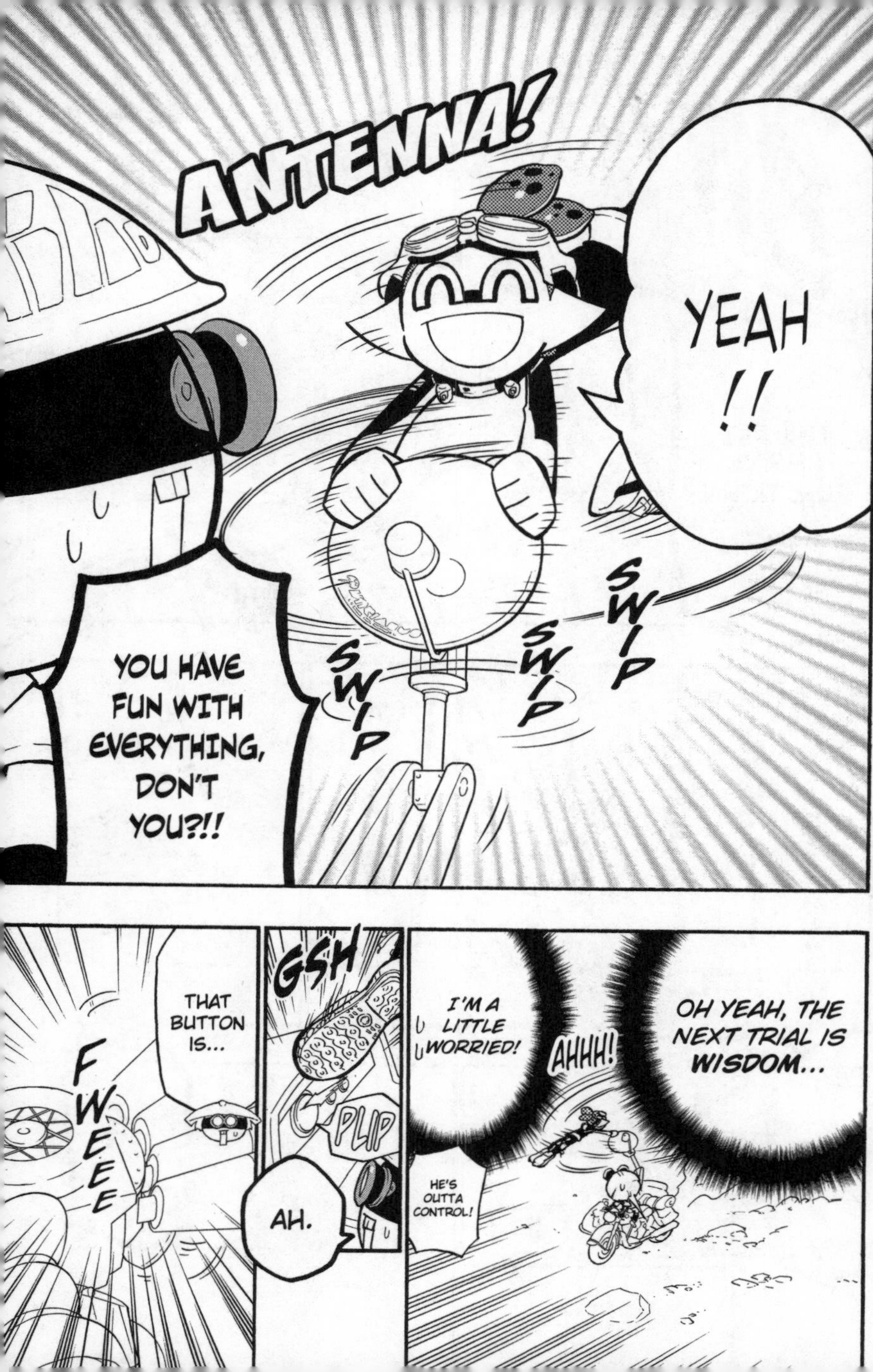
ANTENNA!
YEAH !!
YOU HAVE FUN WITH EVERYTHING, DON'T YOU?!!
SWIP
SWIP
SWIP
OH YEAH, THE NEXT TRIAL IS WISDOM...
AHHH!
I'M A LITTLE WORRIED!
HE'S OUTTA CONTROL!
GSH
PLIP
AH.
THAT BUTTON IS...
FWEEE

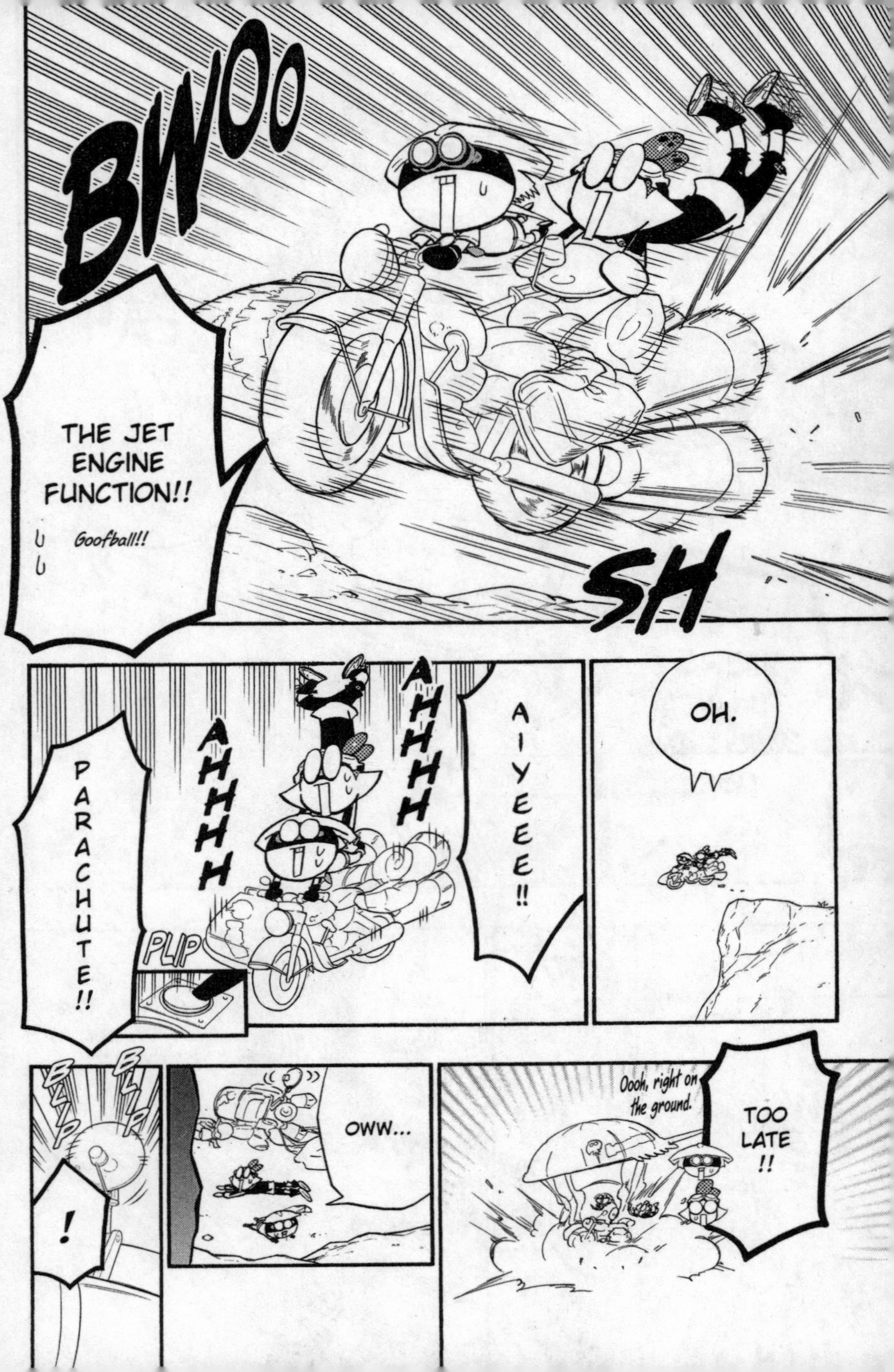
BWOO
THE JET ENGINE FUNCTION!!
Goofball!!
SH
OH.
AIYEEE!!
AHHHHH
AHHHHH
PARACHUTE!!
PLIP
Oooh, right on the ground.
TOO LATE!!
OWW...
BLIP
BLIP
!

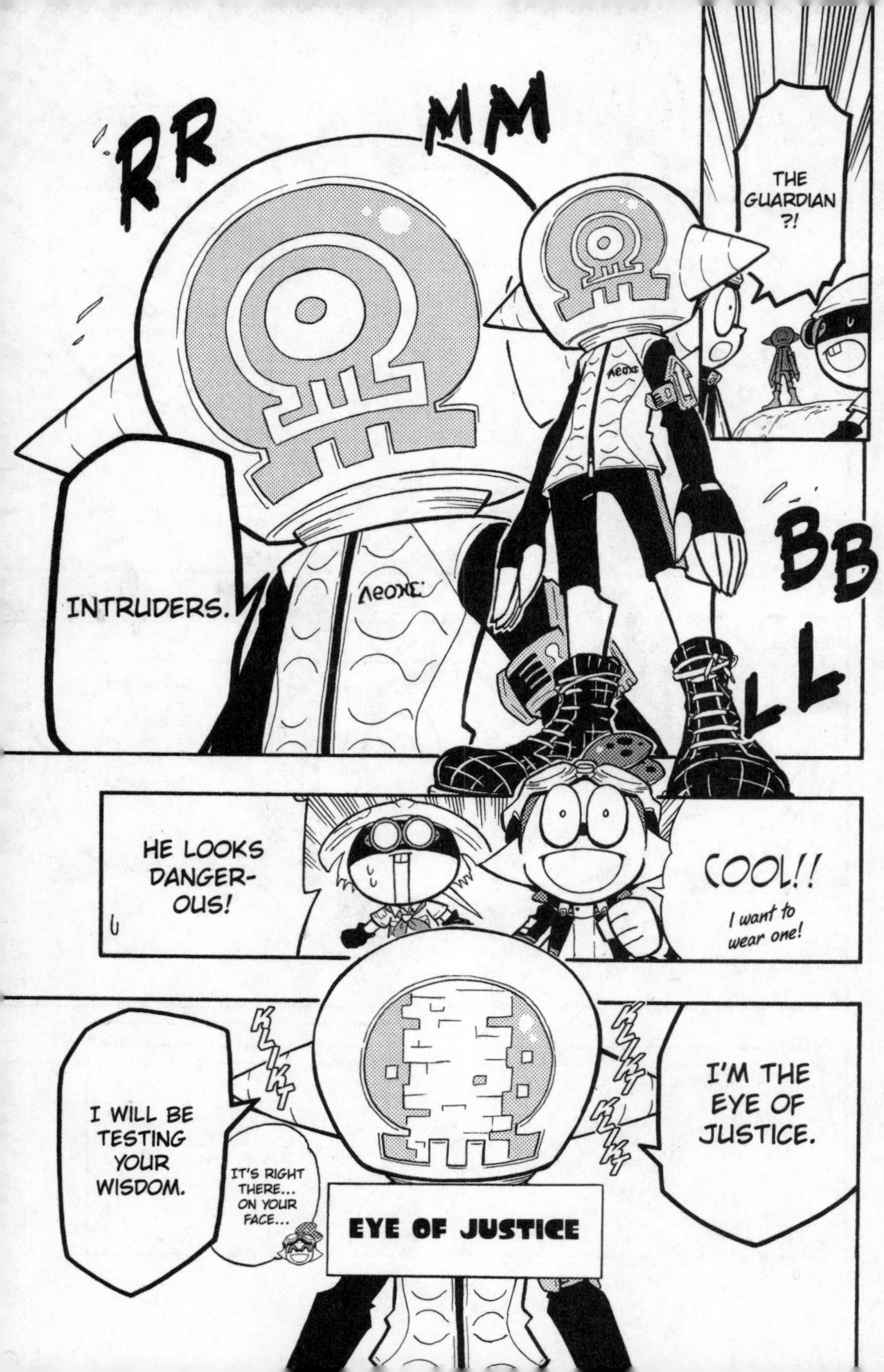
THE GUARDIAN ?!
RR MM BB LL
INTRUDERS.
COOL!!
I want to wear one!
HE LOOKS DANGER-OUS!
I'M THE EYE OF JUSTICE.
KLIK KLIK KLIK
EYE OF JUSTICE
I WILL BE TESTING YOUR WISDOM.
IT'S RIGHT THERE... ON YOUR FACE...

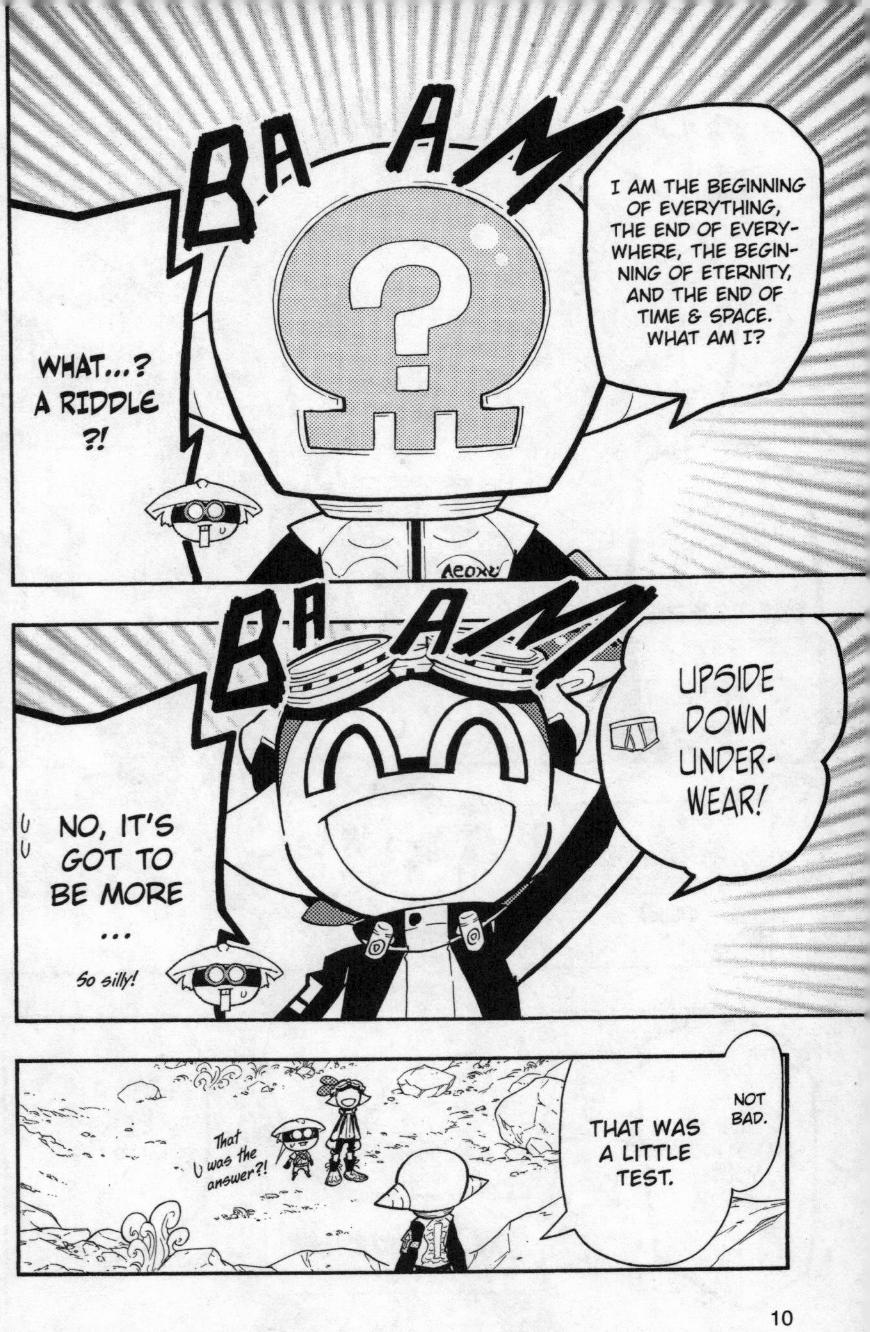
BAAM
I AM THE BEGINNING OF EVERYTHING, THE END OF EVERYWHERE, THE BEGINNING OF ETERNITY, AND THE END OF TIME & SPACE. WHAT AM I?
WHAT...? A RIDDLE ?!
BAAM
UPSIDE DOWN UNDERWEAR!
NO, IT'S GOT TO BE MORE ...
So silly!
NOT BAD.
THAT WAS A LITTLE TEST.
That was the answer?!

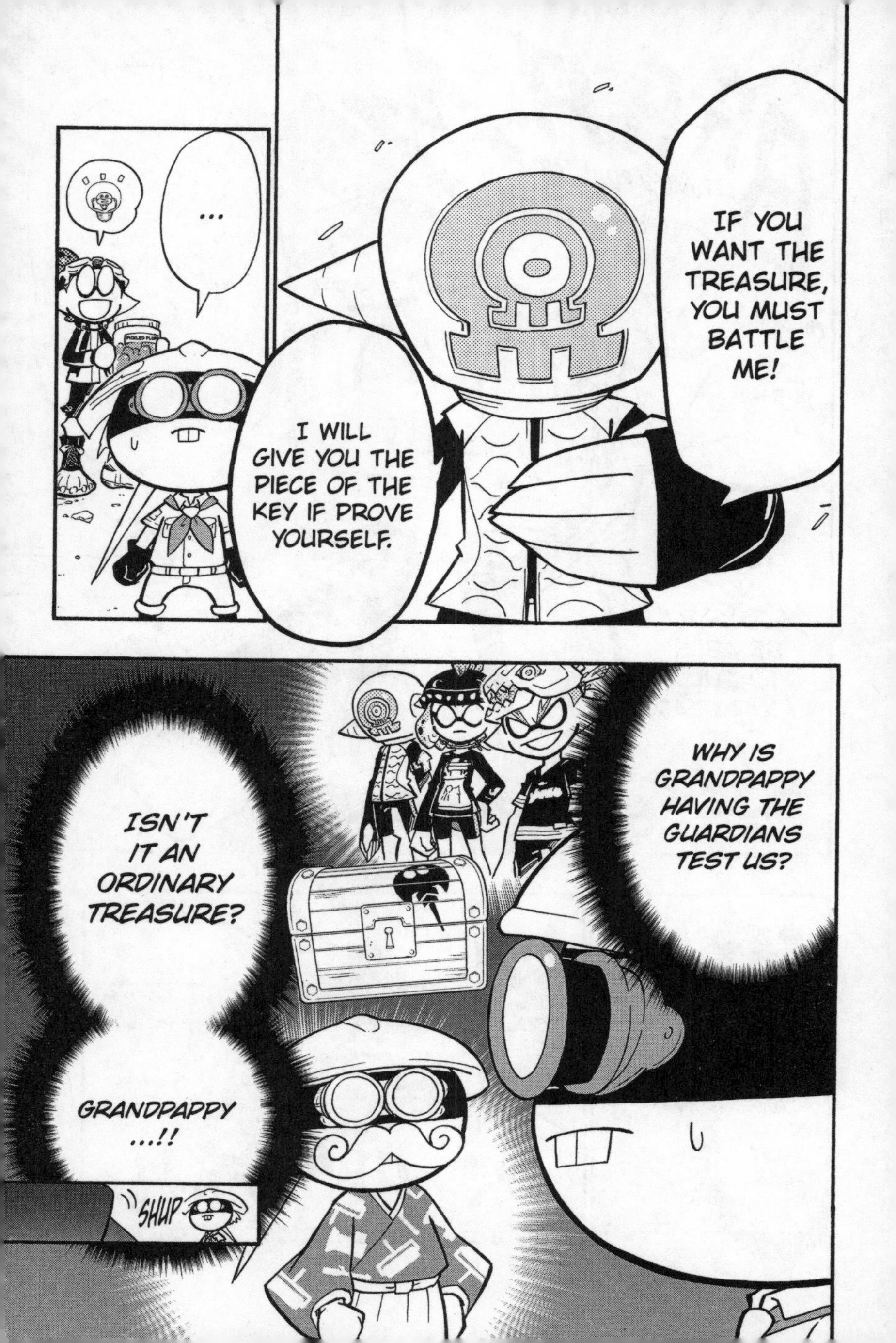
IF YOU WANT THE TREASURE, YOU MUST BATTLE ME!
I WILL GIVE YOU THE PIECE OF THE KEY IF PROVE YOURSELF.
...
WHY IS GRANDPAPPY HAVING THE GUARDIANS TEST US?
ISN'T IT AN ORDINARY TREASURE?
GRANDPAPPY ...!!
SHUP

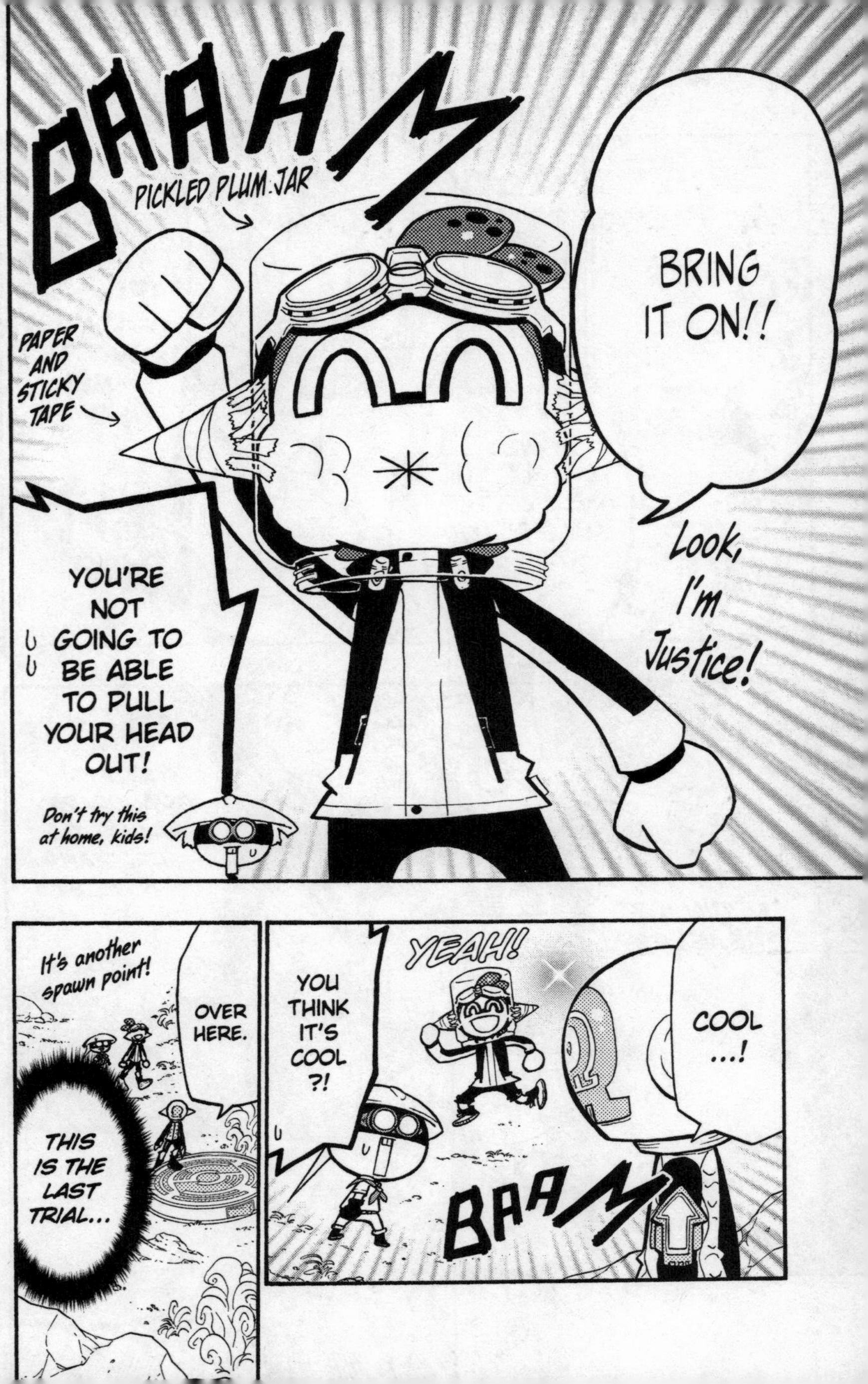
BRING IT ON!!
BAAAM
PICKLED PLUM JAR
PAPER AND STICKY TAPE
Look, I'm Justice!
YOU'RE NOT GOING TO BE ABLE TO PULL YOUR HEAD OUT!
Don't try this at home, kids!
COOL ...!
YEAH!
YOU THINK IT'S COOL ?!
BAAM
OVER HERE.
It's another spawn point!
THIS IS THE LAST TRIAL...

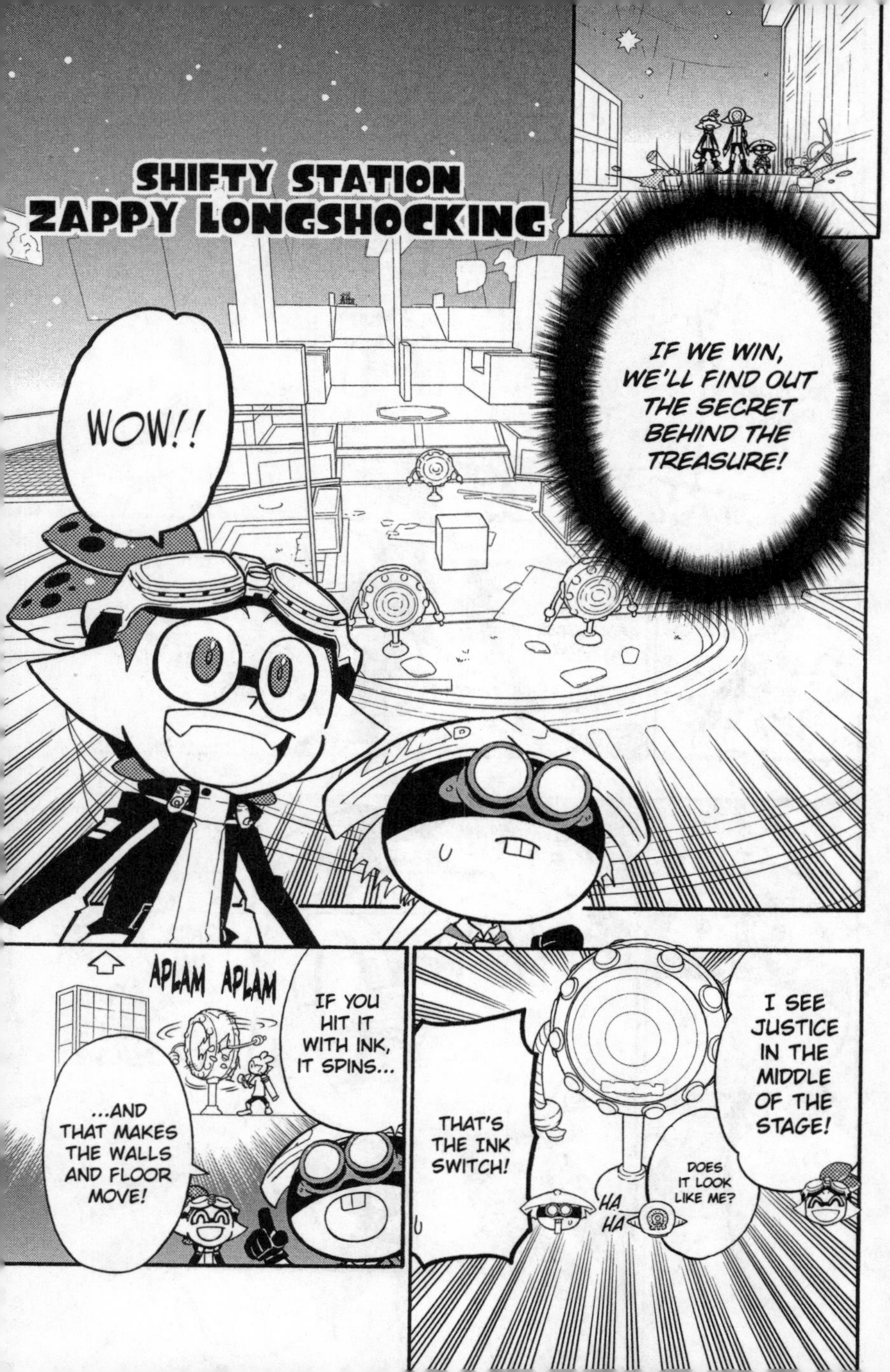
SHIFTY STATION
ZAPPY LONGSHOCKING
IF WE WIN, WE'LL FIND OUT THE SECRET BEHIND THE TREASURE!
WOW!!
I SEE JUSTICE IN THE MIDDLE OF THE STAGE!
THAT'S THE INK SWITCH!
DOES IT LOOK LIKE ME?
HA HA
IF YOU HIT IT WITH INK, IT SPINS...
APLAM APLAM
...AND THAT MAKES THE WALLS AND FLOOR MOVE!

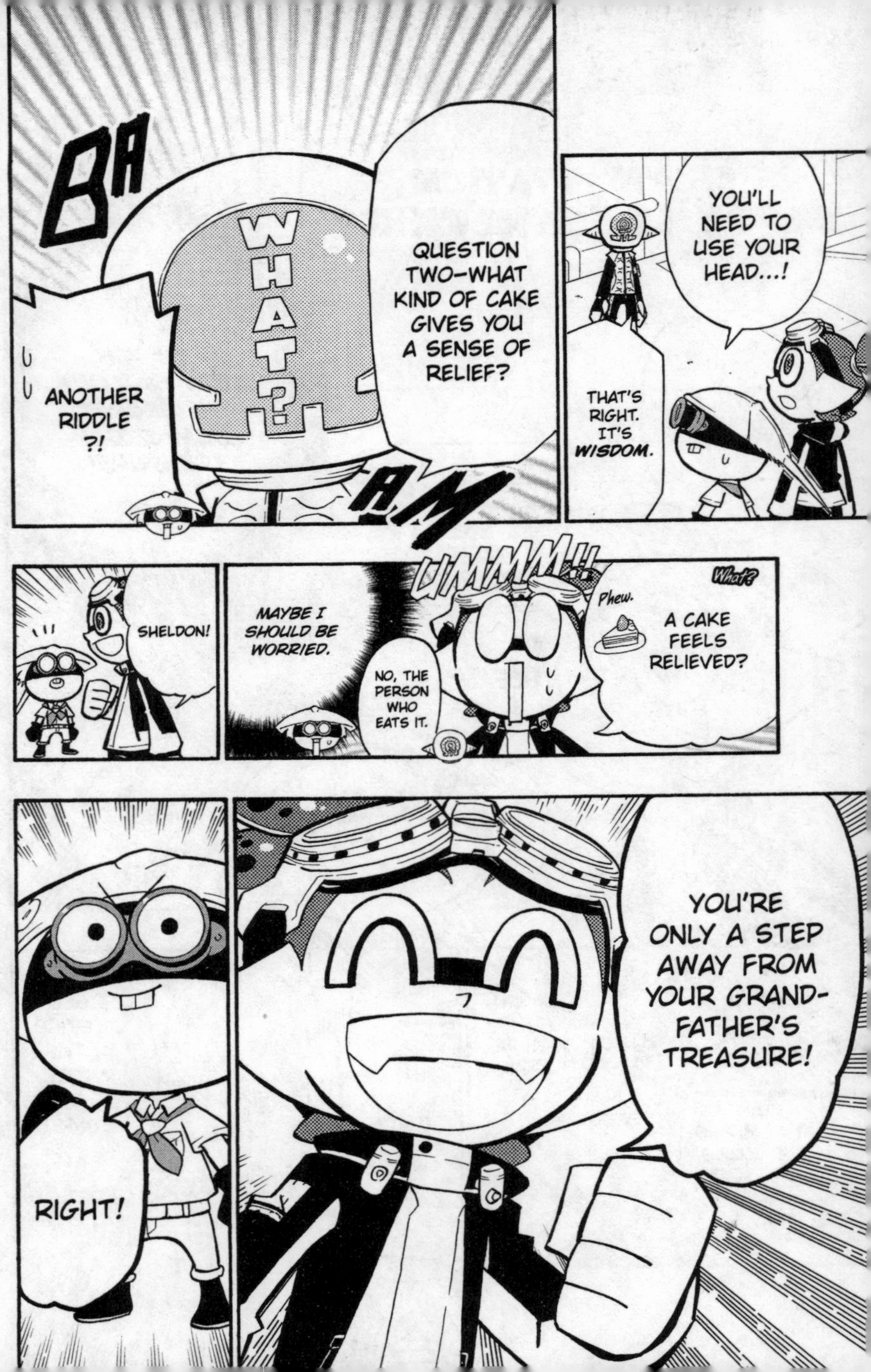
YOU'LL NEED TO USE YOUR HEAD...!
THAT'S RIGHT. IT'S WISDOM.
QUESTION TWO—WHAT KIND OF CAKE GIVES YOU A SENSE OF RELIEF?
WHAT?
BA
ANOTHER RIDDLE ?!
AM
What?
UMMMM!!
A CAKE FEELS RELIEVED?
Phew.
NO, THE PERSON WHO EATS IT.
MAYBE I SHOULD BE WORRIED.
SHELDON!
YOU'RE ONLY A STEP AWAY FROM YOUR GRAND-FATHER'S TREASURE!
RIGHT!

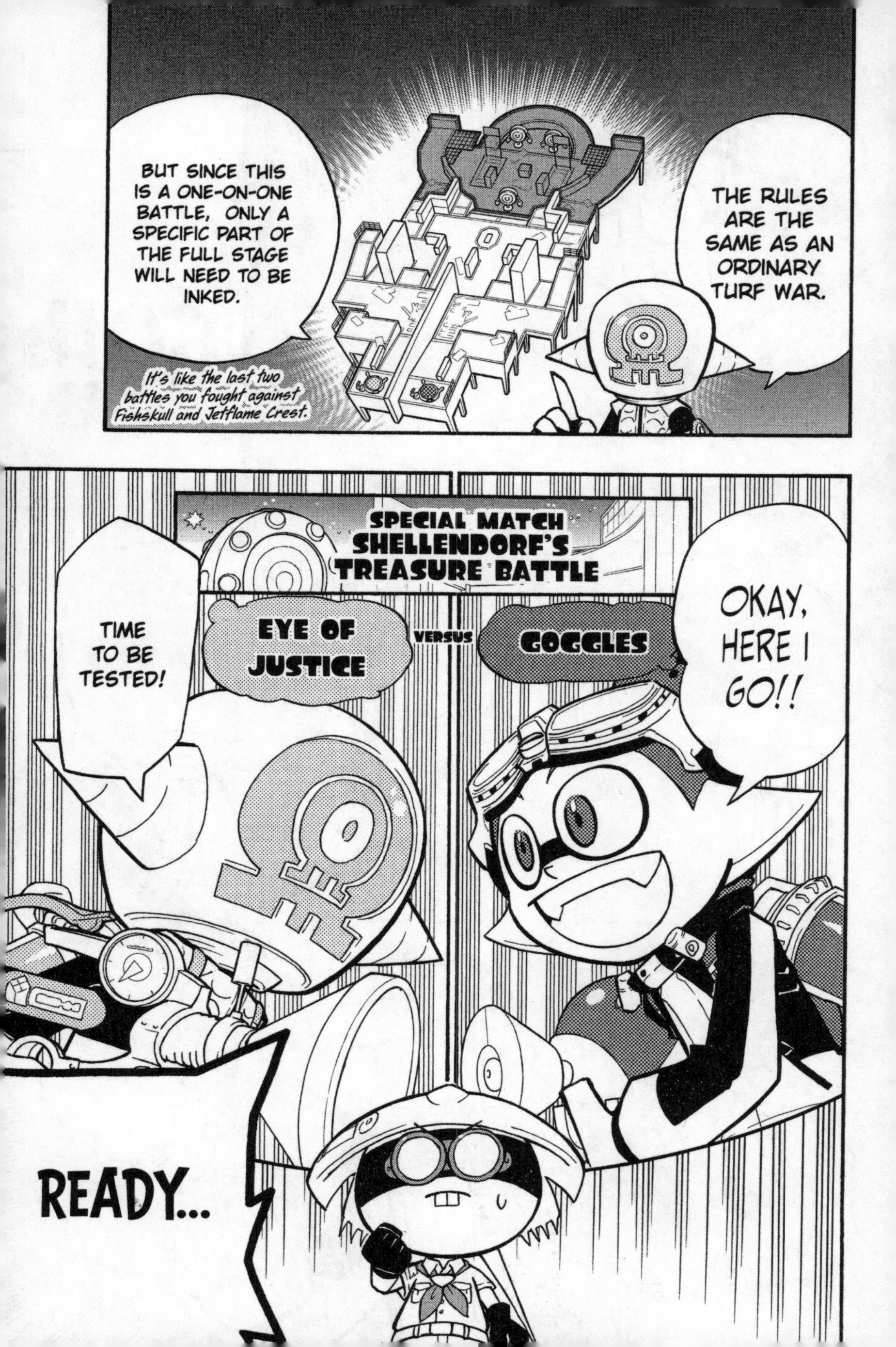
THE RULES ARE THE SAME AS AN ORDINARY TURF WAR.
BUT SINCE THIS IS A ONE-ON-ONE BATTLE, ONLY A SPECIFIC PART OF THE FULL STAGE WILL NEED TO BE INKED.
It's like the last two battles you fought against Fishskull and Jetflame Crest.
SPECIAL MATCH SHELLENDORF'S TREASURE BATTLE
OKAY, HERE I GO!!
GOGGLES
VERSUS
EYE OF JUSTICE
TIME TO BE TESTED!
READY...

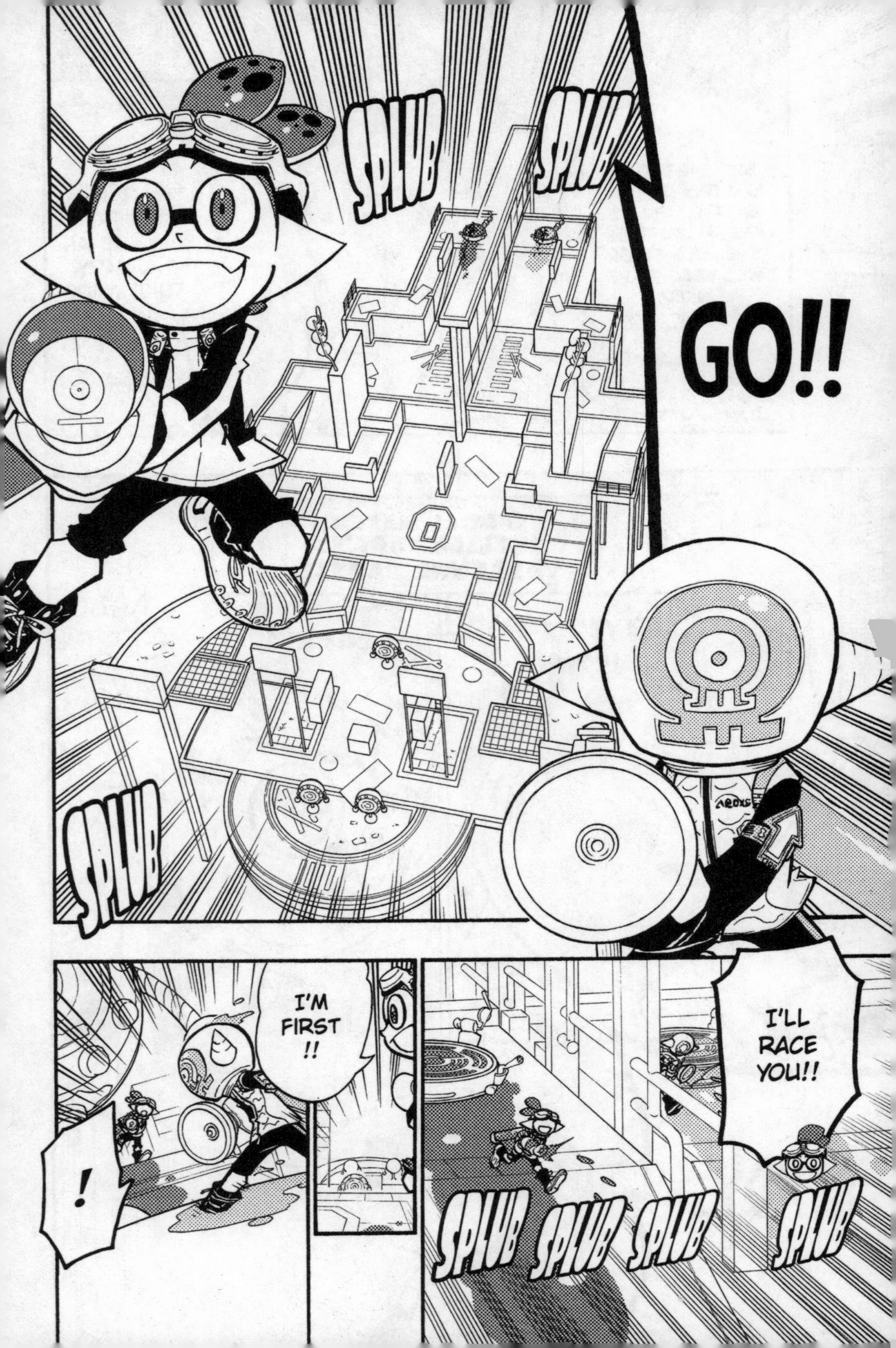
GO!!
SPLUB
SPLUB
SPLUB
I'LL RACE YOU!!
SPLUB
SPLUB
SPLUB
SPLUB
I'M FIRST !!
!

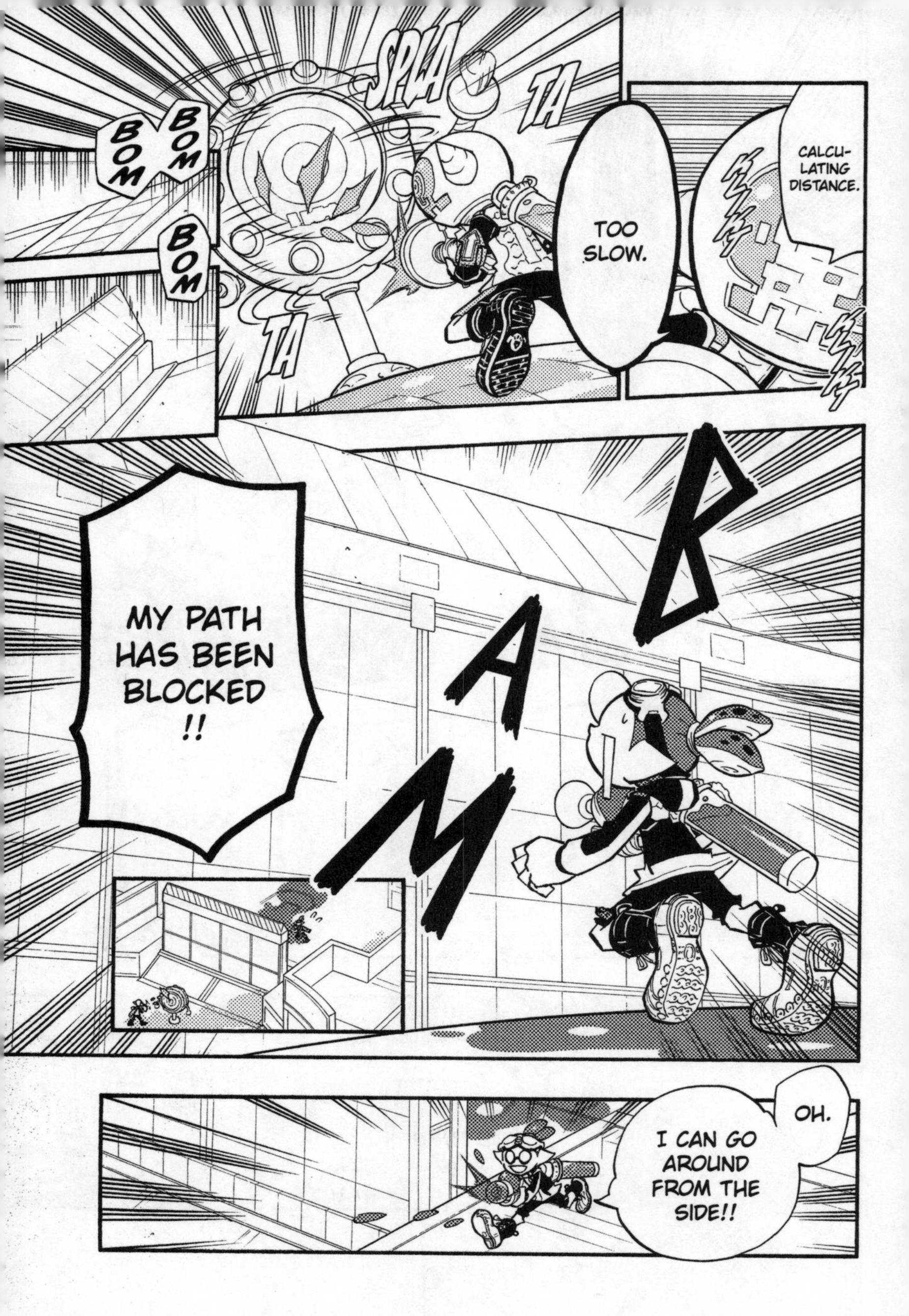
CALCU-
LATING
DISTANCE.
TOO
SLOW.
SPLA
TA
TA
BOM
BOM
BOM
BOM
BAM
MY PATH
HAS BEEN
BLOCKED
!!
OH.
I CAN GO
AROUND
FROM THE
SIDE!!

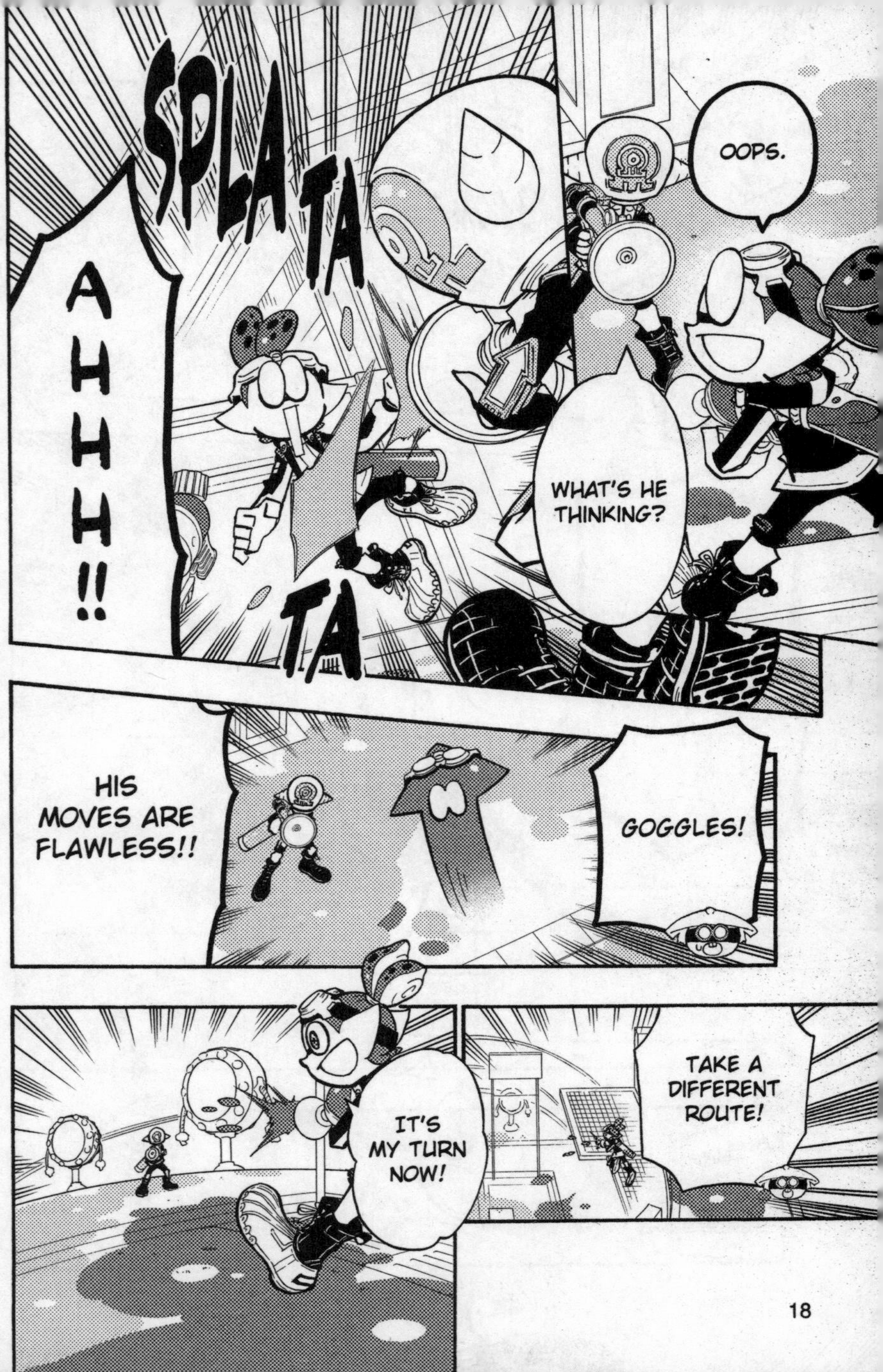
OOPS.
WHAT'S HE THINKING?
SPLATA
AHHHH!!
TA TA
GOGGLES!
HIS MOVES ARE FLAWLESS!!
TAKE A DIFFERENT ROUTE!
IT'S MY TURN NOW!

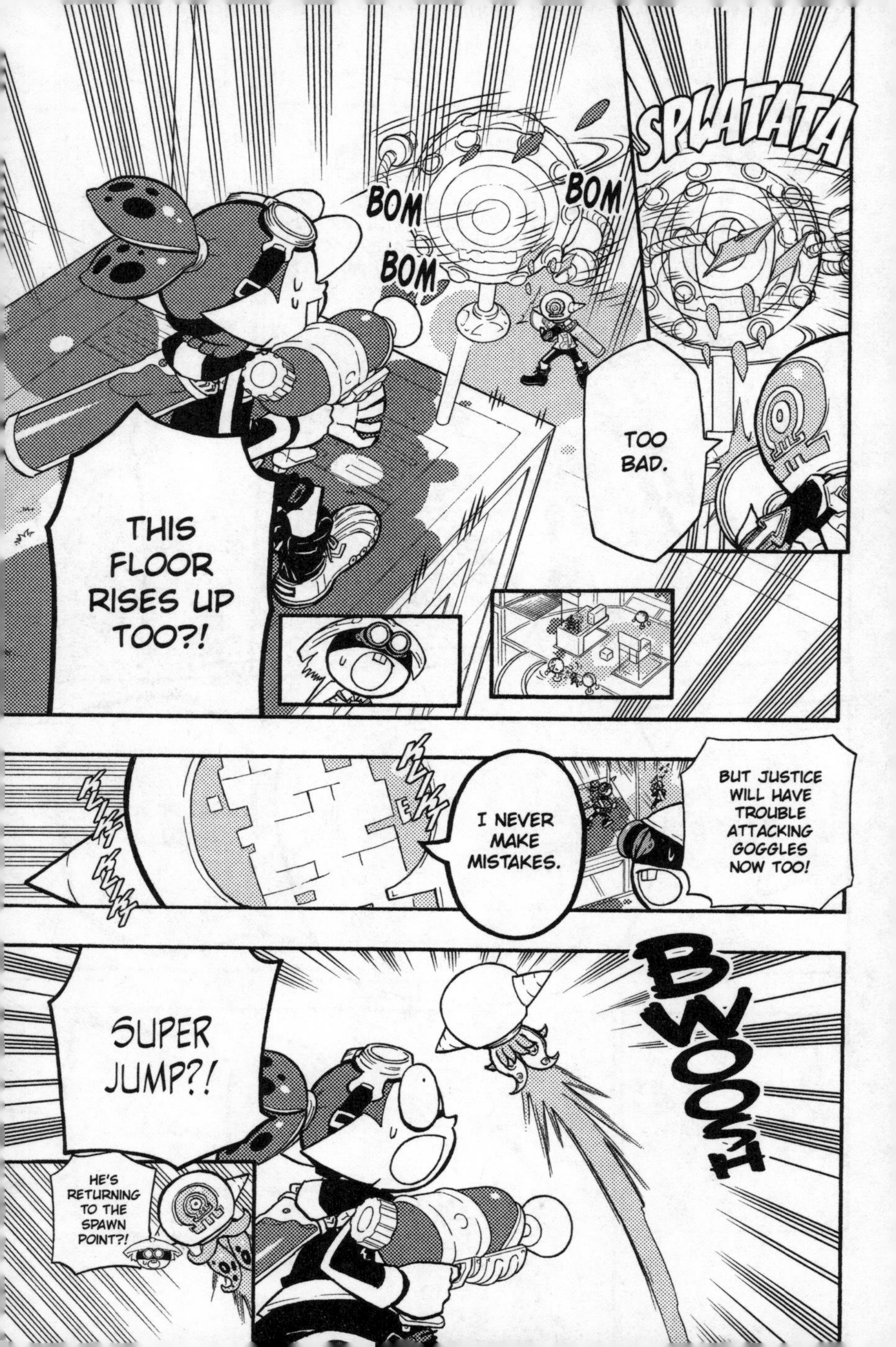
SPLATATA
TOO BAD.
BOM
BOM
BOM
THIS FLOOR RISES UP TOO?!
BUT JUSTICE WILL HAVE TROUBLE ATTACKING GOGGLES NOW TOO!
I NEVER MAKE MISTAKES.
BWOOSH
SUPER JUMP?!
HE'S RETURNING TO THE SPAWN POINT?!

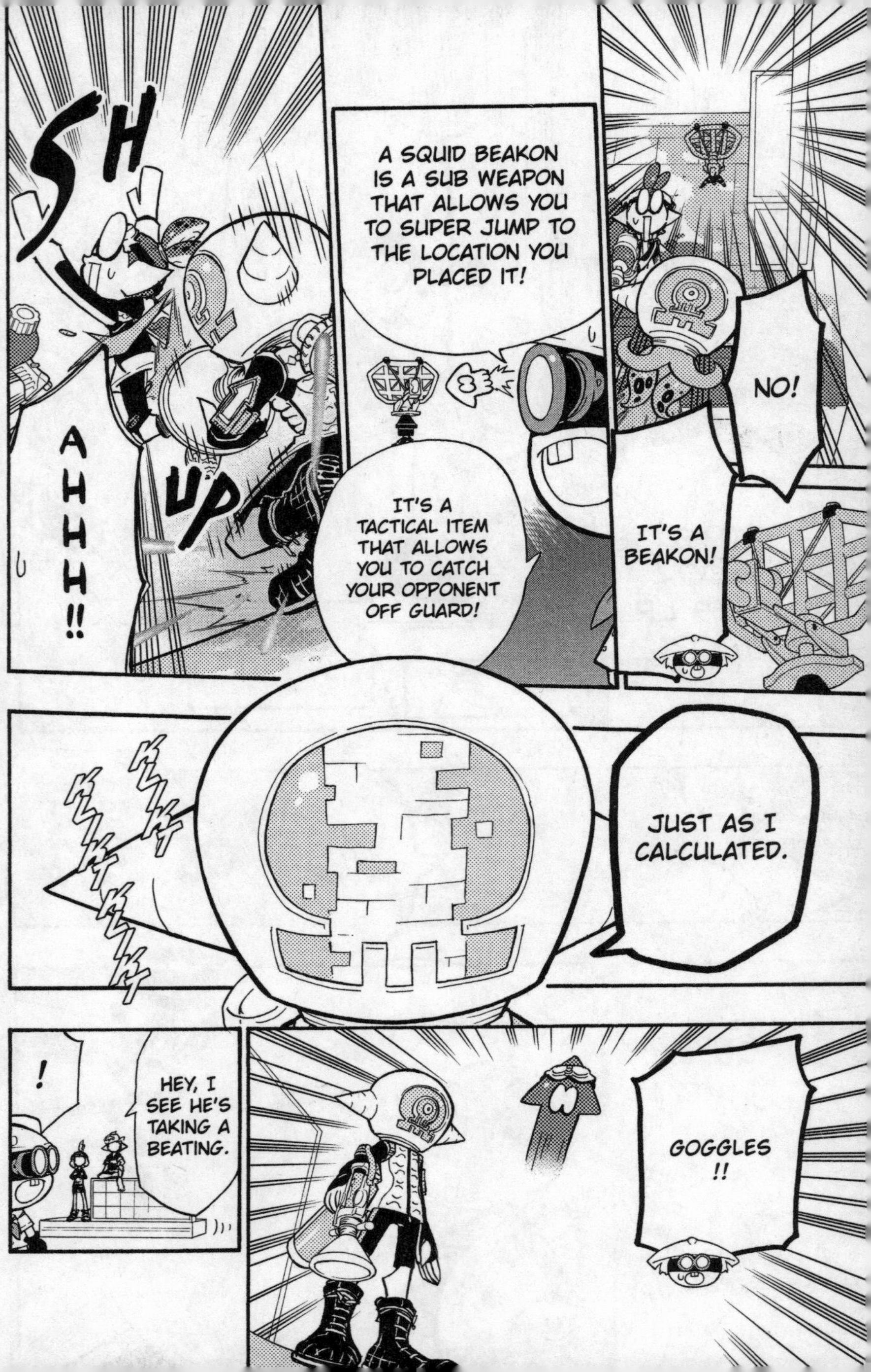
NO!
IT'S A BEAKON!
A SQUID BEAKON IS A SUB WEAPON THAT ALLOWS YOU TO SUPER JUMP TO THE LOCATION YOU PLACED IT!
IT'S A TACTICAL ITEM THAT ALLOWS YOU TO CATCH YOUR OPPONENT OFF GUARD!
SHUP
AHHHH!!
JUST AS I CALCULATED.
GOGGLES !!
HEY, I SEE HE'S TAKING A BEATING.
!

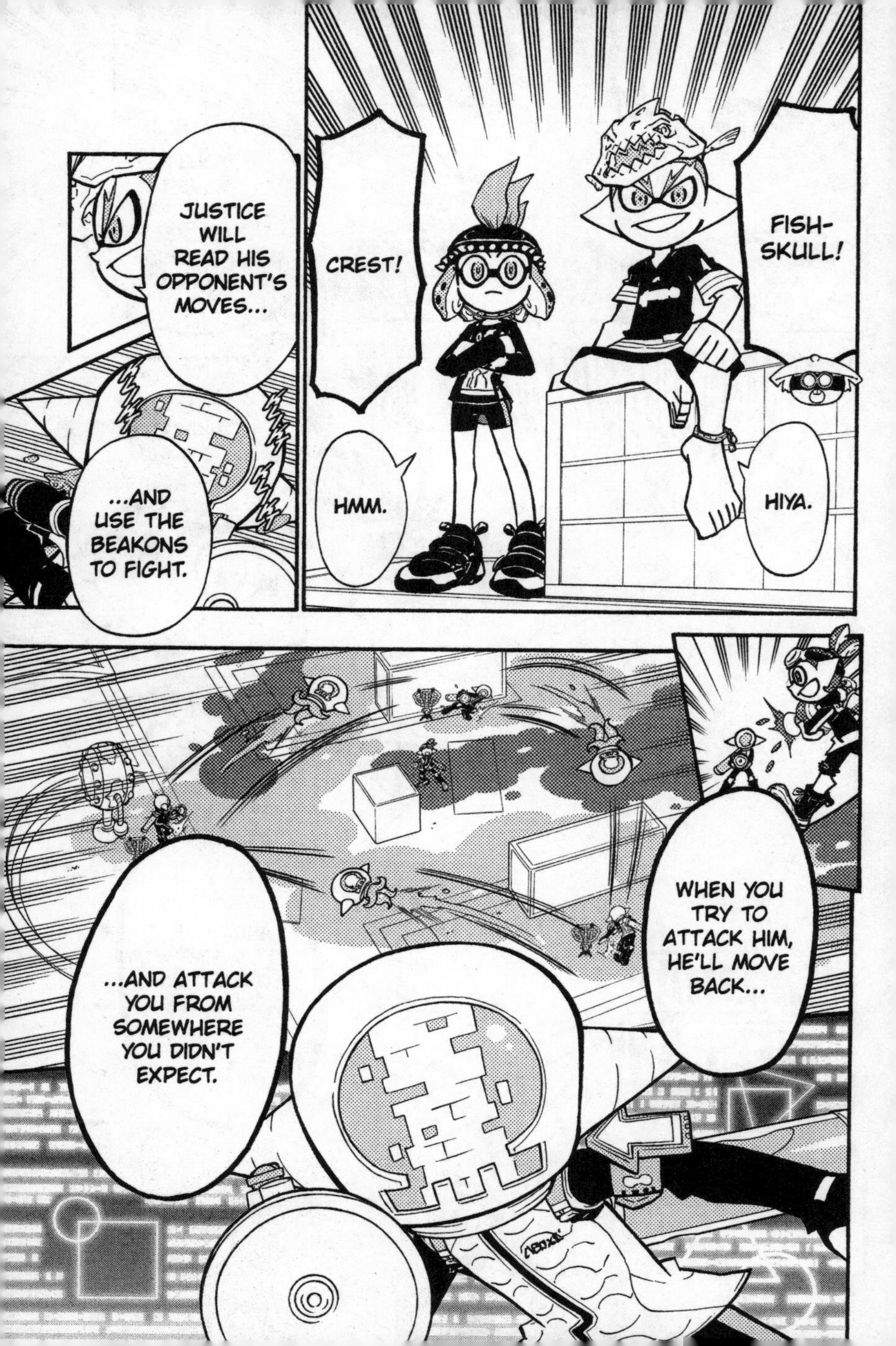
FISH-SKULL!
CREST!
HIYA.
HMM.
JUSTICE WILL READ HIS OPPONENT'S MOVES...
...AND USE THE BEAKONS TO FIGHT.
WHEN YOU TRY TO ATTACK HIM, HE'LL MOVE BACK...
...AND ATTACK YOU FROM SOMEWHERE YOU DIDN'T EXPECT.

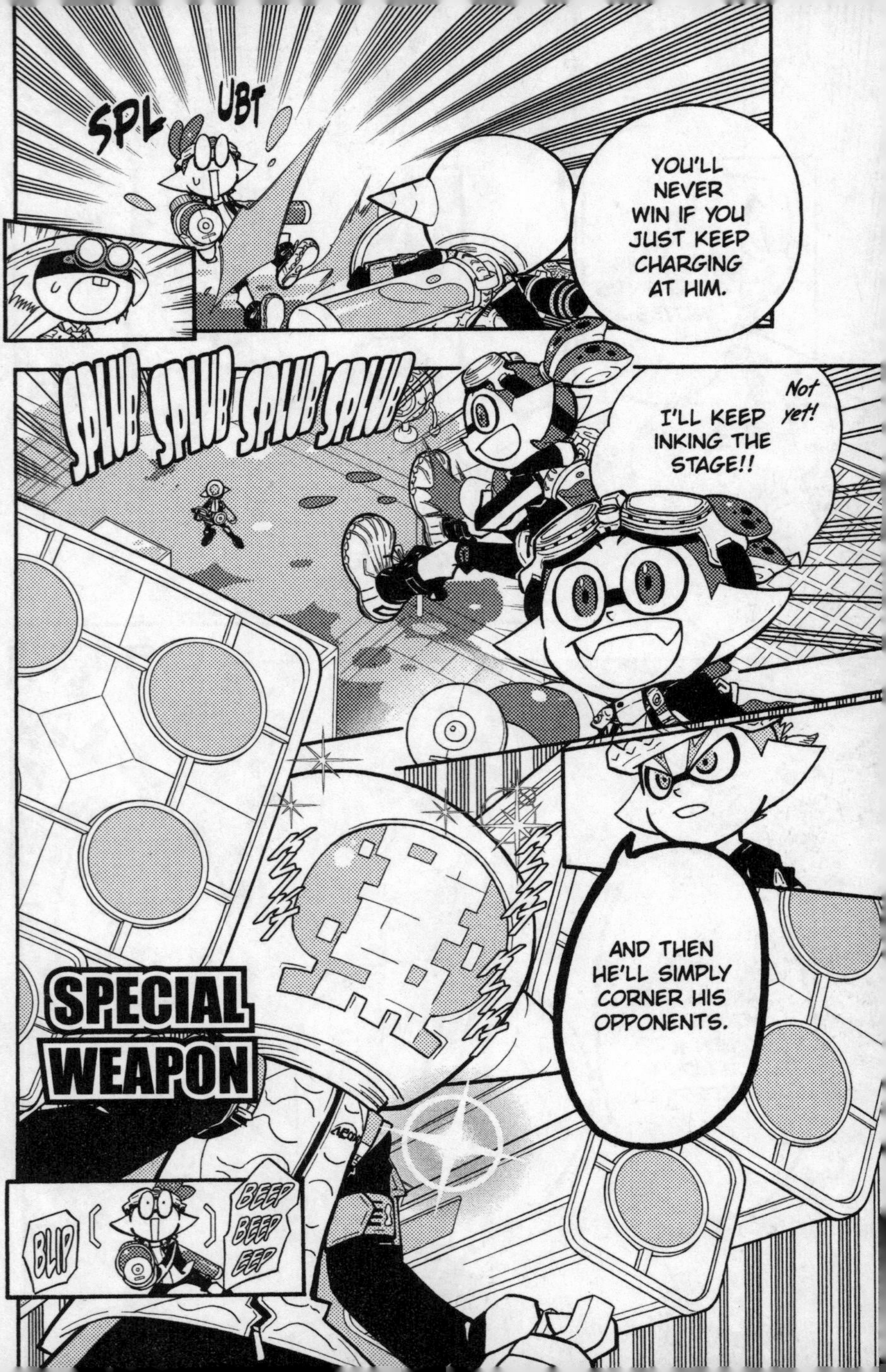

YOU'LL NEVER WIN IF YOU JUST KEEP CHARGING AT HIM.
SPL UBT
Not yet!
I'LL KEEP INKING THE STAGE!!
SPLUB SPLUB SPLUB SPLUB
AND THEN HE'LL SIMPLY CORNER HIS OPPONENTS.
SPECIAL WEAPON
BEEP BEEP EEP
BLIP

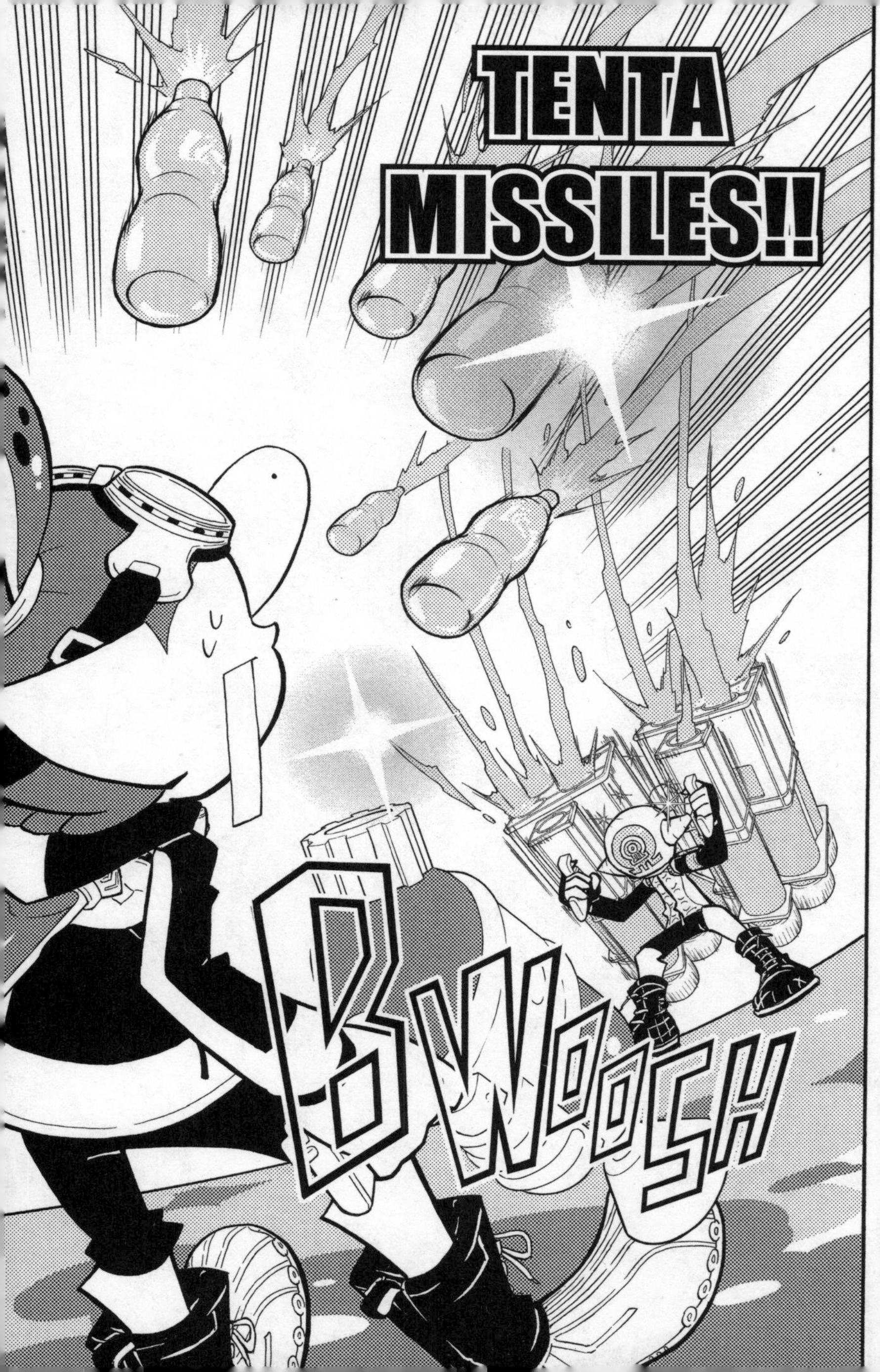
TENTA MISSILES!!
BWOOSH

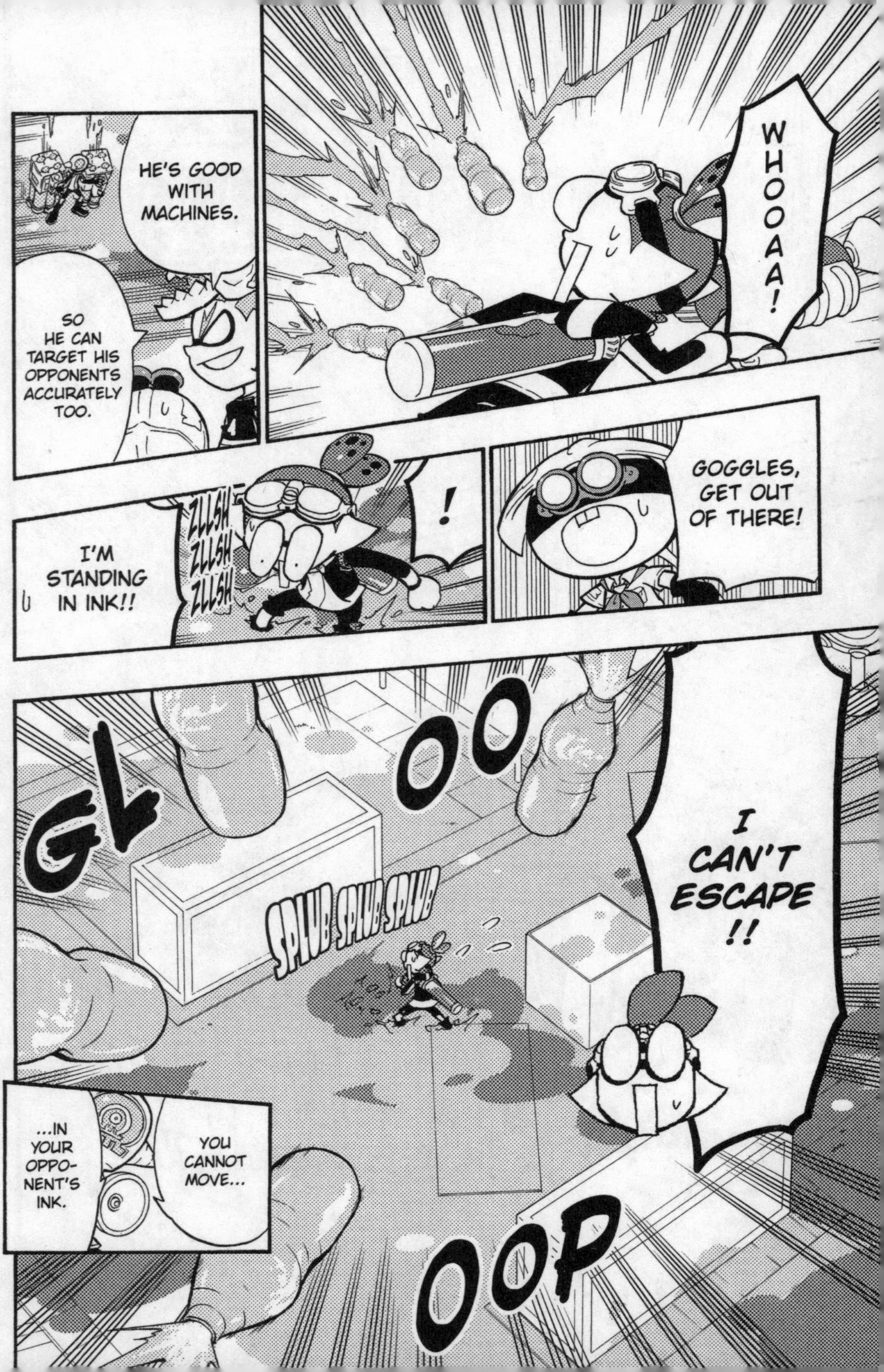
WHOOAA!
HE'S GOOD WITH MACHINES.
SO HE CAN TARGET HIS OPPONENTS ACCURATELY TOO.
GOGGLES, GET OUT OF THERE!
!
ZLLSH ZLLSH ZLLSH
I'M STANDING IN INK!!
GLOOOOP
I CAN'T ESCAPE!!
SPLUB SPLUB SPLUB
YOU CANNOT MOVE...
...IN YOUR OPPO-NENT'S INK.

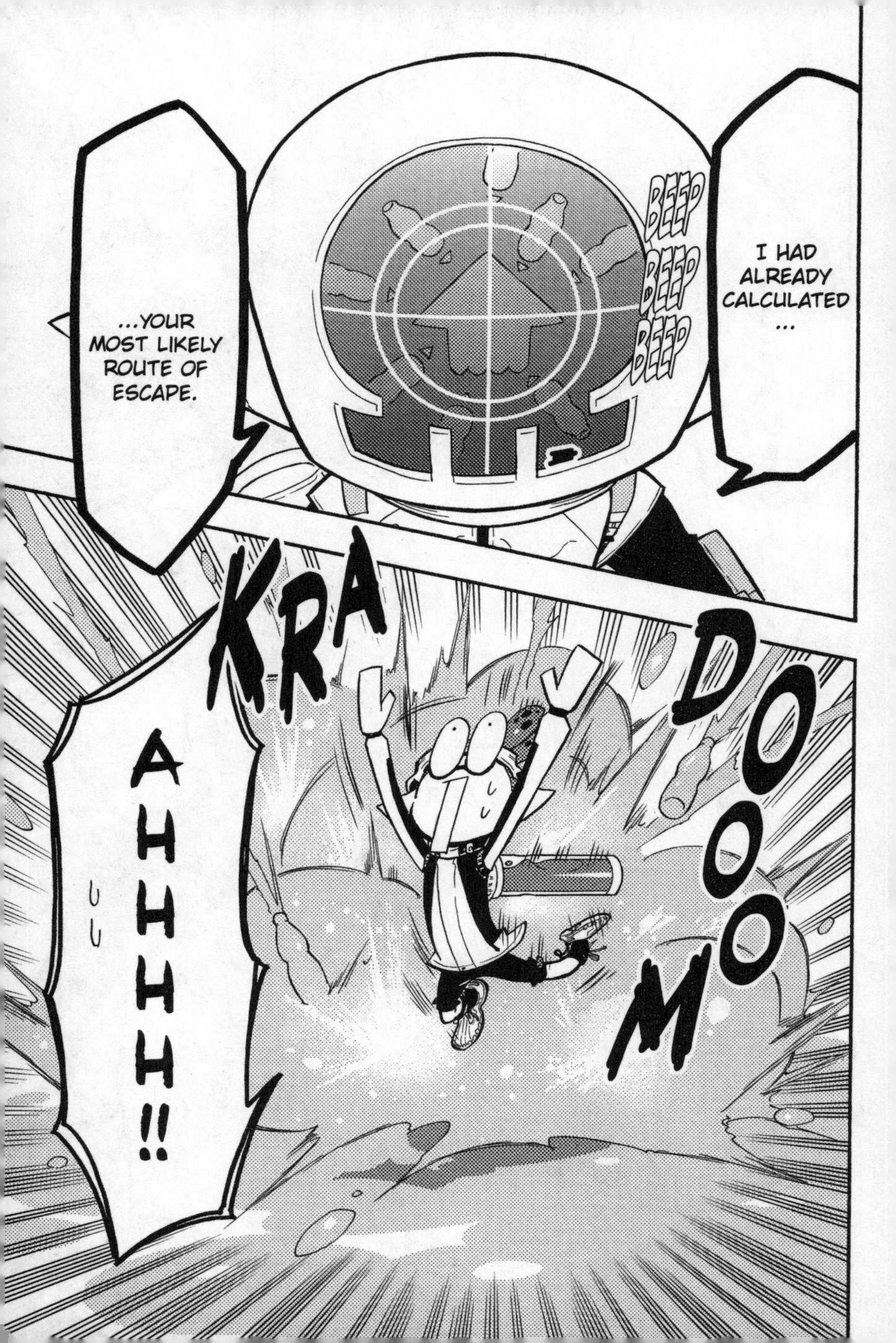

I HAD ALREADY CALCULATED ...
BEEP BEEP BEEP
...YOUR MOST LIKELY ROUTE OF ESCAPE.
KRA
DOOOM
AHHHH!!

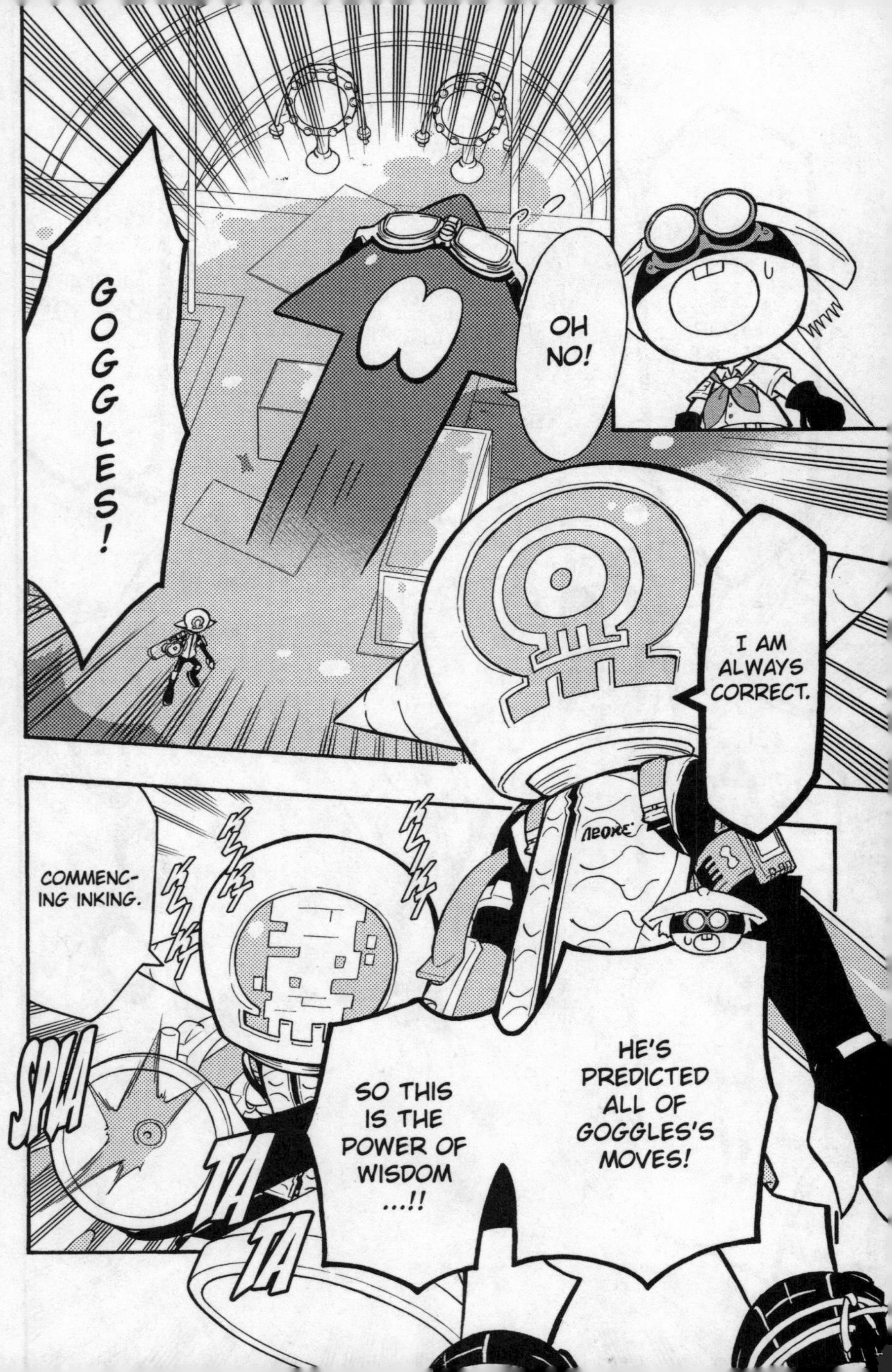
OH NO!
GOGGLES!
I AM ALWAYS CORRECT.
HE'S PREDICTED ALL OF GOGGLES'S MOVES!
SO THIS IS THE POWER OF WISDOM ...!!
COMMENCING INKING.
SPLA
TA
TA

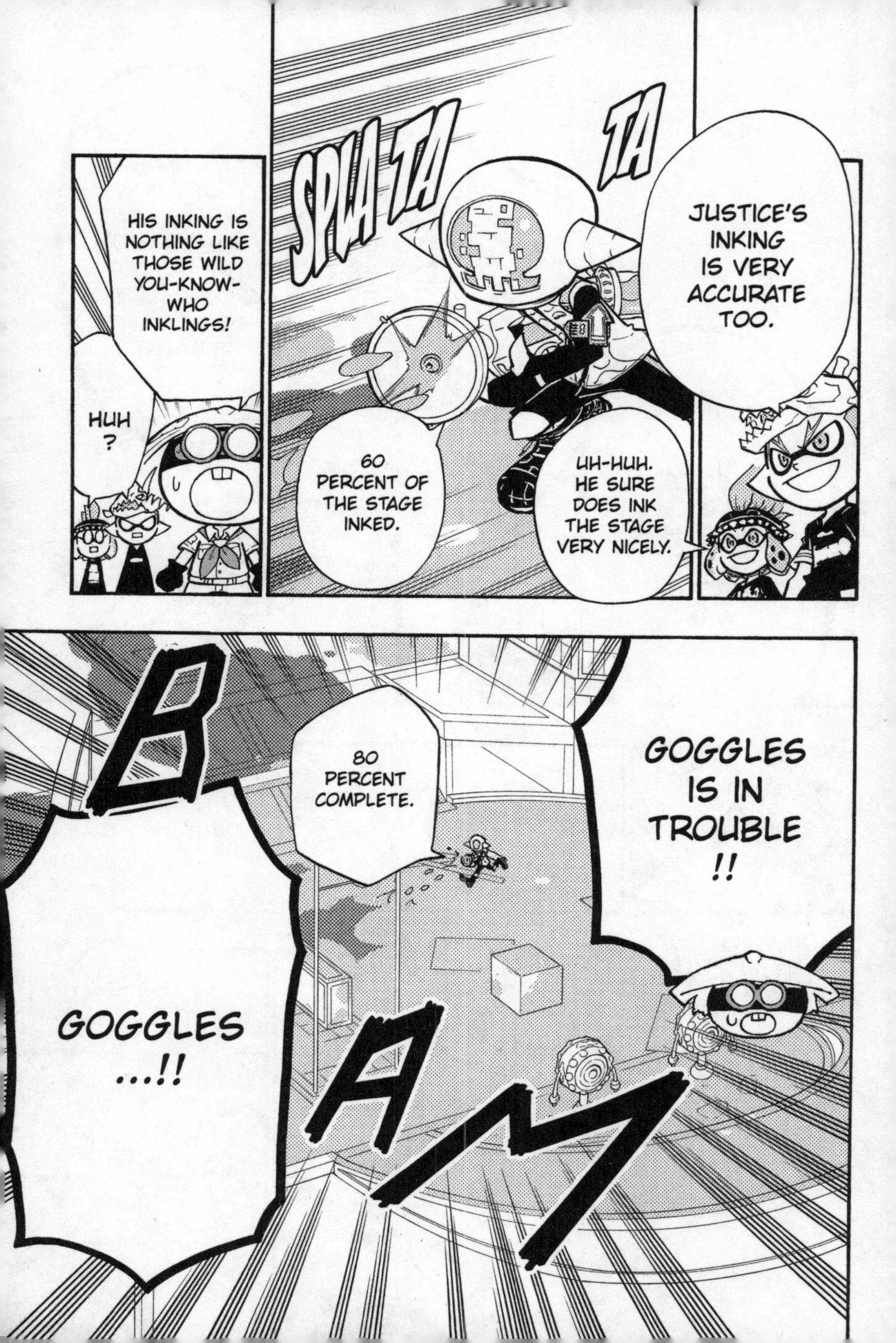
JUSTICE'S INKING IS VERY ACCURATE TOO.
UH-HUH. HE SURE DOES INK THE STAGE VERY NICELY.
SPLA TA TA
60 PERCENT OF THE STAGE INKED.
HIS INKING IS NOTHING LIKE THOSE WILD YOU-KNOW-WHO INKLINGS!
HUH?
GOGGLES IS IN TROUBLE!!
80 PERCENT COMPLETE.
BAM
GOGGLES...!!

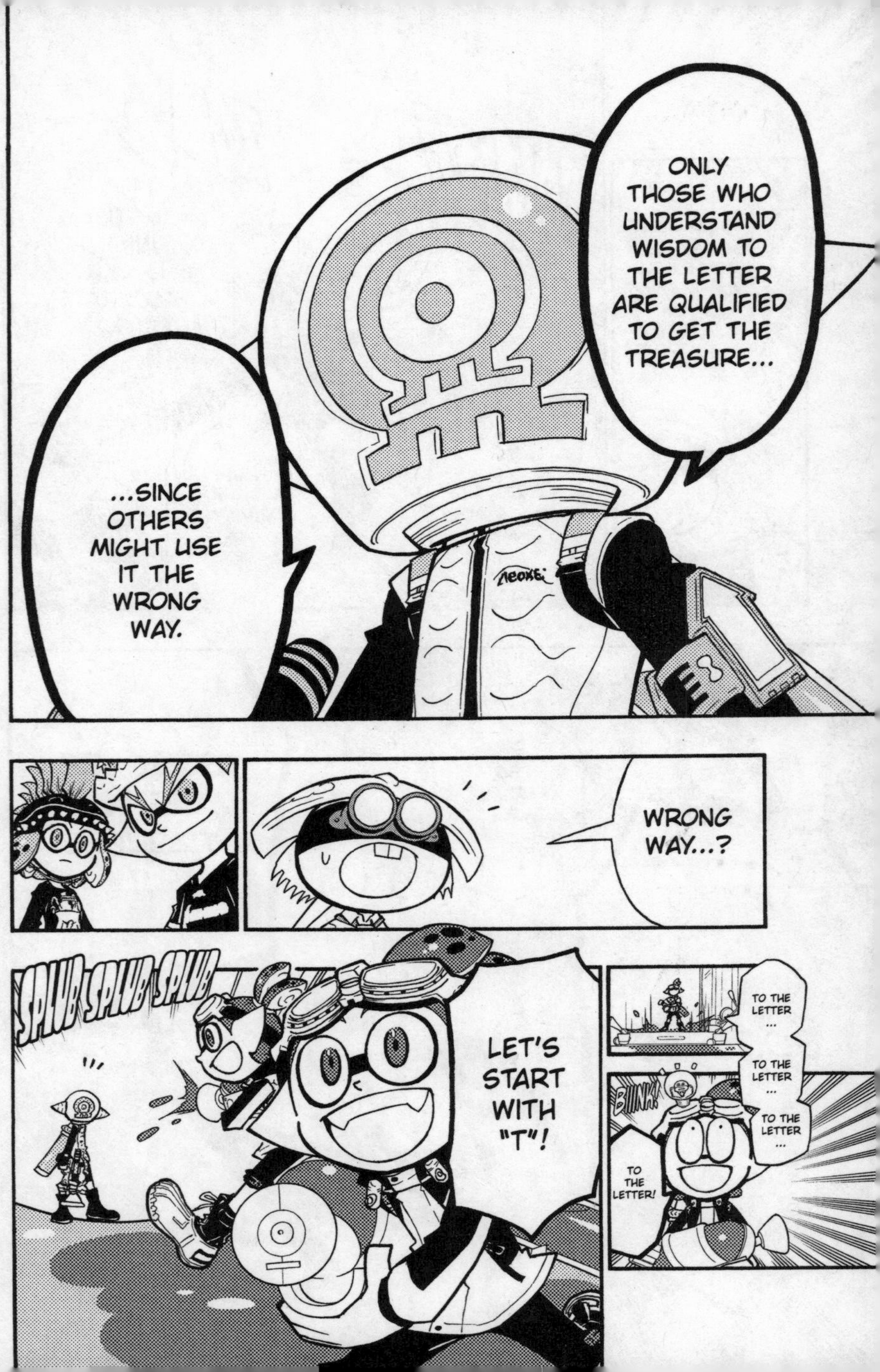
ONLY THOSE WHO UNDERSTAND WISDOM TO THE LETTER ARE QUALIFIED TO GET THE TREASURE...
...SINCE OTHERS MIGHT USE IT THE WRONG WAY.
WRONG WAY...?
TO THE LETTER ...
TO THE LETTER ...
TO THE LETTER ...
BIIINK!
TO THE LETTER!
LET'S START WITH "T"!
SPLUB SPLUB SPLUB

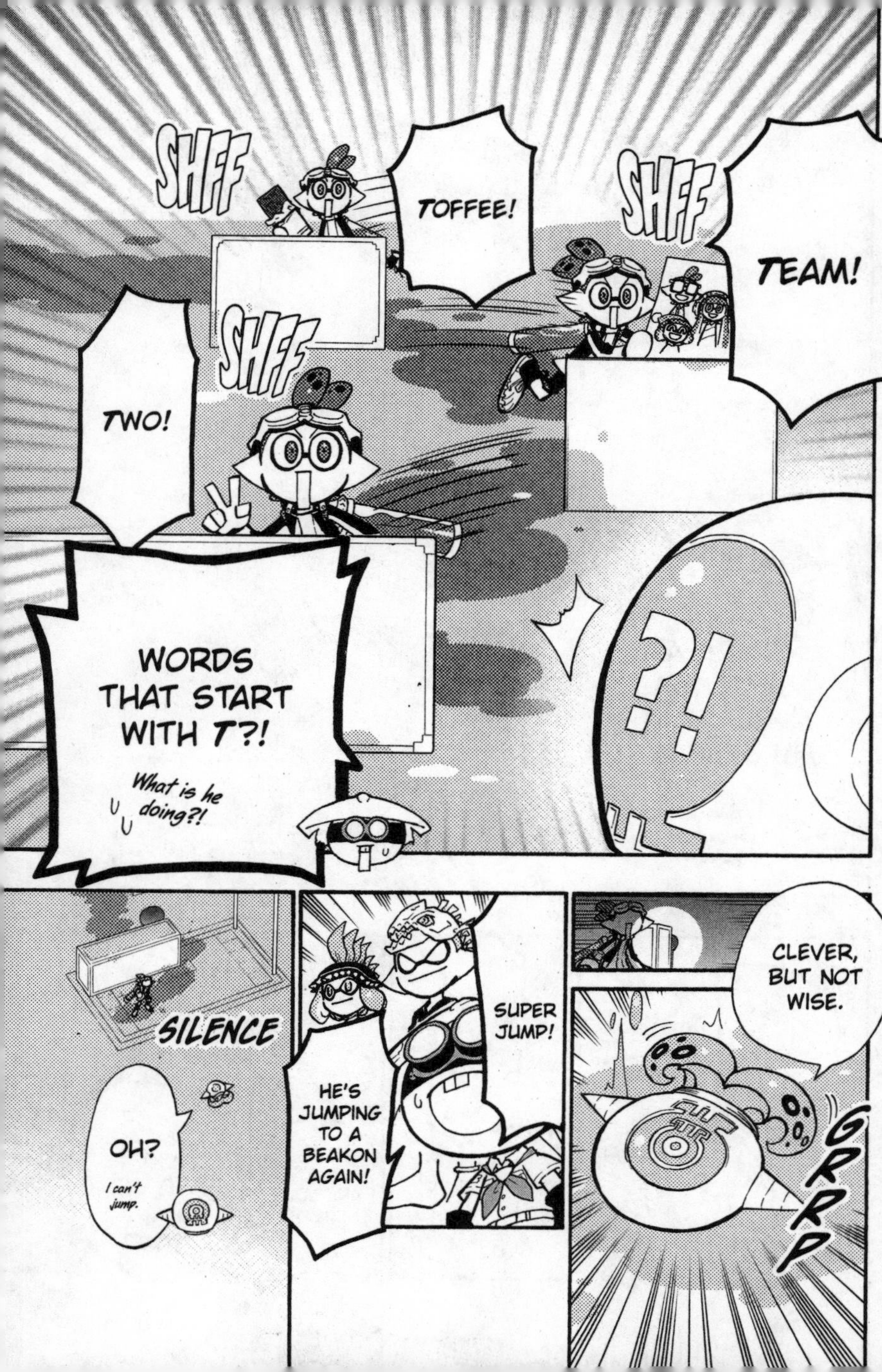
TEAM!
SHFF
TOFFEE!
SHFF
SHFF
TWO!
?!
WORDS THAT START WITH T?!
What is he doing?!
CLEVER, BUT NOT WISE.
GRRP
SUPER JUMP!
HE'S JUMPING TO A BEAKON AGAIN!
SILENCE
OH?
I can't jump.

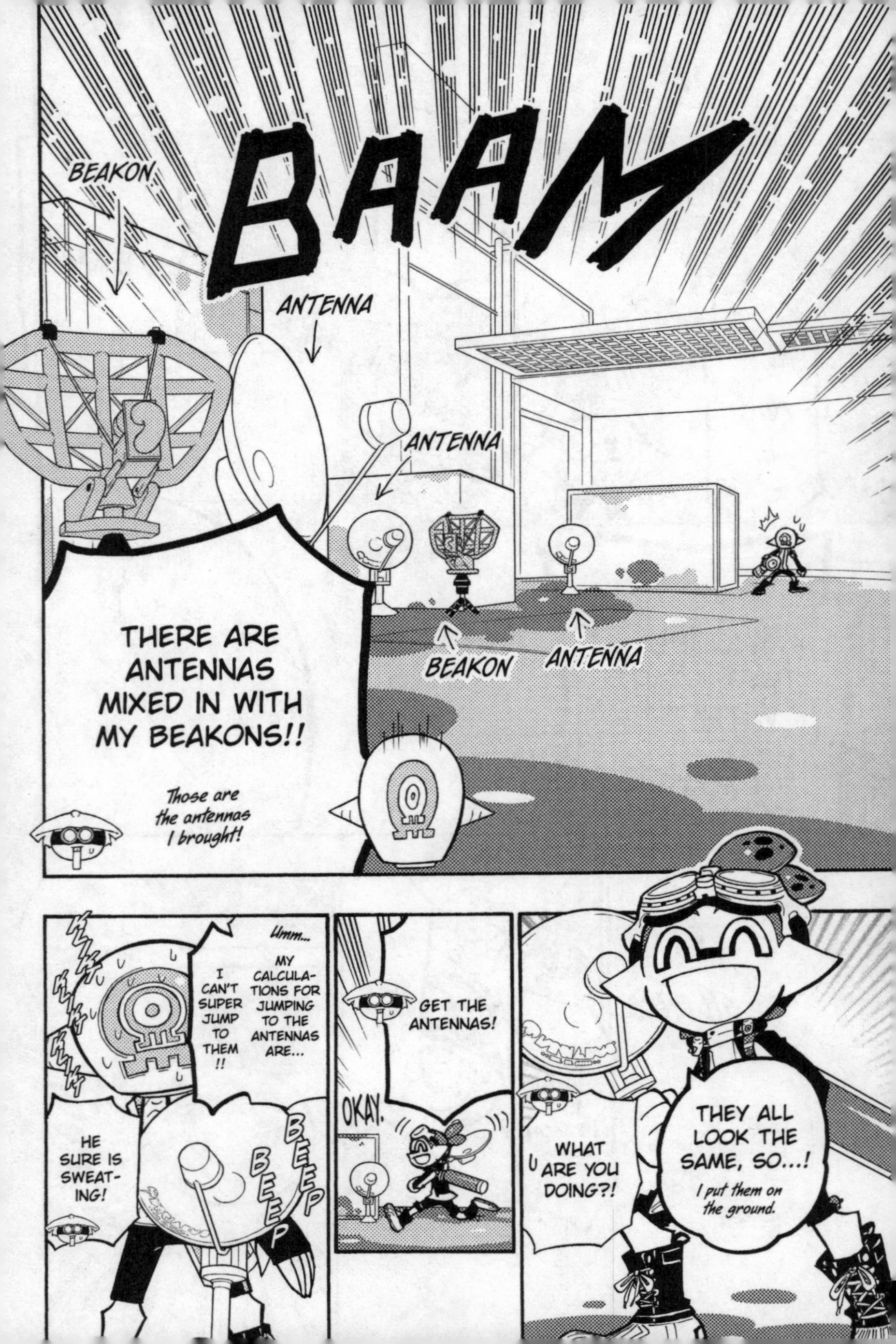
BAAM
BEAKON
ANTENNA
ANTENNA
BEAKON
ANTENNA
THERE ARE ANTENNAS MIXED IN WITH MY BEAKONS!!
Those are the antennas I brought!
THEY ALL LOOK THE SAME, SO...!
I put them on the ground.
WHAT ARE YOU DOING?!
GET THE ANTENNAS!
OKAY.
Umm... MY CALCULATIONS FOR JUMPING TO THE ANTENNAS ARE...
I CAN'T SUPER JUMP TO THEM!!
BEEP BEEP
HE SURE IS SWEATING!

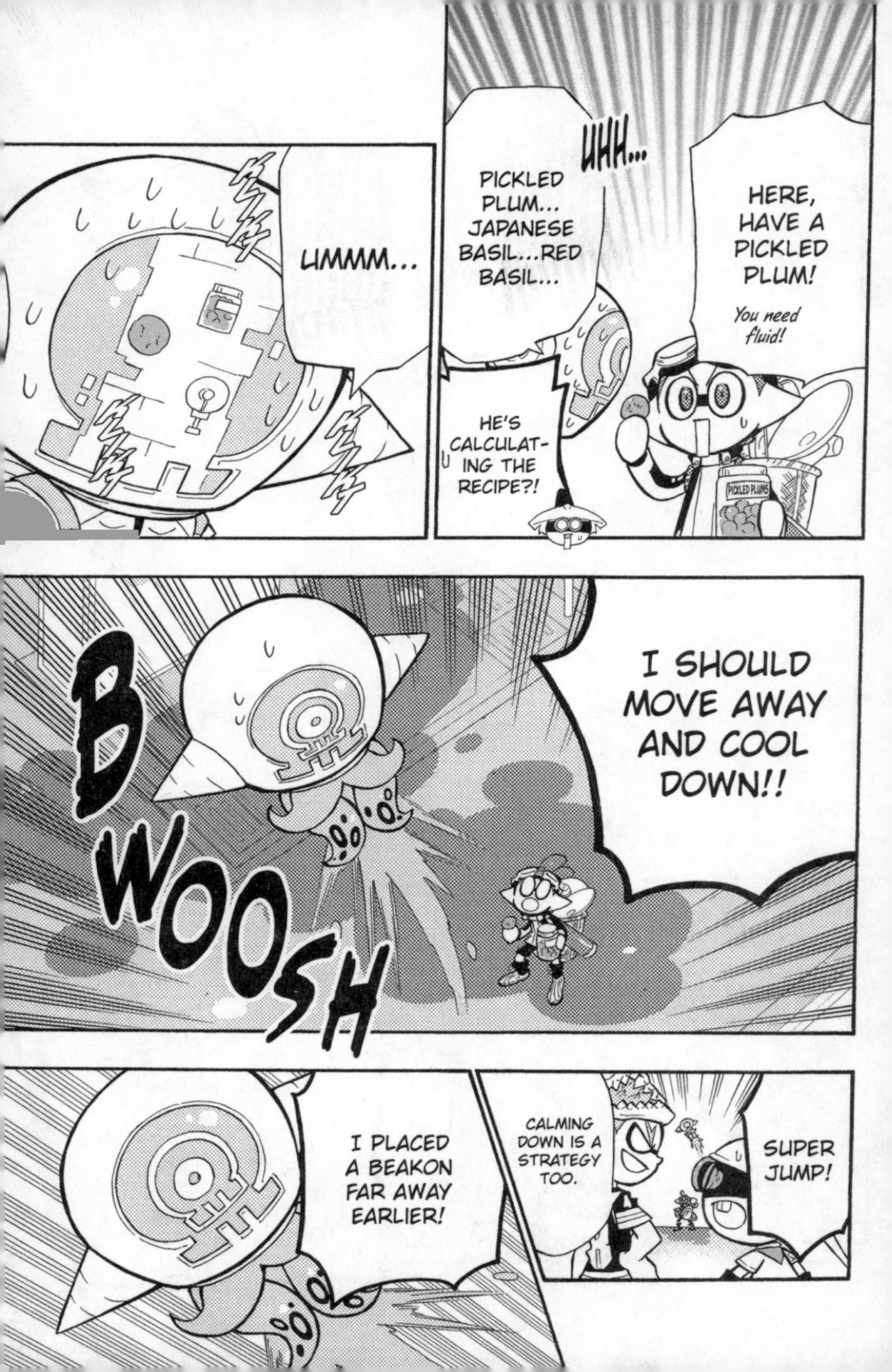
HERE, HAVE A PICKLED PLUM!
You need fluid!
PICKLED PLUMS
UHH...
PICKLED PLUM... JAPANESE BASIL...RED BASIL...
HE'S CALCULAT-ING THE RECIPE?!
UMMM...
I SHOULD MOVE AWAY AND COOL DOWN!!
BWOOSH
SUPER JUMP!
CALMING DOWN IS A STRATEGY TOO.
I PLACED A BEAKON FAR AWAY EARLIER!

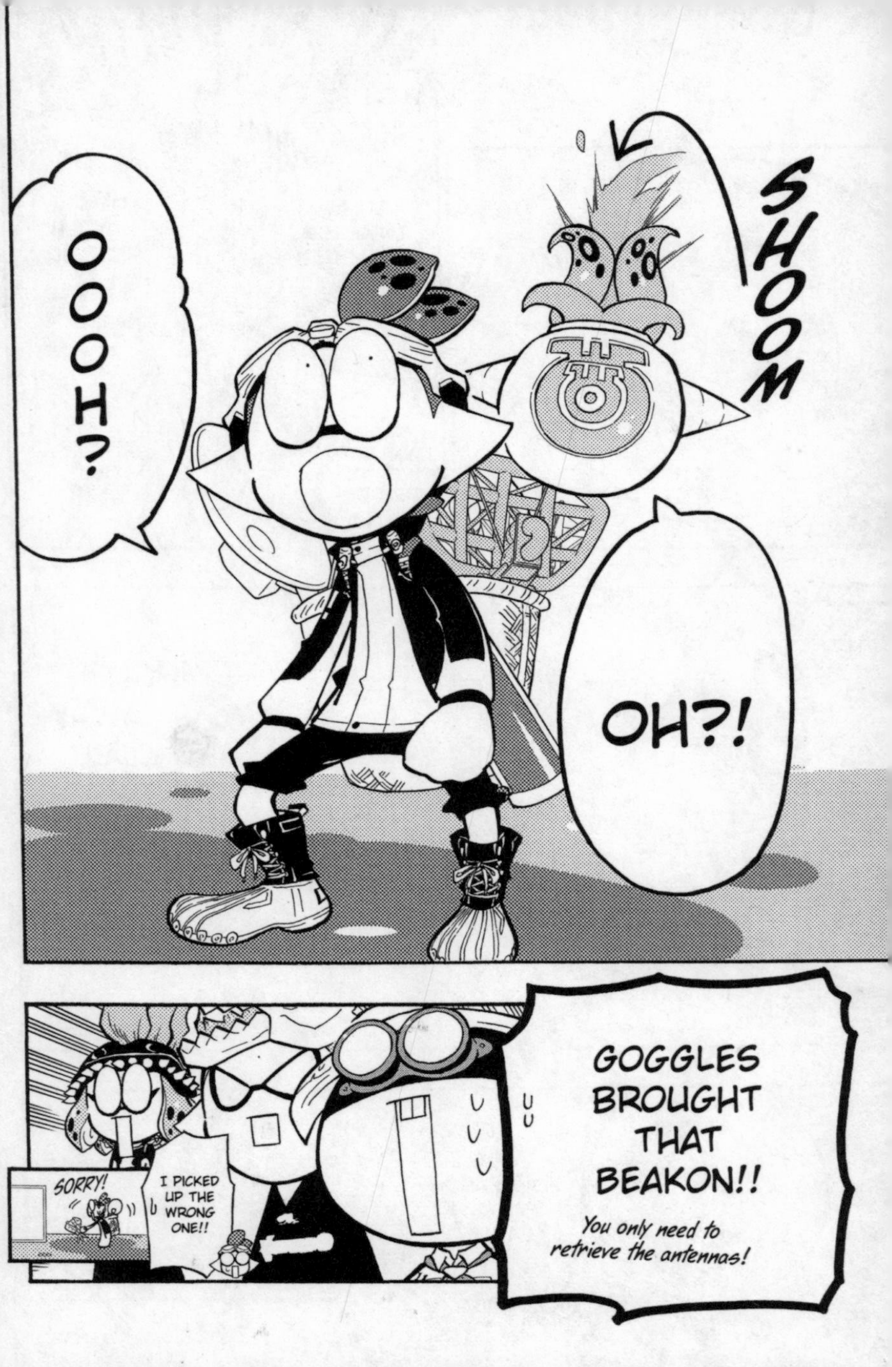
SHOOM
OH?!
OOOH?
GOGGLES BROUGHT THAT BEAKON!!
You only need to retrieve the antennas!
I PICKED UP THE WRONG ONE!!
SORRY!

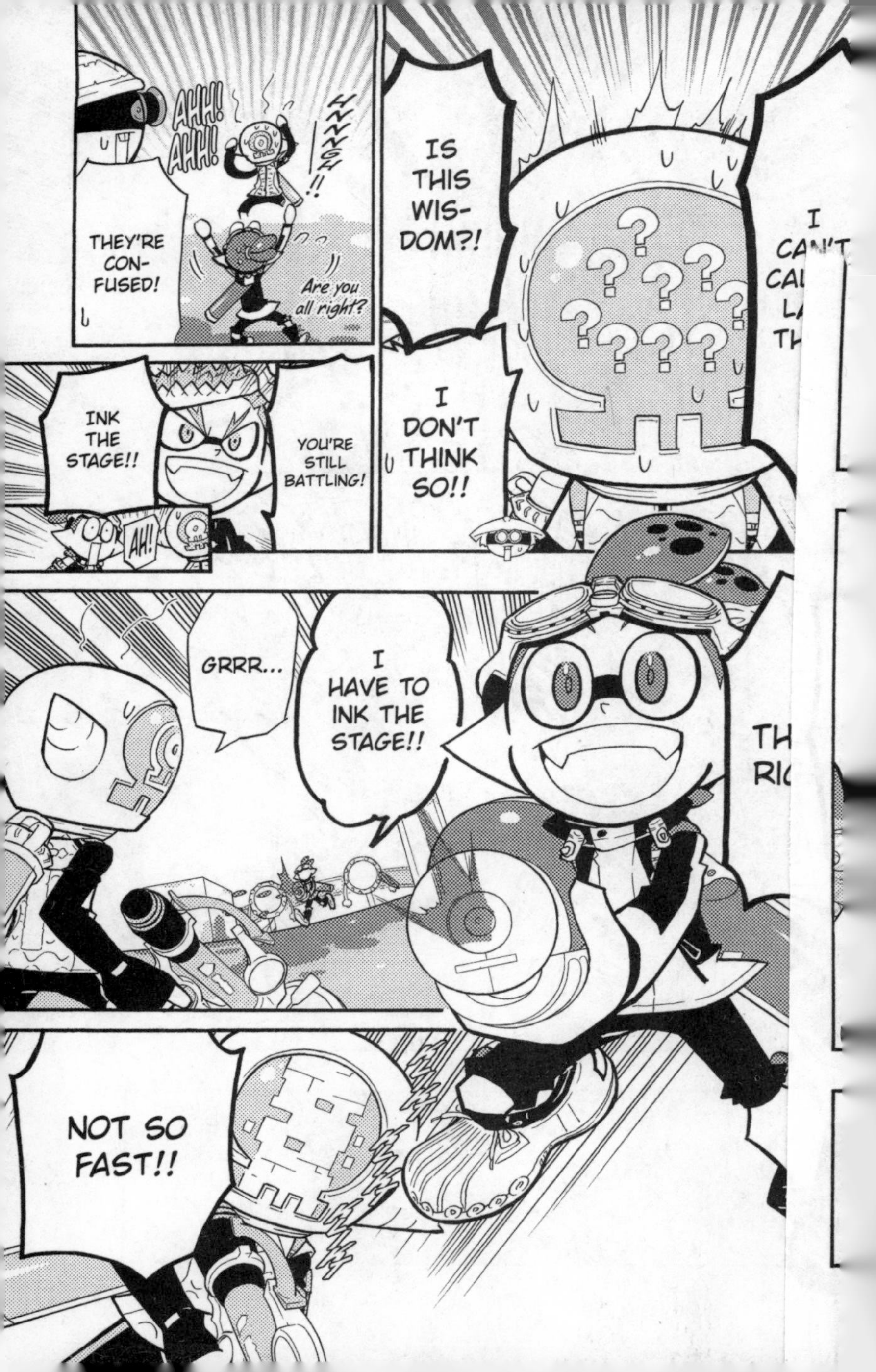
IS THIS WIS-DOM?!
I DON'T THINK SO!!
HNNNGH!!
AHH! AHH!
THEY'RE CON-FUSED!
Are you all right?
YOU'RE STILL BATTLING!
INK THE STAGE!!
AH!
I HAVE TO INK THE STAGE!!
GRRR...
NOT SO FAST!!

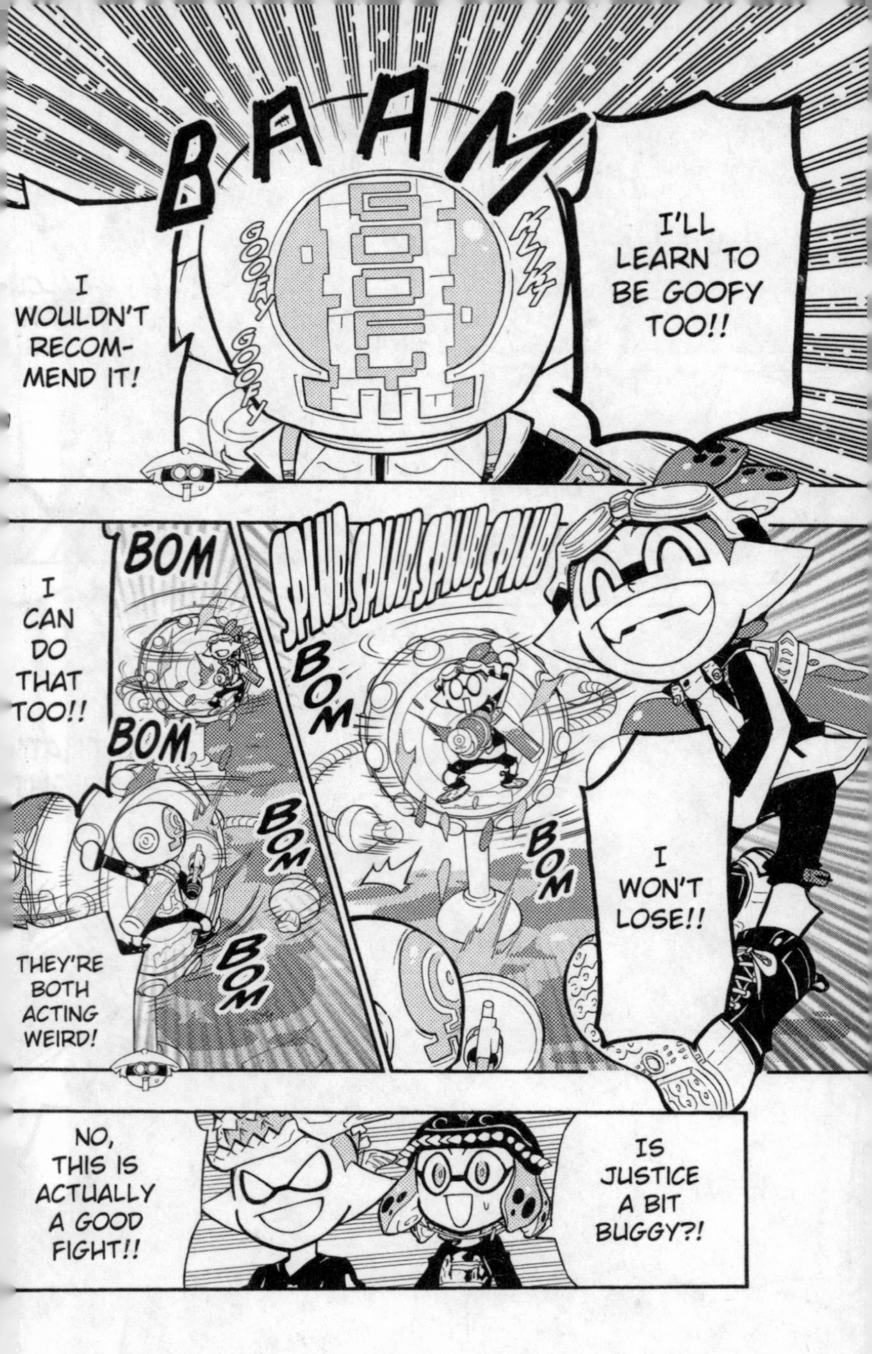
I'LL LEARN TO BE GOOFY TOO!!
BAAM
GOOFY
GOOFY GOOFY GOOFY
I WOULDN'T RECOM-MEND IT!
I WON'T LOSE!!
SPLUB SPLUB SPLUB SPLUB
BOM
BOM
BOM
BOM
I CAN DO THAT TOO!!
BOM
BOM
THEY'RE BOTH ACTING WEIRD!
IS JUSTICE A BIT BUGGY?!
NO, THIS IS ACTUALLY A GOOD FIGHT!!

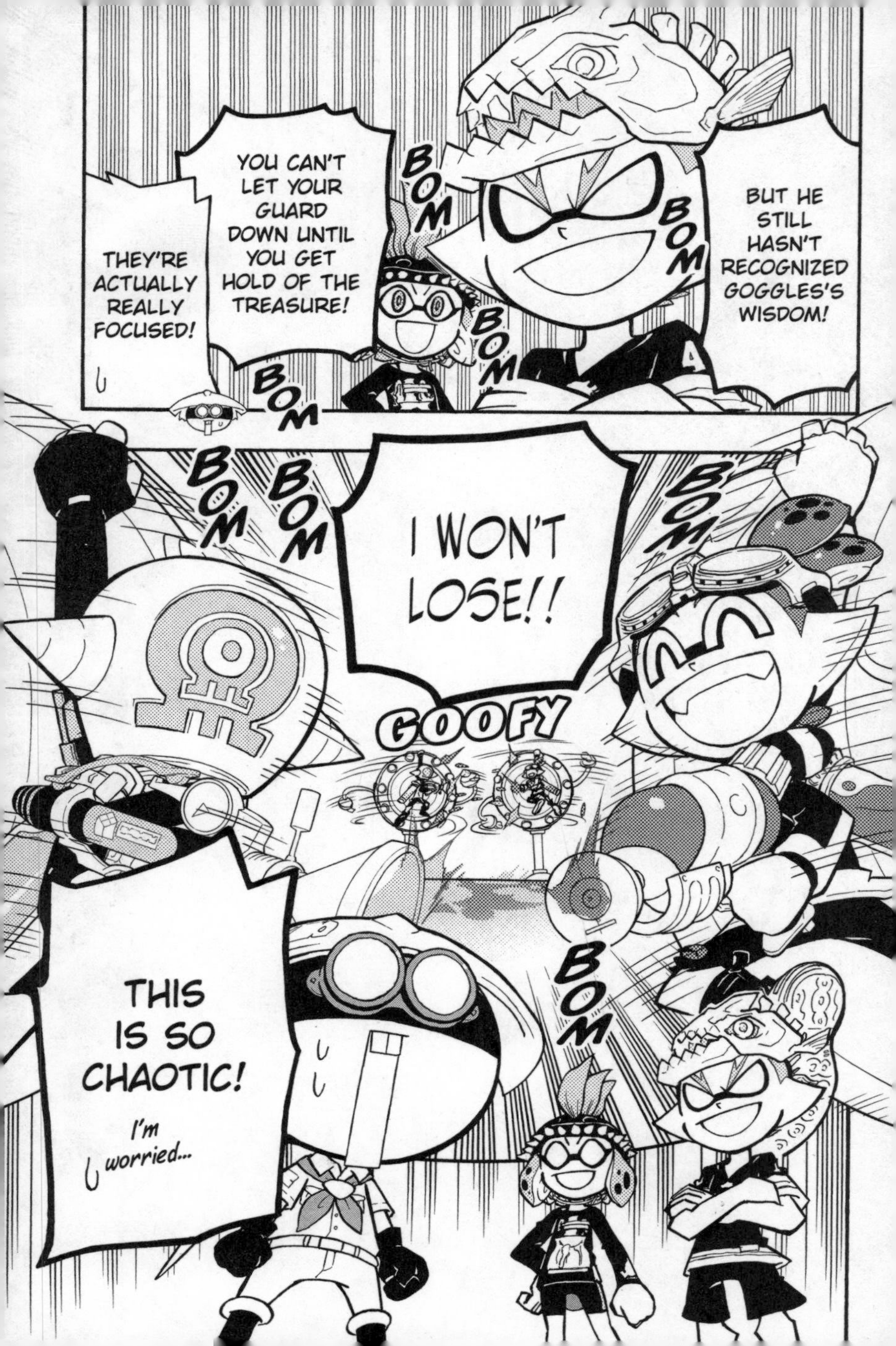
BUT HE STILL HASN'T RECOGNIZED GOGGLES'S WISDOM!
BOM BOM
YOU CAN'T LET YOUR GUARD DOWN UNTIL YOU GET HOLD OF THE TREASURE!
BOM BOM
THEY'RE ACTUALLY REALLY FOCUSED!
BOM
BOM
I WON'T LOSE!!
BOM BOM
GOOFY
BOM
THIS IS SO CHAOTIC!
I'm worried...

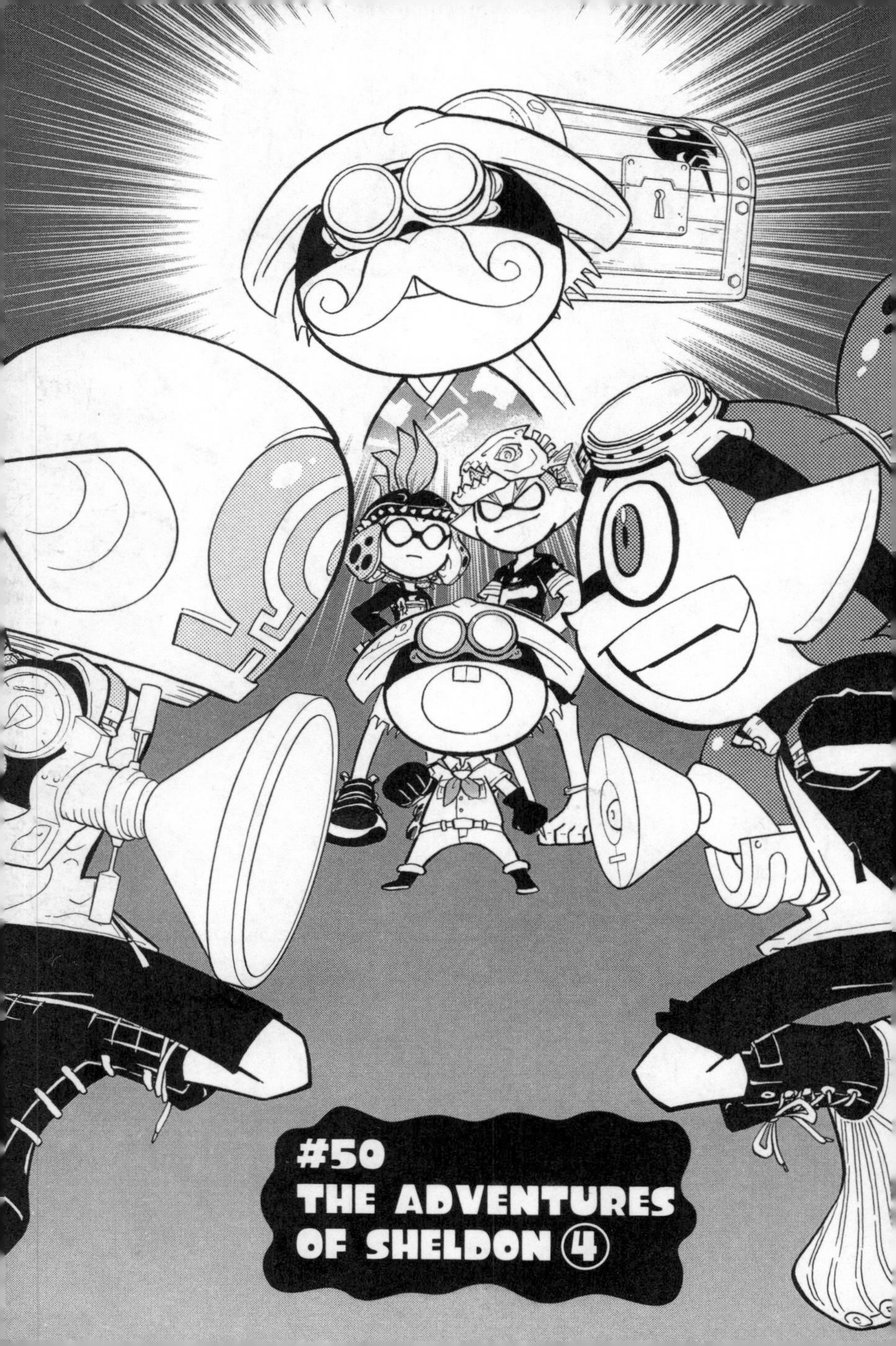
#50
THE ADVENTURES OF SHELDON ④

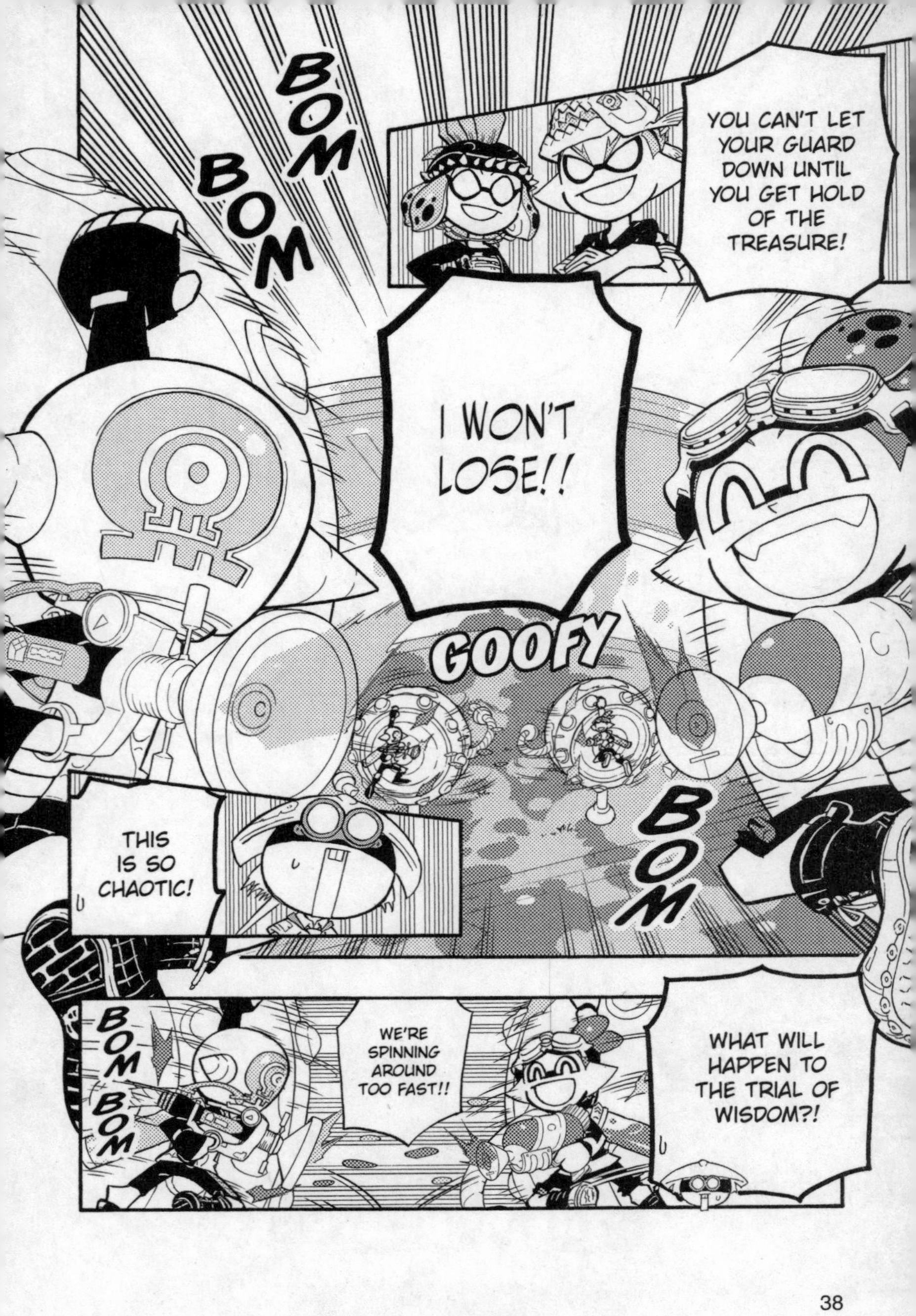

YOU CAN'T LET YOUR GUARD DOWN UNTIL YOU GET HOLD OF THE TREASURE!
BOM BOM BOM
I WON'T LOSE!!
GOOFY
BOM BOM
THIS IS SO CHAOTIC!
WHAT WILL HAPPEN TO THE TRIAL OF WISDOM?!
WE'RE SPINNING AROUND TOO FAST!!
BOM BOM

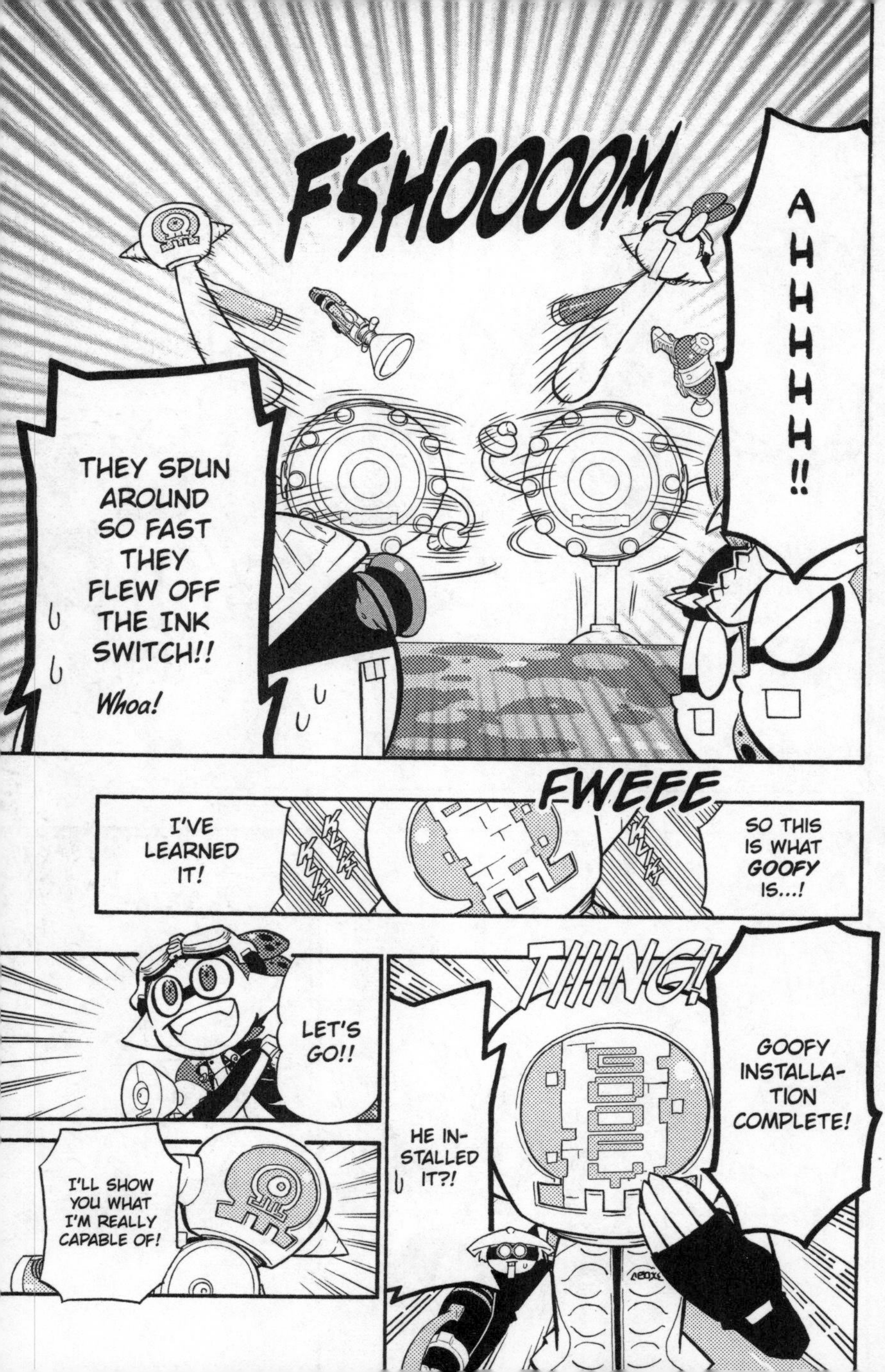
AHHHHHH!!
FSHOOOOM
THEY SPUN AROUND SO FAST THEY FLEW OFF THE INK SWITCH!!
Whoa!
FWEEE
SO THIS IS WHAT GOOFY IS...!
I'VE LEARNED IT!
THIIING!
GOOFY INSTALLA-TION COMPLETE!
HE IN-STALLED IT?!
LET'S GO!!
I'LL SHOW YOU WHAT I'M REALLY CAPABLE OF!

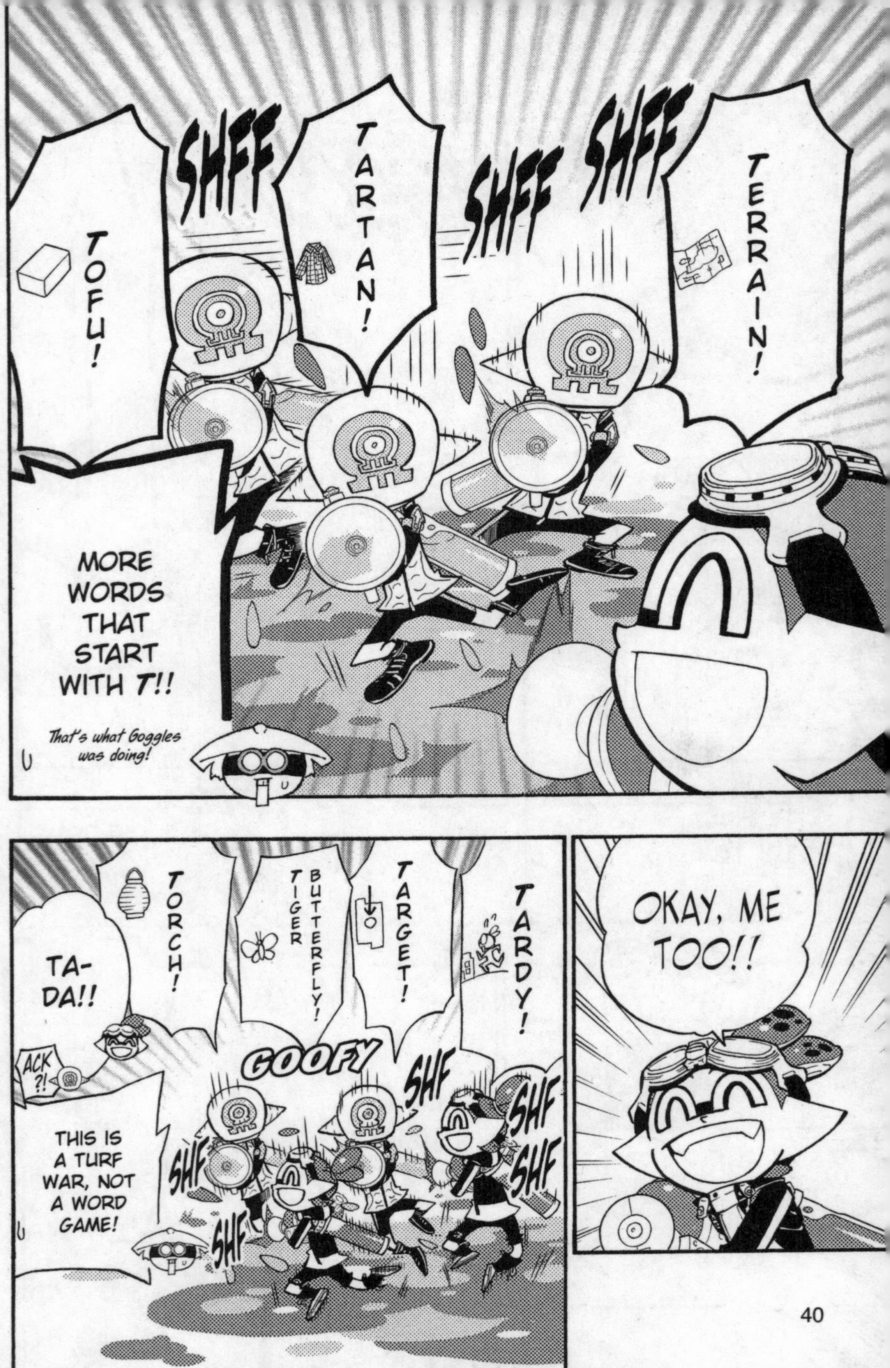
TERRAIN!
SHFF SHFF
TARTAN!
SHFF
TOFU!
MORE WORDS THAT START WITH *T*!!
That's what Goggles was doing!
OKAY, ME TOO!!
TARDY!
TARGET!
BUTTERFLY!
TIGER
TORCH!
TA-DA!!
GOOFY
SHF
SHF
SHF
ACK ?!
SHF
SHF
THIS IS A TURF WAR, NOT A WORD GAME!

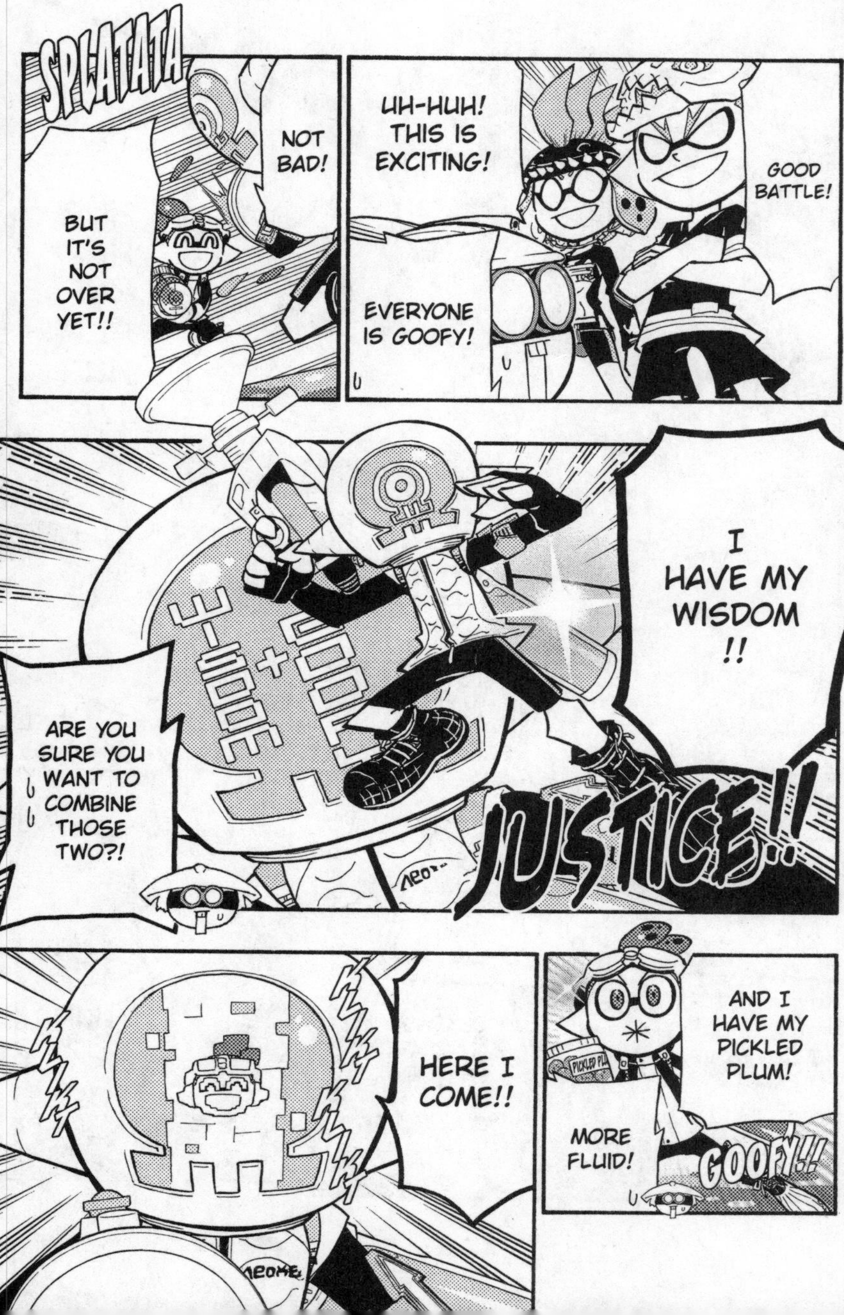
GOOD BATTLE!
UH-HUH! THIS IS EXCITING!
EVERYONE IS GOOFY!
SPLATATA
NOT BAD!
BUT IT'S NOT OVER YET!!
I HAVE MY WISDOM!!
JUSTICE!!
ARE YOU SURE YOU WANT TO COMBINE THOSE TWO?!
AND I HAVE MY PICKLED PLUM!
GOOFY!!
MORE FLUID!
HERE I COME!!

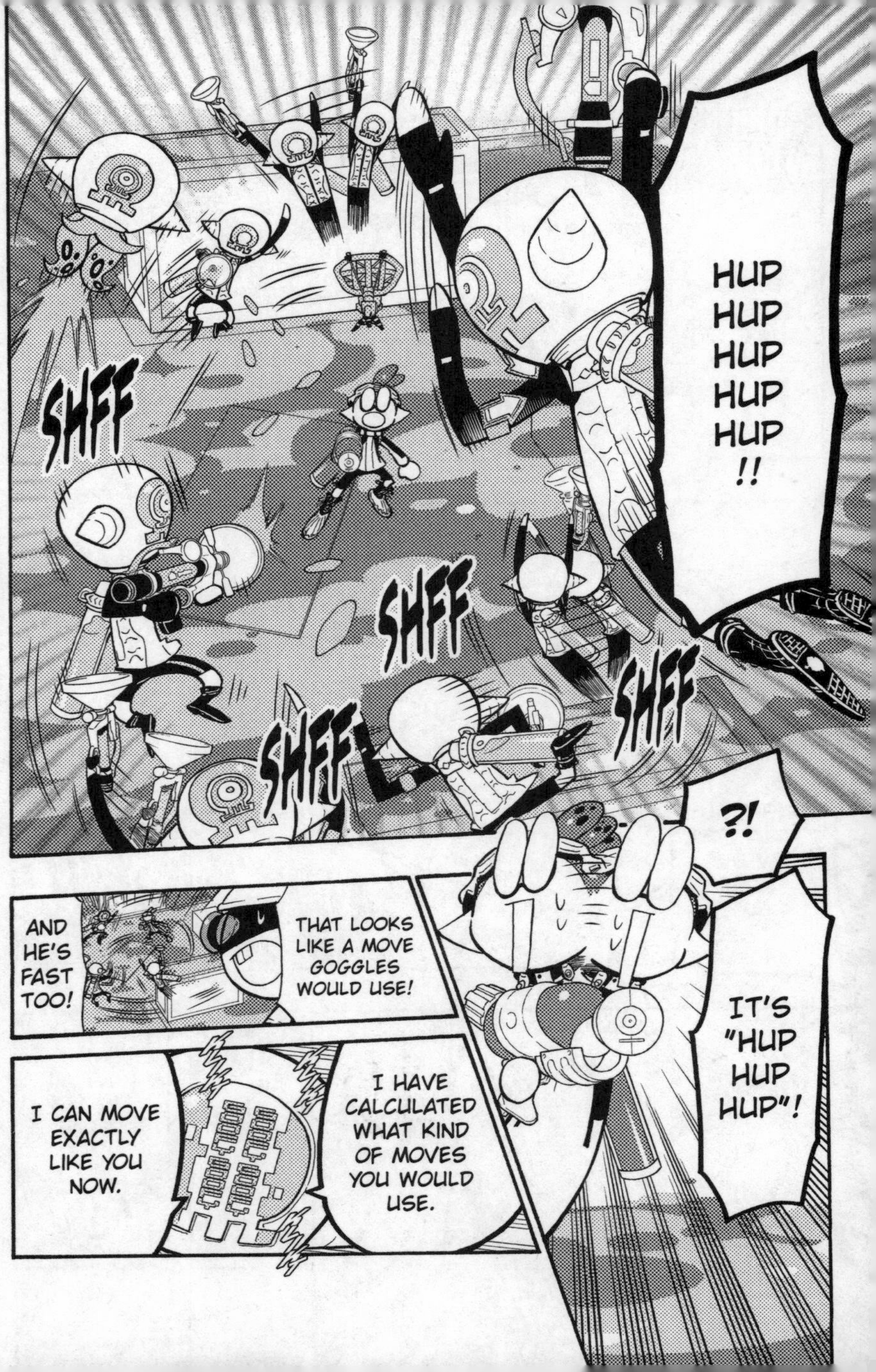
HUP HUP HUP HUP HUP !!
SHFF
SHFF
SHFF
SHFF
?!
IT'S "HUP HUP HUP"!
THAT LOOKS LIKE A MOVE GOGGLES WOULD USE!
AND HE'S FAST TOO!
I HAVE CALCULATED WHAT KIND OF MOVES YOU WOULD USE.
I CAN MOVE EXACTLY LIKE YOU NOW.

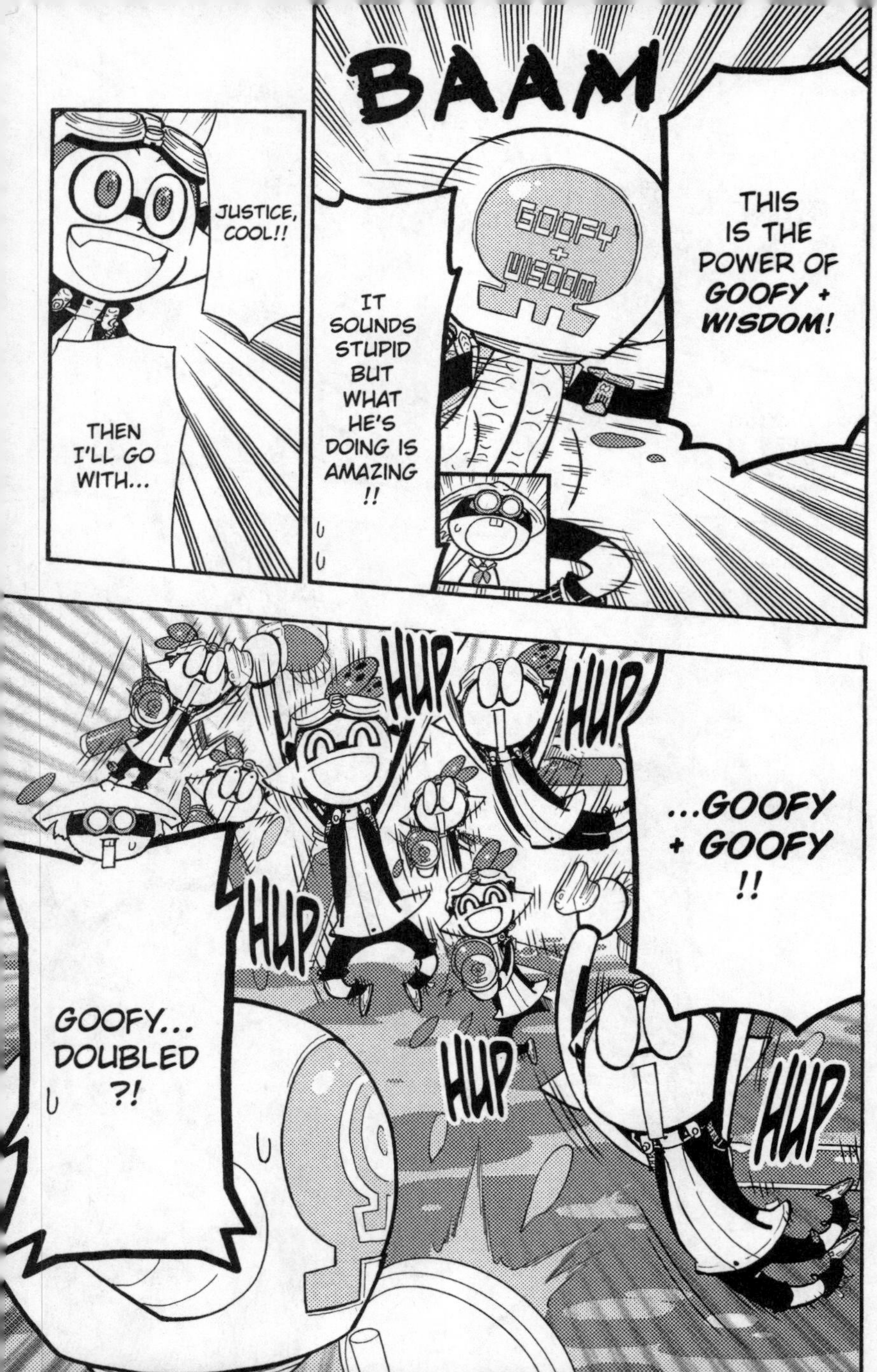
BAAM
THIS IS THE POWER OF GOOFY + WISDOM!
GOOFY + WISDOM
IT SOUNDS STUPID BUT WHAT HE'S DOING IS AMAZING!!
JUSTICE, COOL!!
THEN I'LL GO WITH...
...GOOFY + GOOFY!!
HUP
HUP
HUP
HUP
HUP
GOOFY... DOUBLED?!

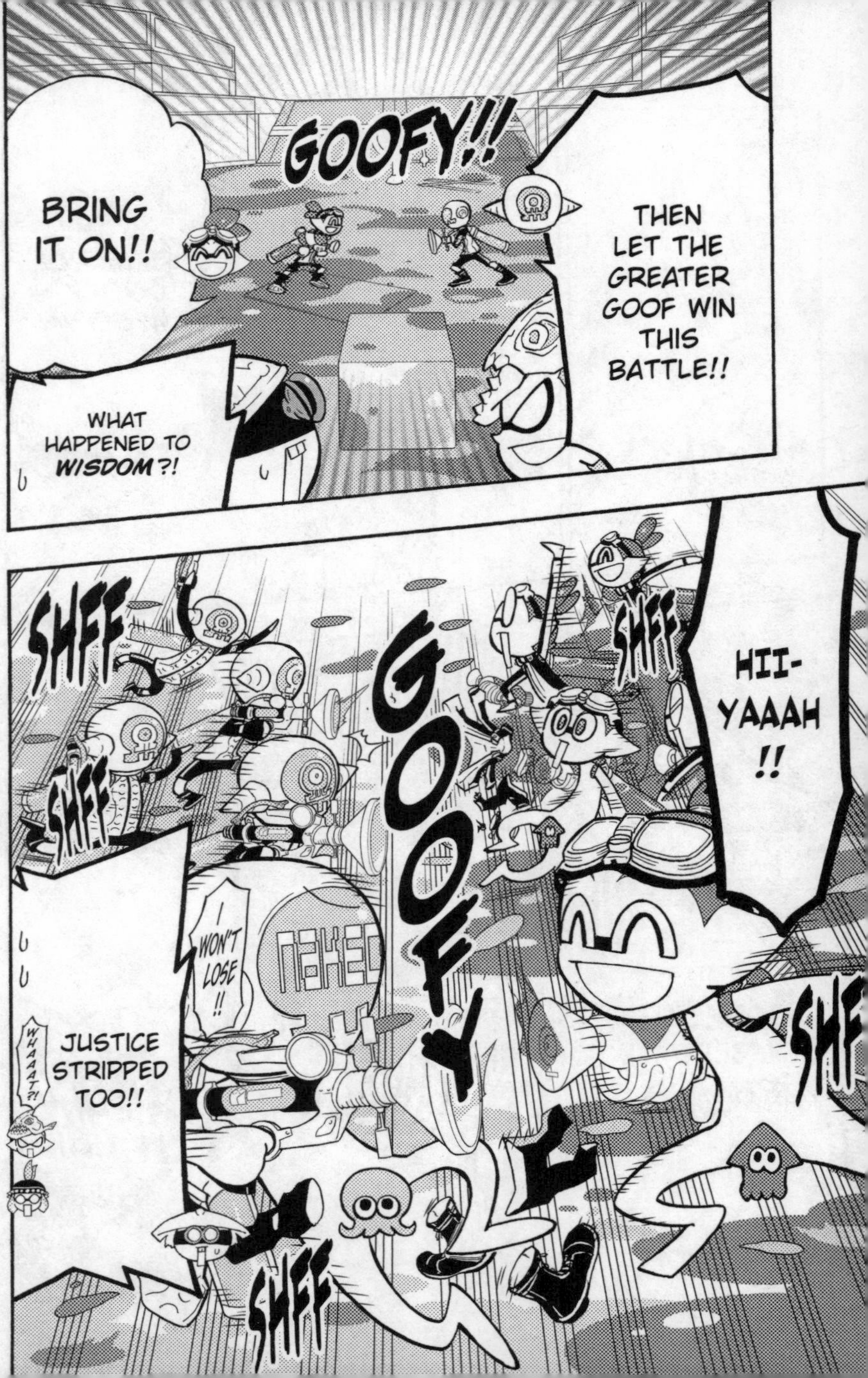
THEN LET THE GREATER GOOF WIN THIS BATTLE!!
GOOFY!!
BRING IT ON!!
WHAT HAPPENED TO WISDOM?!
HII-YAAAH!!
SHFF
SHFF
GOOFY
SHFF
SHFF
I WON'T LOSE!!
NAKED
JUSTICE STRIPPED TOO!!
WHAAAAT?!
SHFF
SHFF

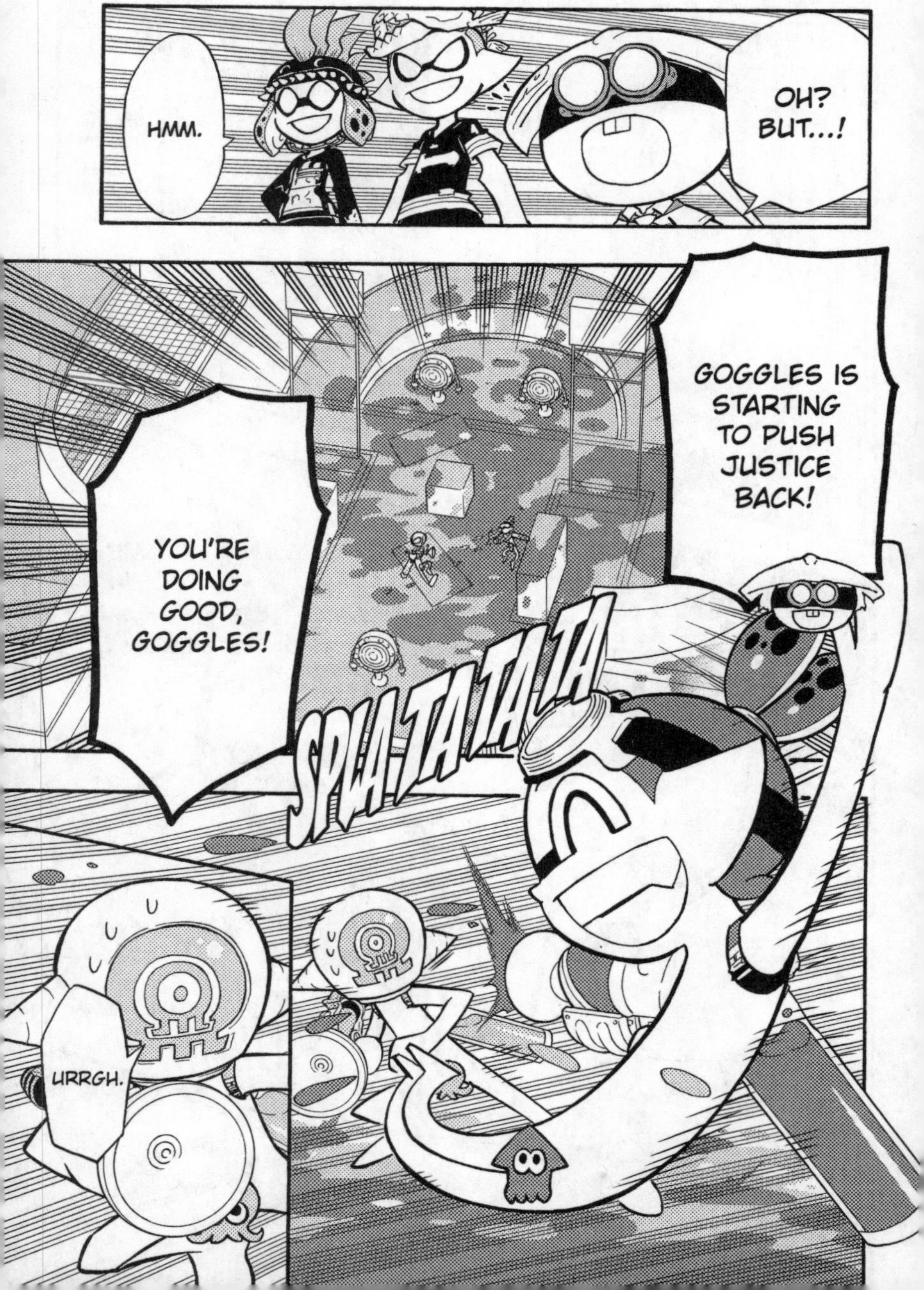
OH? BUT...!
HMM.
GOGGLES IS STARTING TO PUSH JUSTICE BACK!
YOU'RE DOING GOOD, GOGGLES!
SPLA-TA-TA-TA-TA
URRGH.

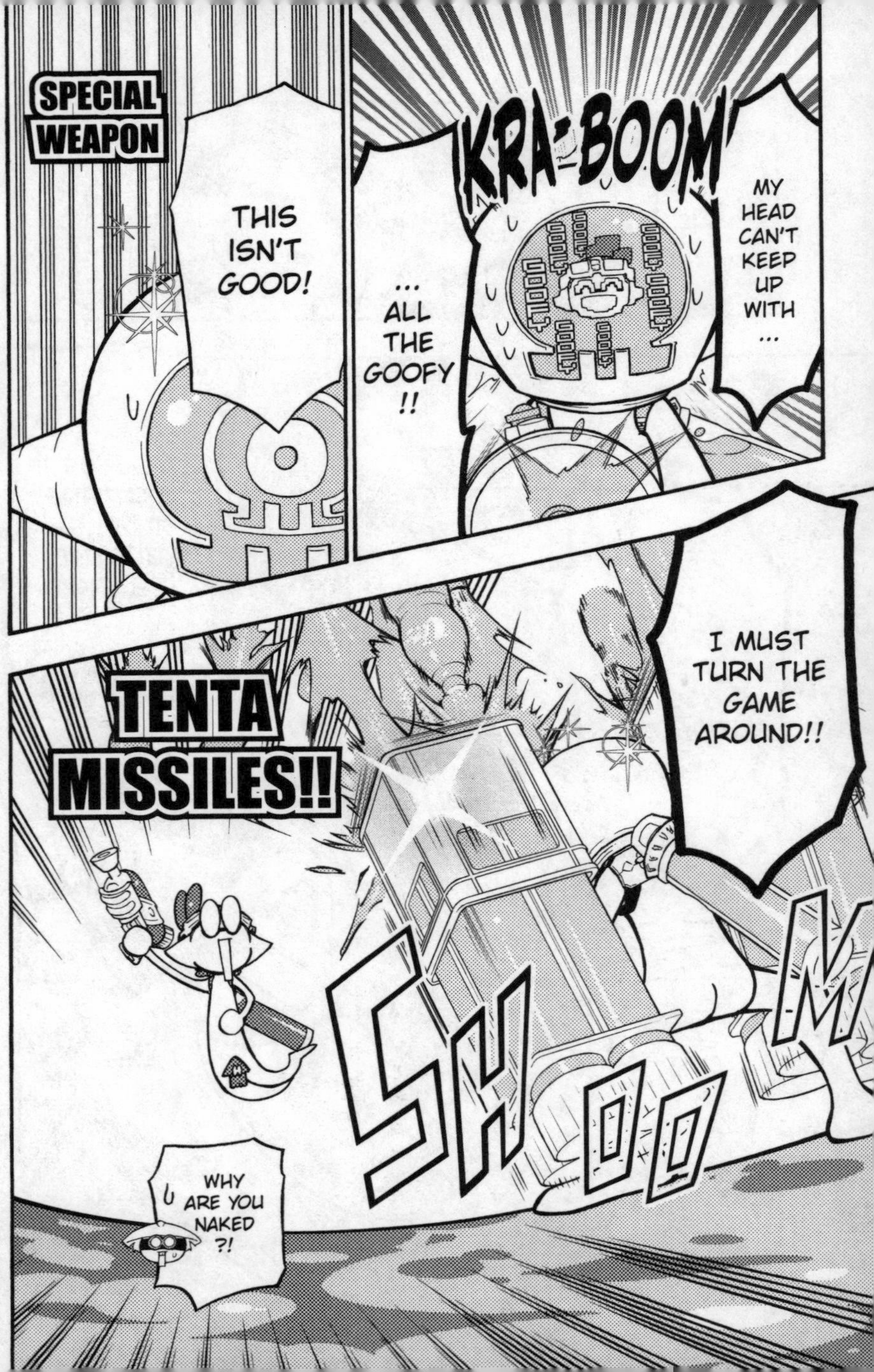
KRA-BOOM
MY HEAD CAN'T KEEP UP WITH ...
... ALL THE GOOFY !!
SPECIAL WEAPON
THIS ISN'T GOOD!
I MUST TURN THE GAME AROUND!!
TENTA MISSILES!!
SHOOM
WHY ARE YOU NAKED ?!

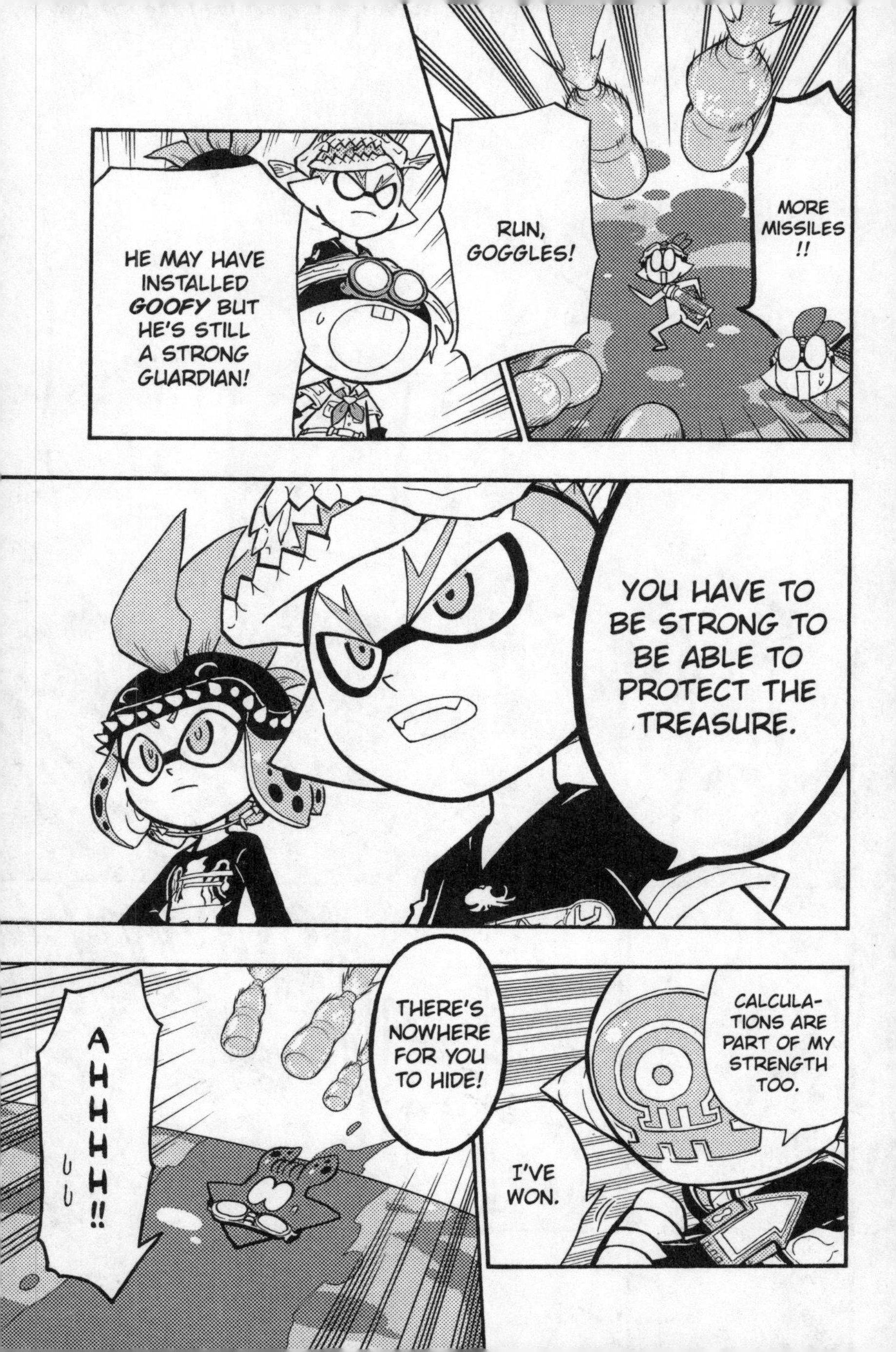
MORE MISSILES !!
RUN, GOGGLES!
HE MAY HAVE INSTALLED *GOOFY* BUT HE'S STILL A STRONG GUARDIAN!
YOU HAVE TO BE STRONG TO BE ABLE TO PROTECT THE TREASURE.
CALCULATIONS ARE PART OF MY STRENGTH TOO.
I'VE WON.
THERE'S NOWHERE FOR YOU TO HIDE!
AHHHH!!

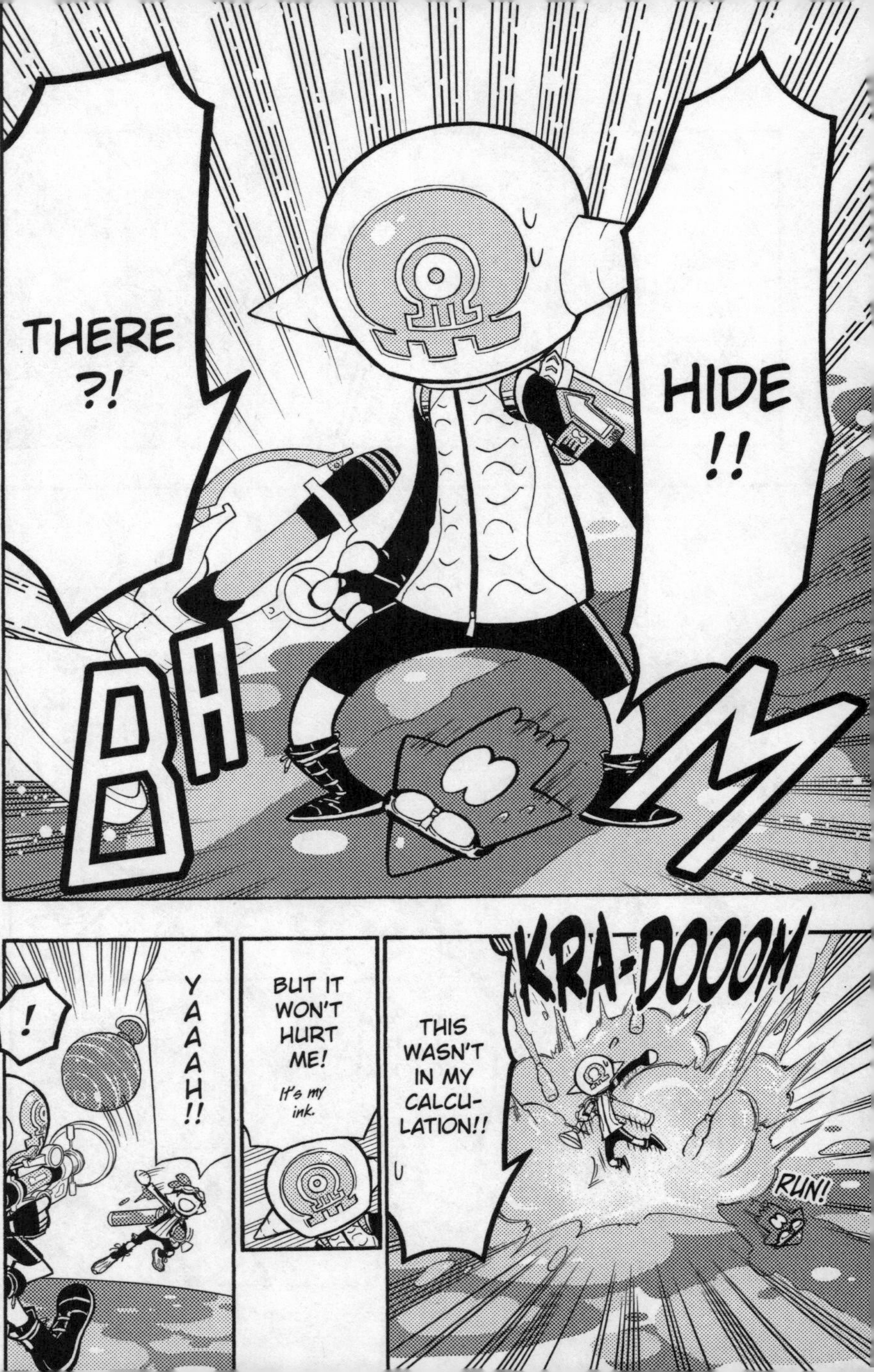
HIDE!!
THERE?!
BAM
KRA-DOOOM
THIS WASN'T IN MY CALCULATION!!
RUN!
BUT IT WON'T HURT ME!
It's my ink.
YAAAAH!!
!

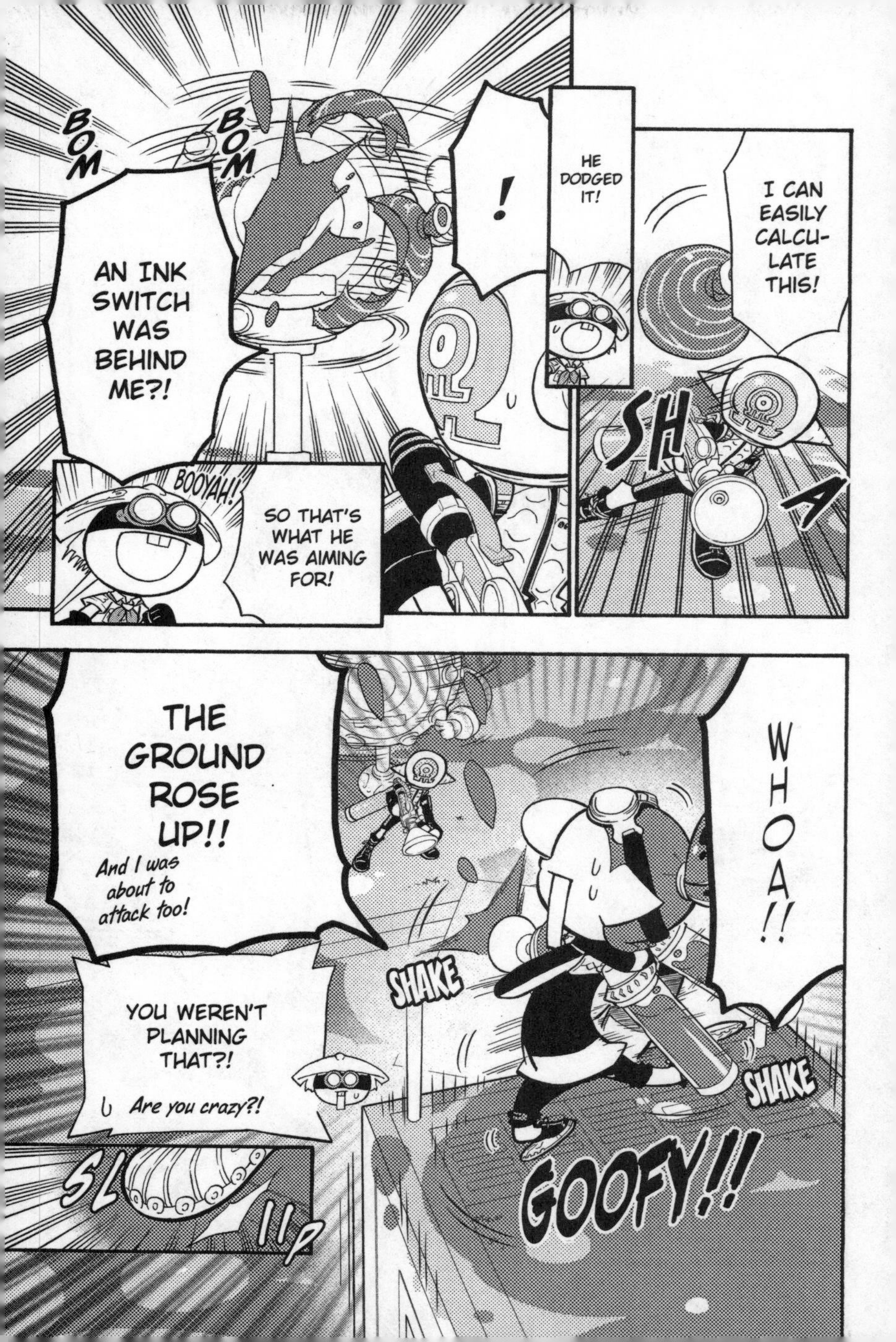
I CAN EASILY CALCULATE THIS!
SHA
HE DODGED IT!
!
BOM
BOM
AN INK SWITCH WAS BEHIND ME?!
BOOYAH!!
SO THAT'S WHAT HE WAS AIMING FOR!
WHOA!!
THE GROUND ROSE UP!!
And I was about to attack too!
SHAKE
SHAKE
YOU WEREN'T PLANNING THAT?!
Are you crazy?!
GOOFY!!
SLIP

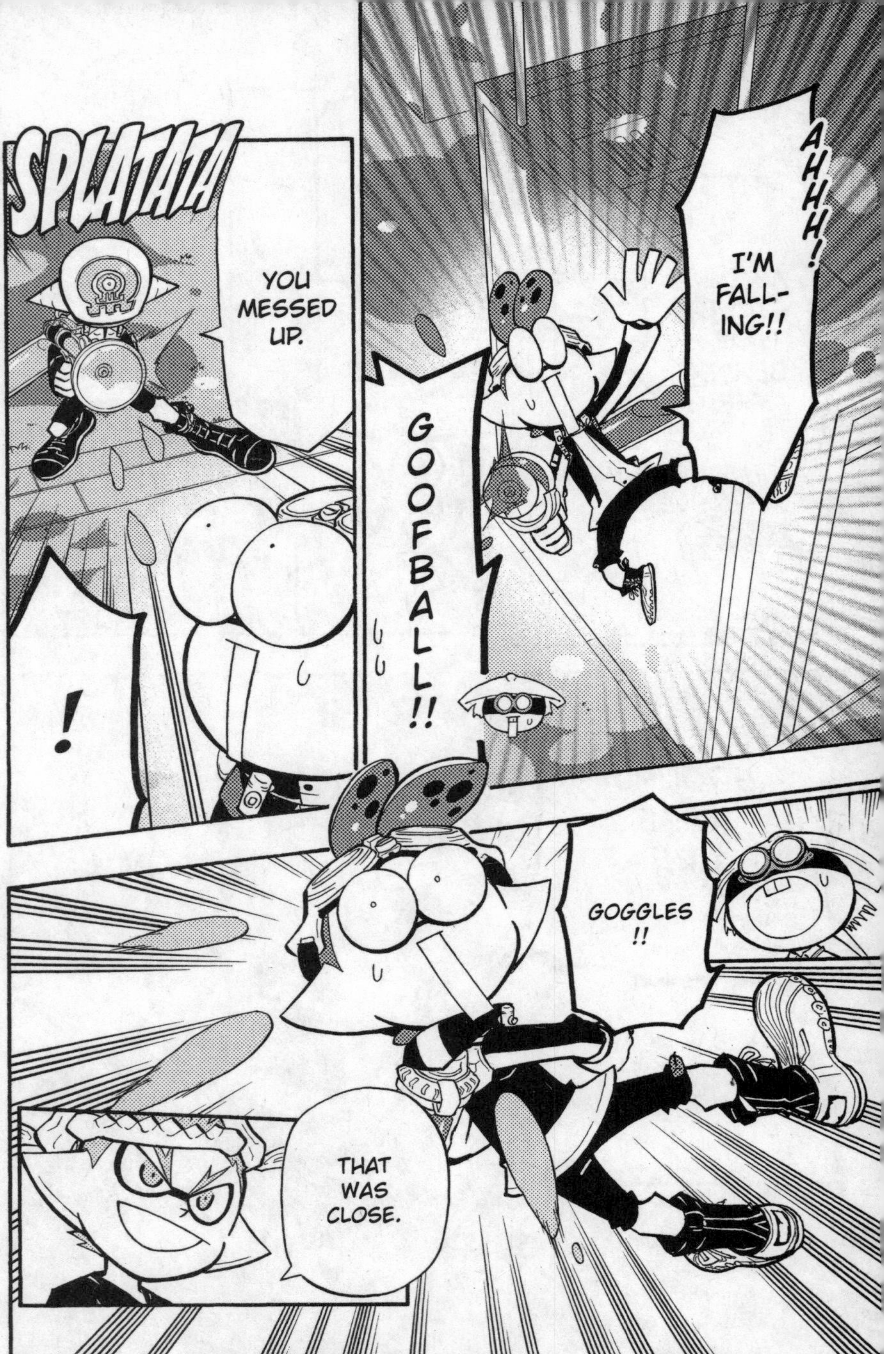
AHHHH!
I'M FALLING!!
GOOOFBALL!!
SPLATATA
YOU MESSED UP.
!
GOGGLES!!
THAT WAS CLOSE.

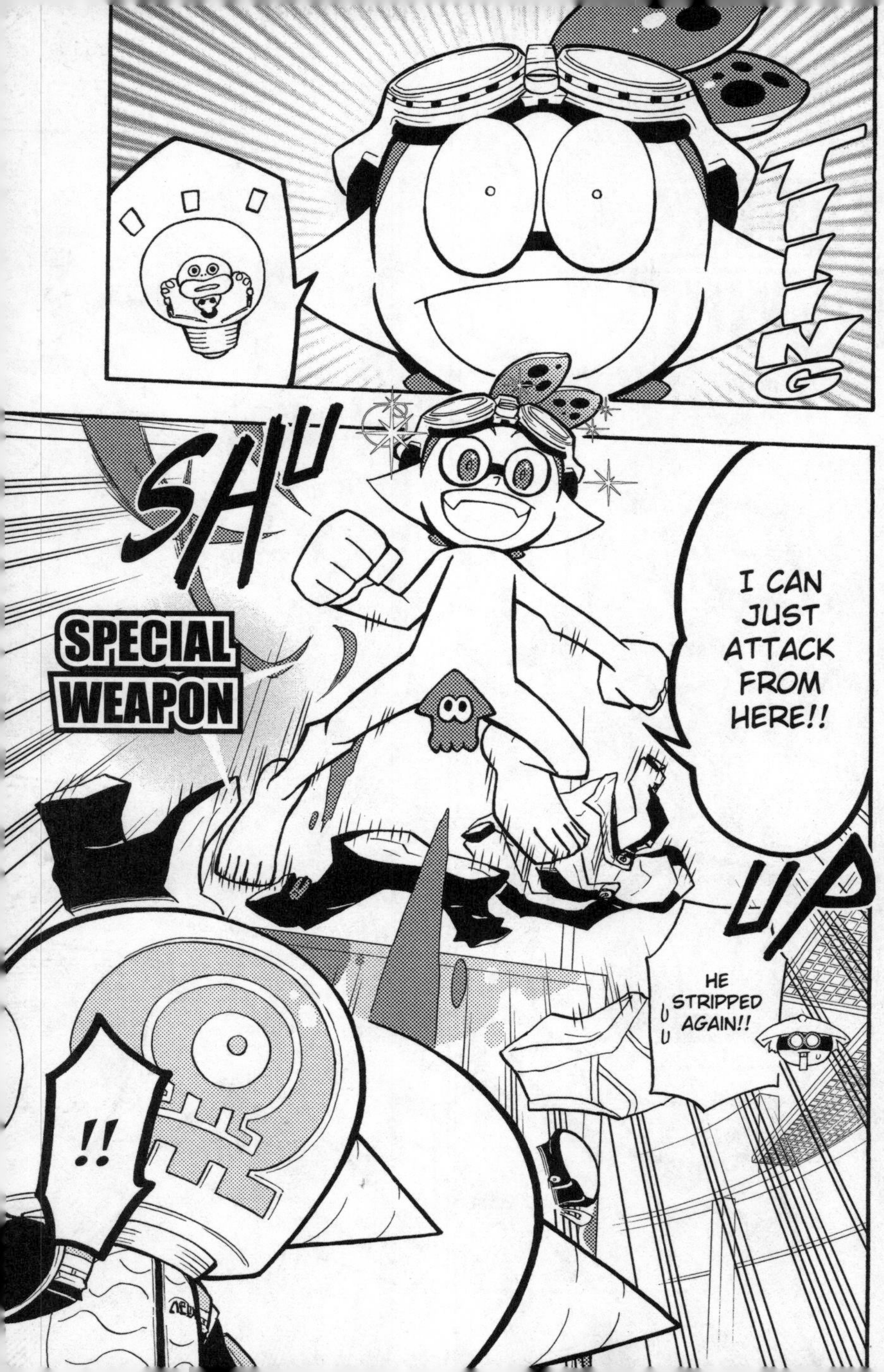

TIING
I CAN JUST ATTACK FROM HERE!!
SHU
UP
SPECIAL WEAPON
HE STRIPPED AGAIN!!
!!

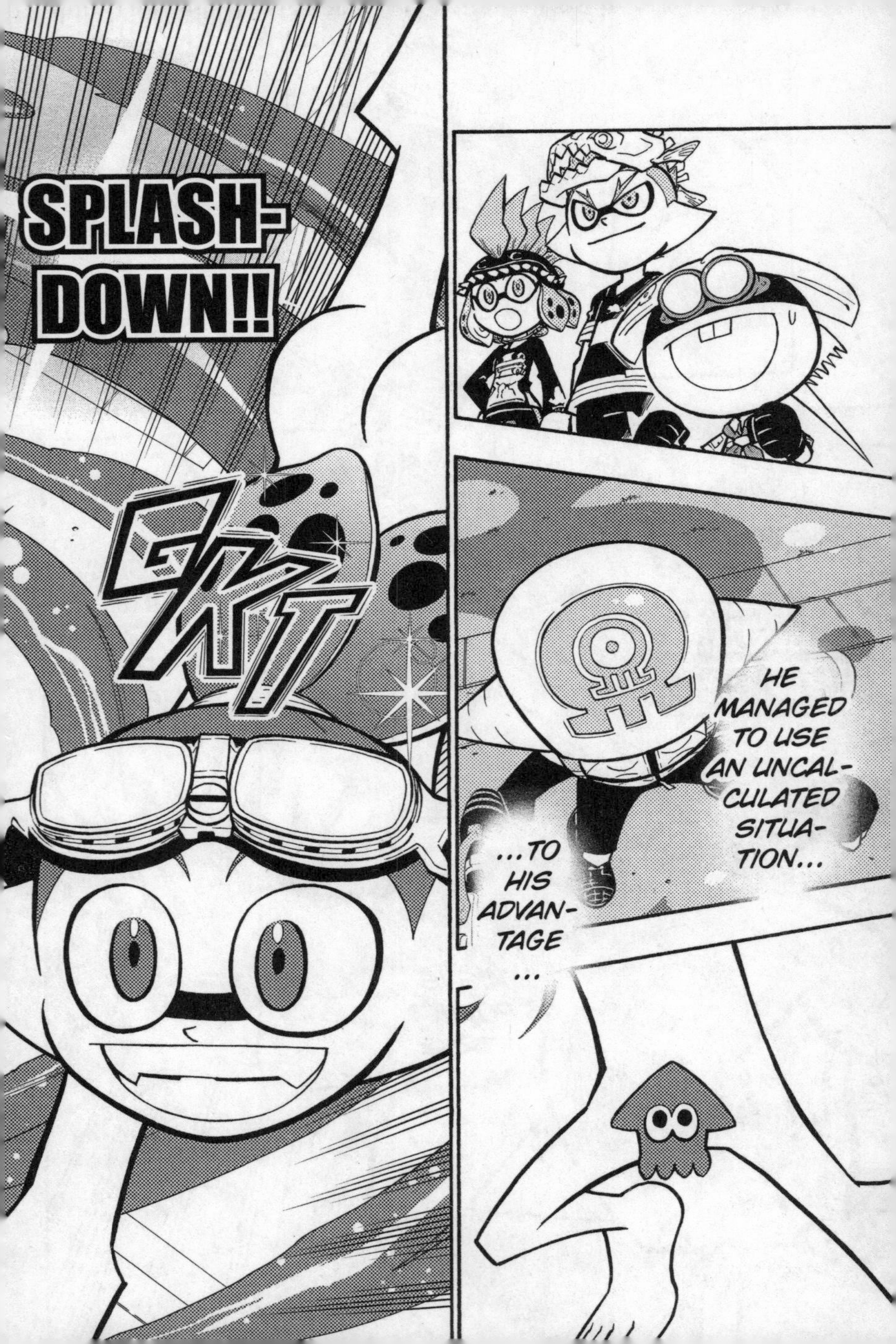
HE MANAGED TO USE AN UNCAL-CULATED SITUA-TION...
...TO HIS ADVAN-TAGE...
SPLASH-DOWN!!

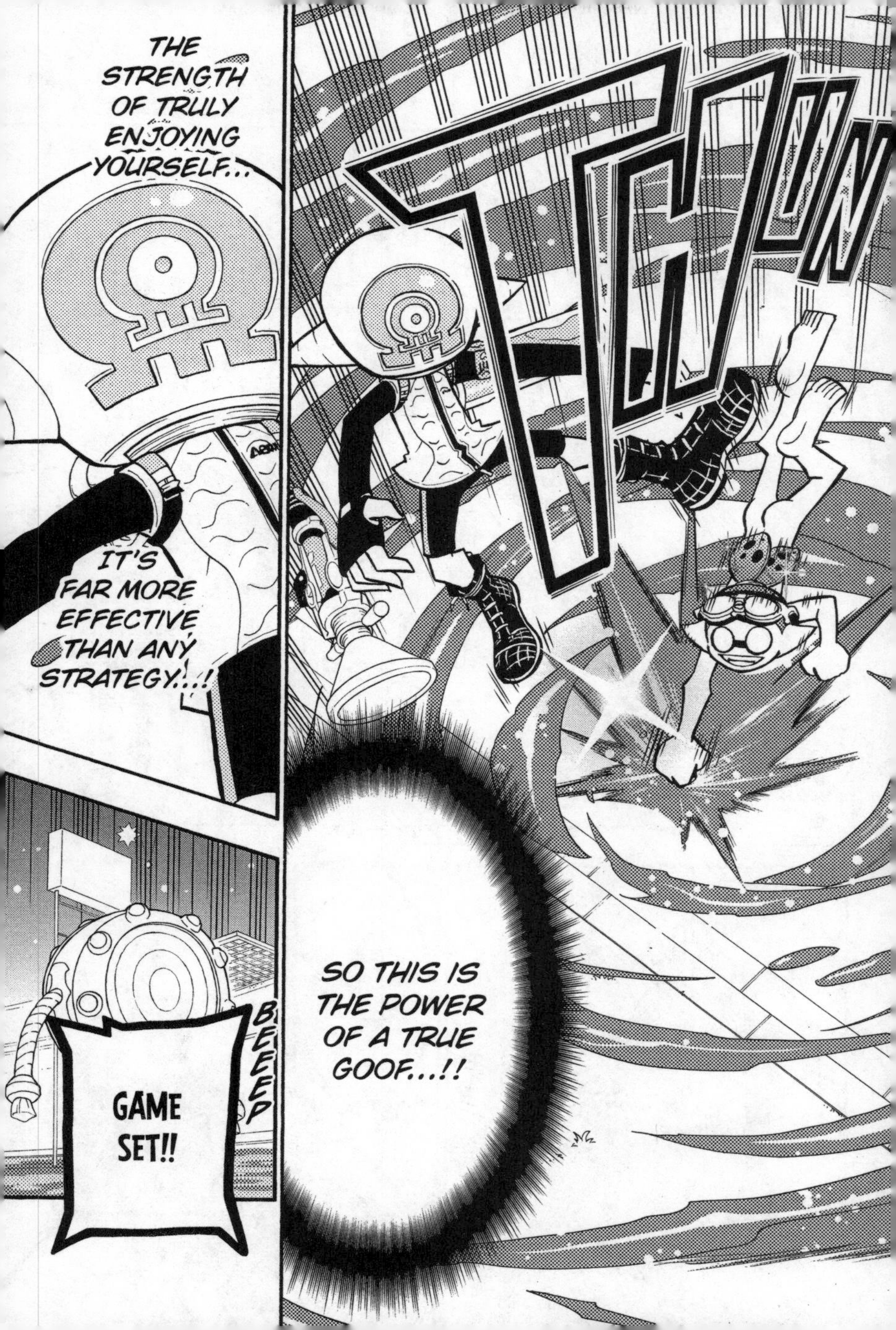
SO THIS IS THE POWER OF A TRUE GOOF...!!
THE STRENGTH OF TRULY ENJOYING YOURSELF...
IT'S FAR MORE EFFECTIVE THAN ANY STRATEGY...!
BEEEEP
GAME SET!!

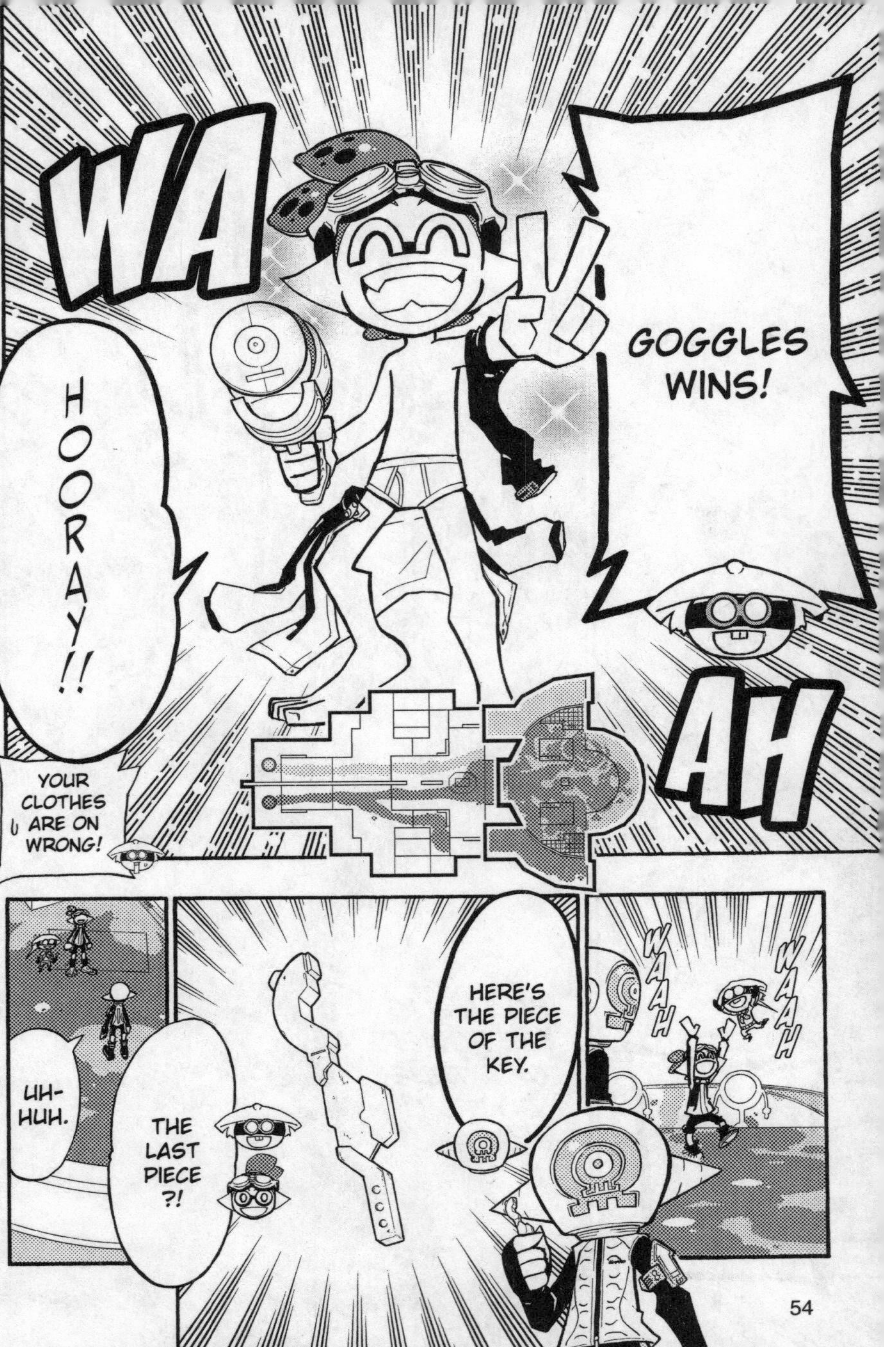
GOGGLES WINS!
WA
HOORAY!!
AH
YOUR CLOTHES ARE ON WRONG!
WAAH
WAAH
HERE'S THE PIECE OF THE KEY.
THE LAST PIECE?!
UH-HUH.

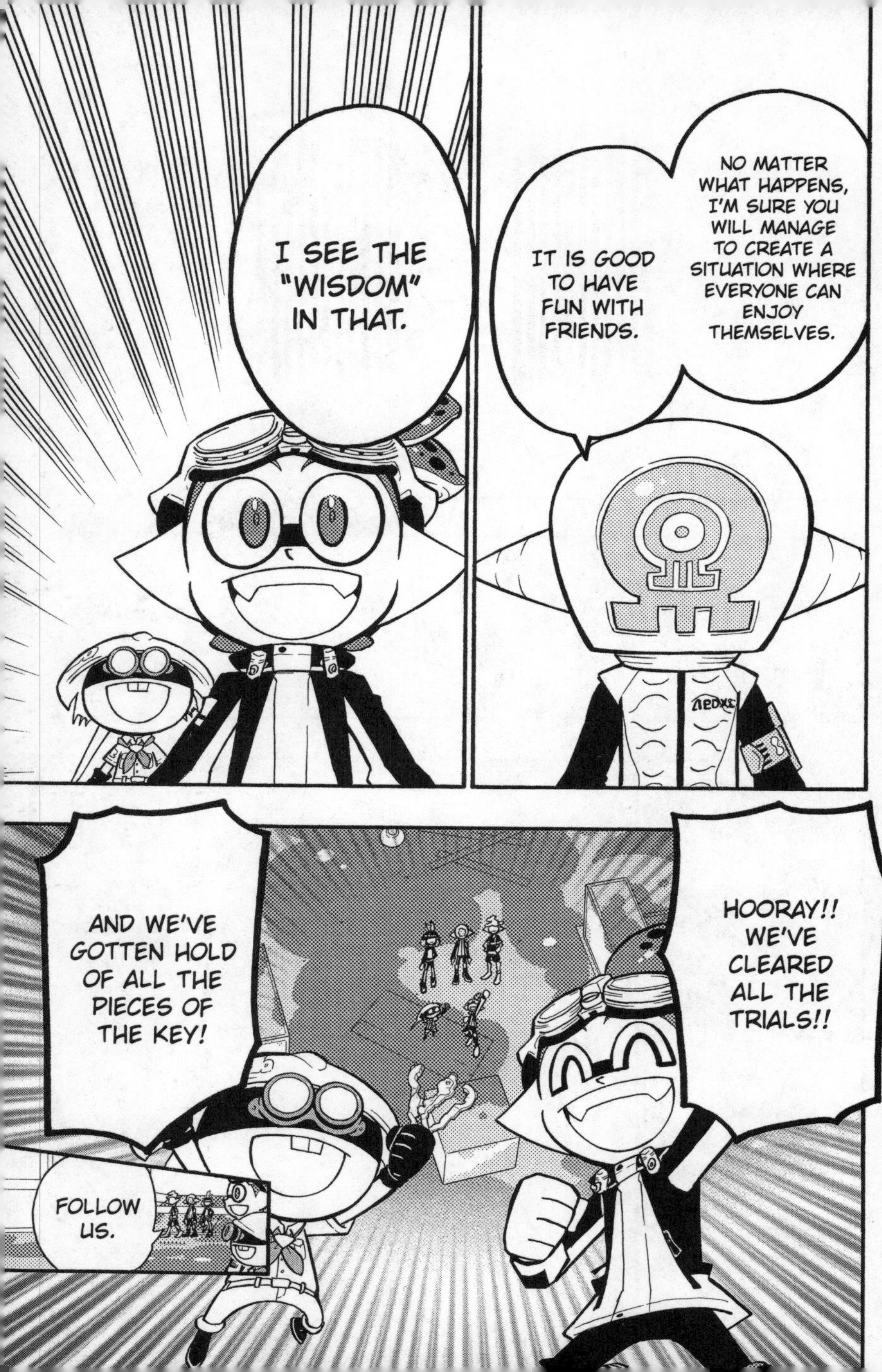
NO MATTER WHAT HAPPENS, I'M SURE YOU WILL MANAGE TO CREATE A SITUATION WHERE EVERYONE CAN ENJOY THEMSELVES.
IT IS GOOD TO HAVE FUN WITH FRIENDS.
I SEE THE "WISDOM" IN THAT.
HOORAY!! WE'VE CLEARED ALL THE TRIALS!!
AND WE'VE GOTTEN HOLD OF ALL THE PIECES OF THE KEY!
FOLLOW US.

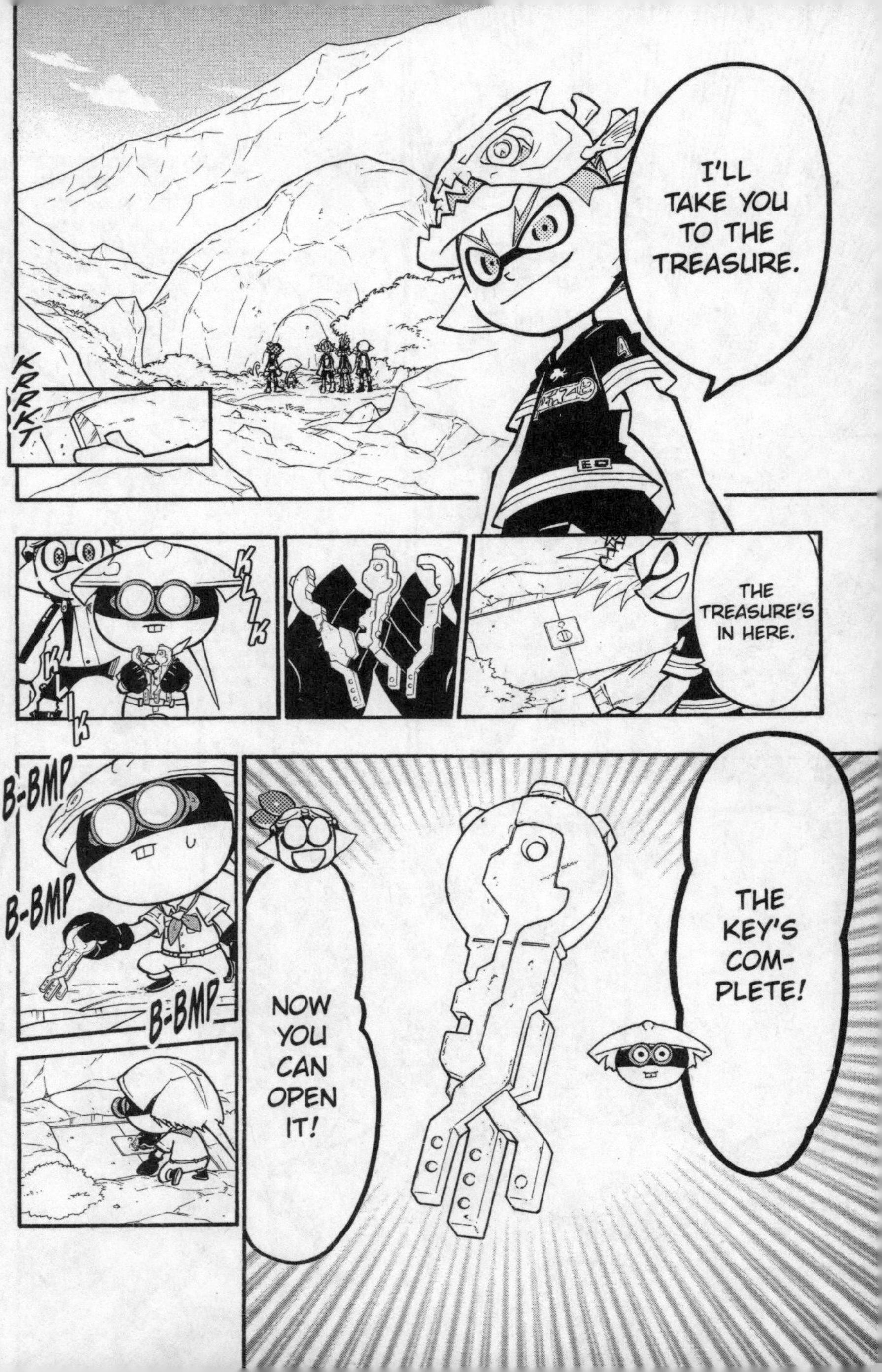
I'LL TAKE YOU TO THE TREASURE.
KRRKT
THE TREASURE'S IN HERE.
KLIK
KLIK
THE KEY'S COM- PLETE!
NOW YOU CAN OPEN IT!
B-BMP
B-BMP
B-BMP

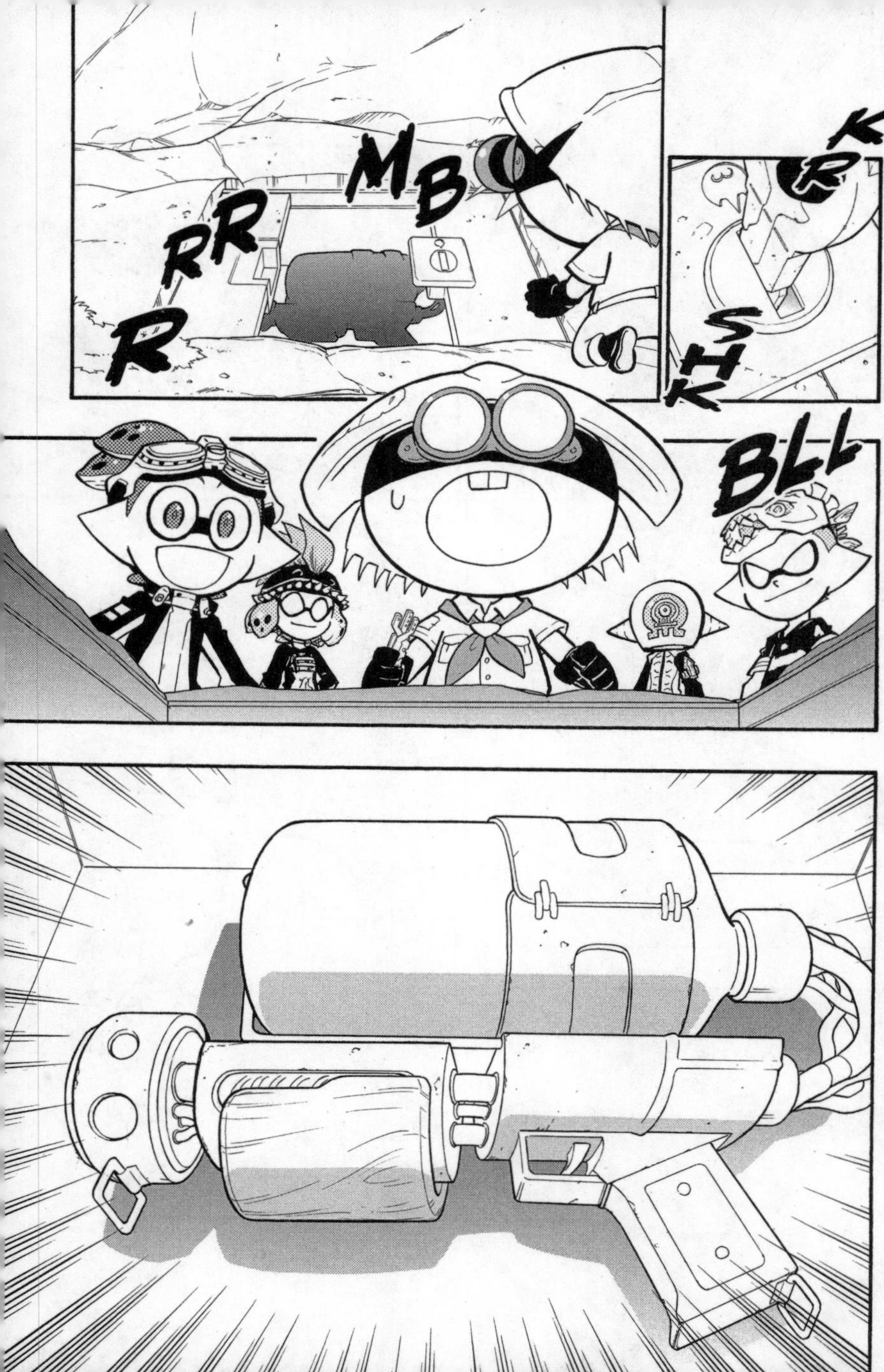

KR
SHK
RRRMB
BLL

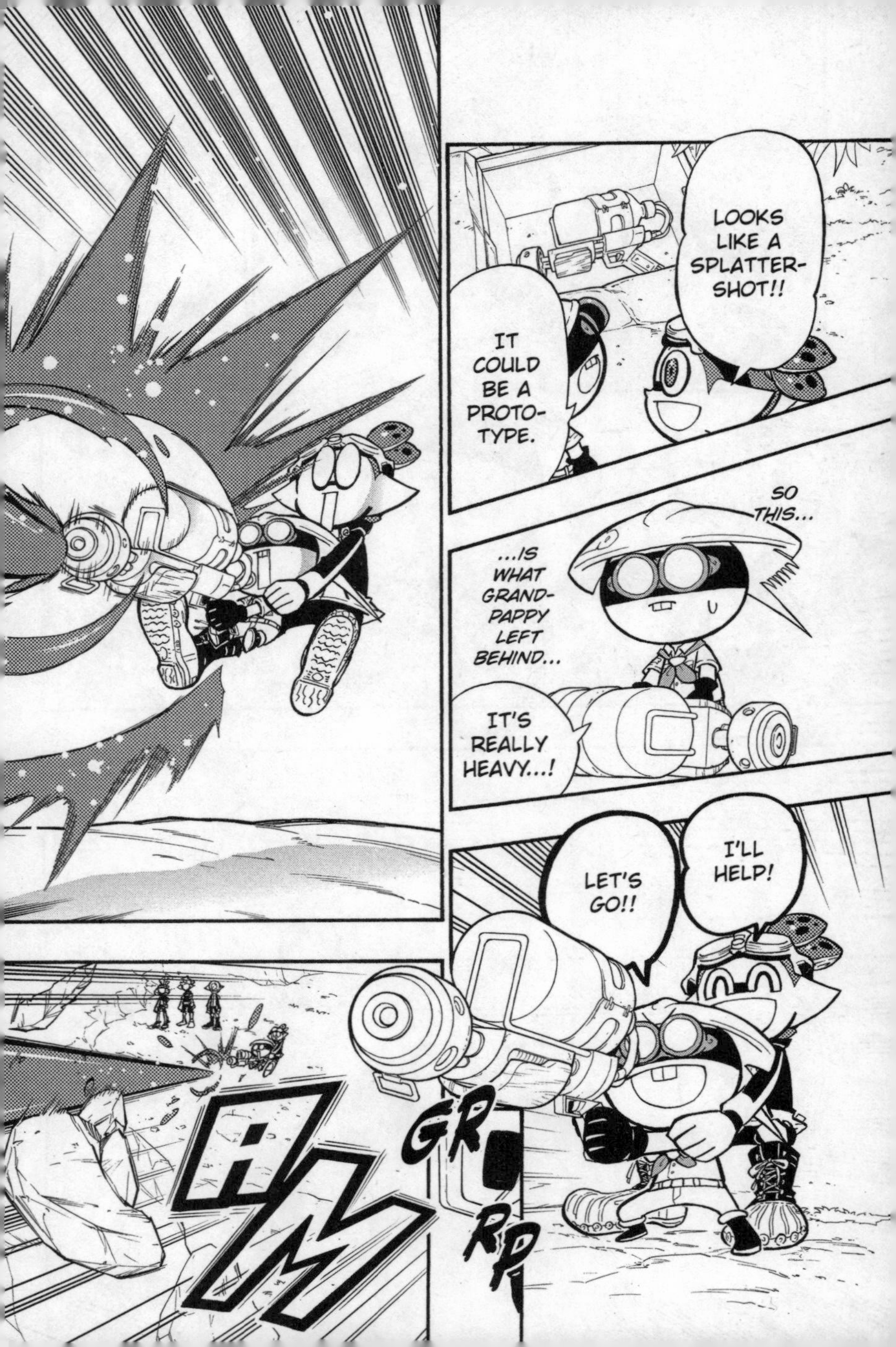
LOOKS LIKE A SPLATTER-SHOT!!
IT COULD BE A PROTO-TYPE.
SO THIS...
...IS WHAT GRAND-PAPPY LEFT BEHIND...
IT'S REALLY HEAVY...!
I'LL HELP!
LET'S GO!!

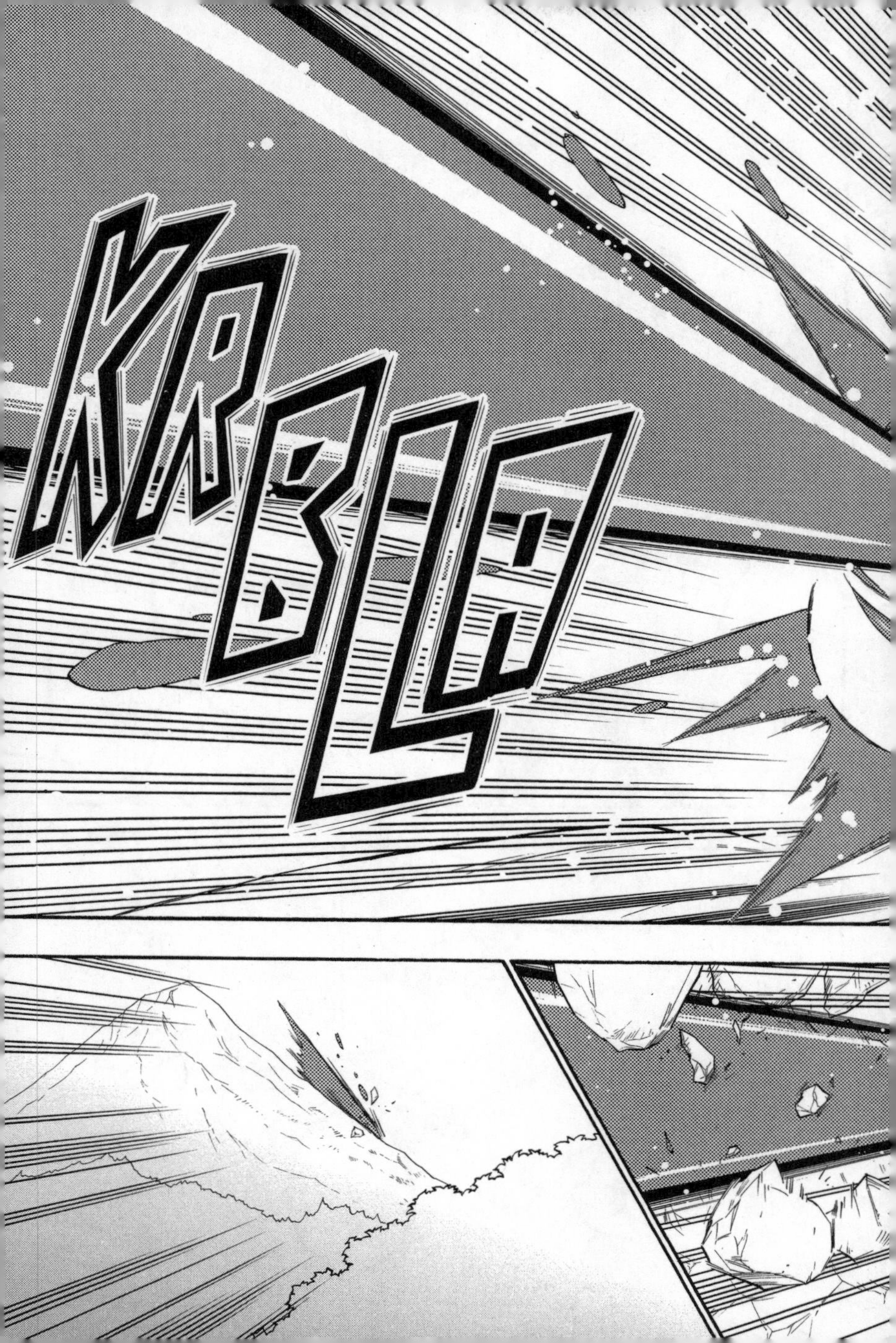
KRBLA

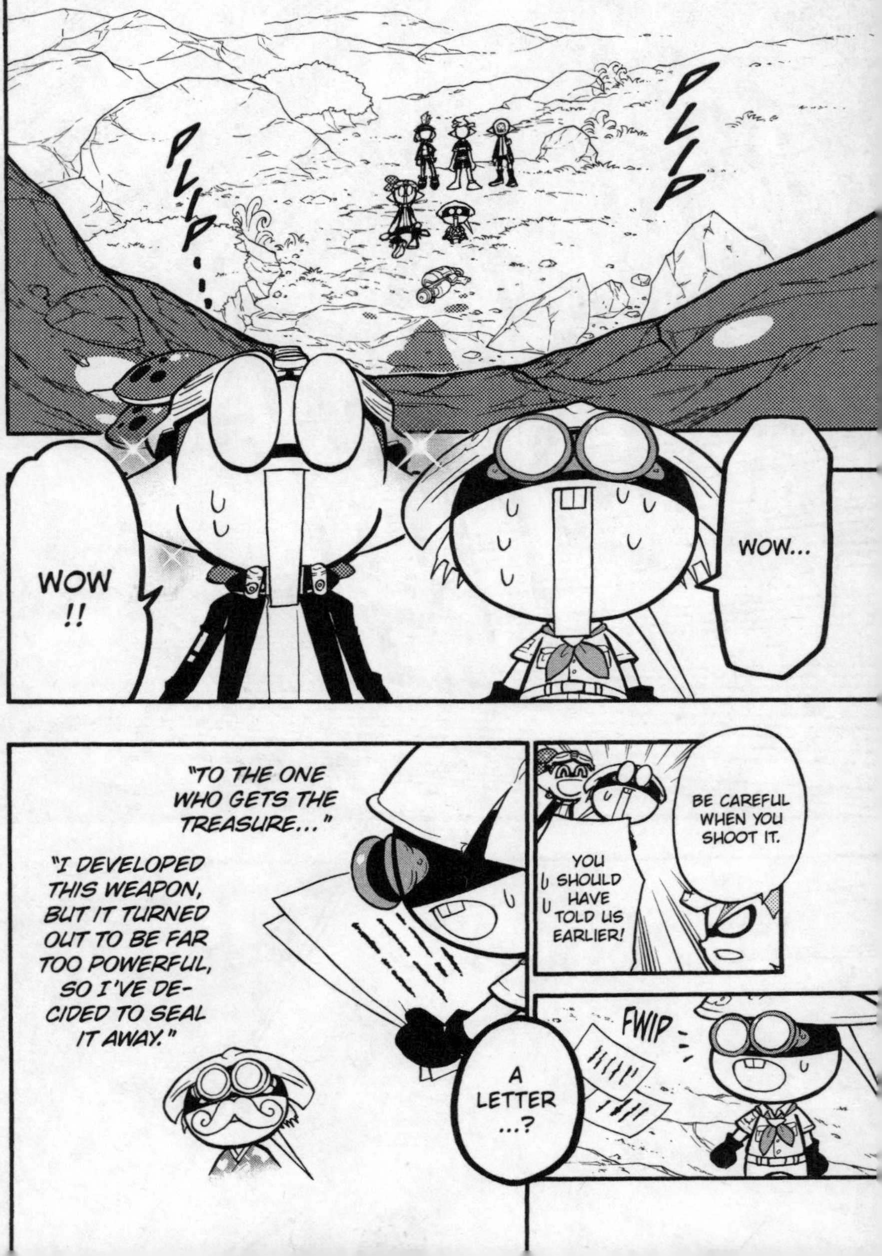
PLIP
PLIP...
WOW...
WOW !!
BE CAREFUL WHEN YOU SHOOT IT.
YOU SHOULD HAVE TOLD US EARLIER!
FWIP
A LETTER ...?
"TO THE ONE WHO GETS THE TREASURE..."
"I DEVELOPED THIS WEAPON, BUT IT TURNED OUT TO BE FAR TOO POWERFUL, SO I'VE DE-CIDED TO SEAL IT AWAY."

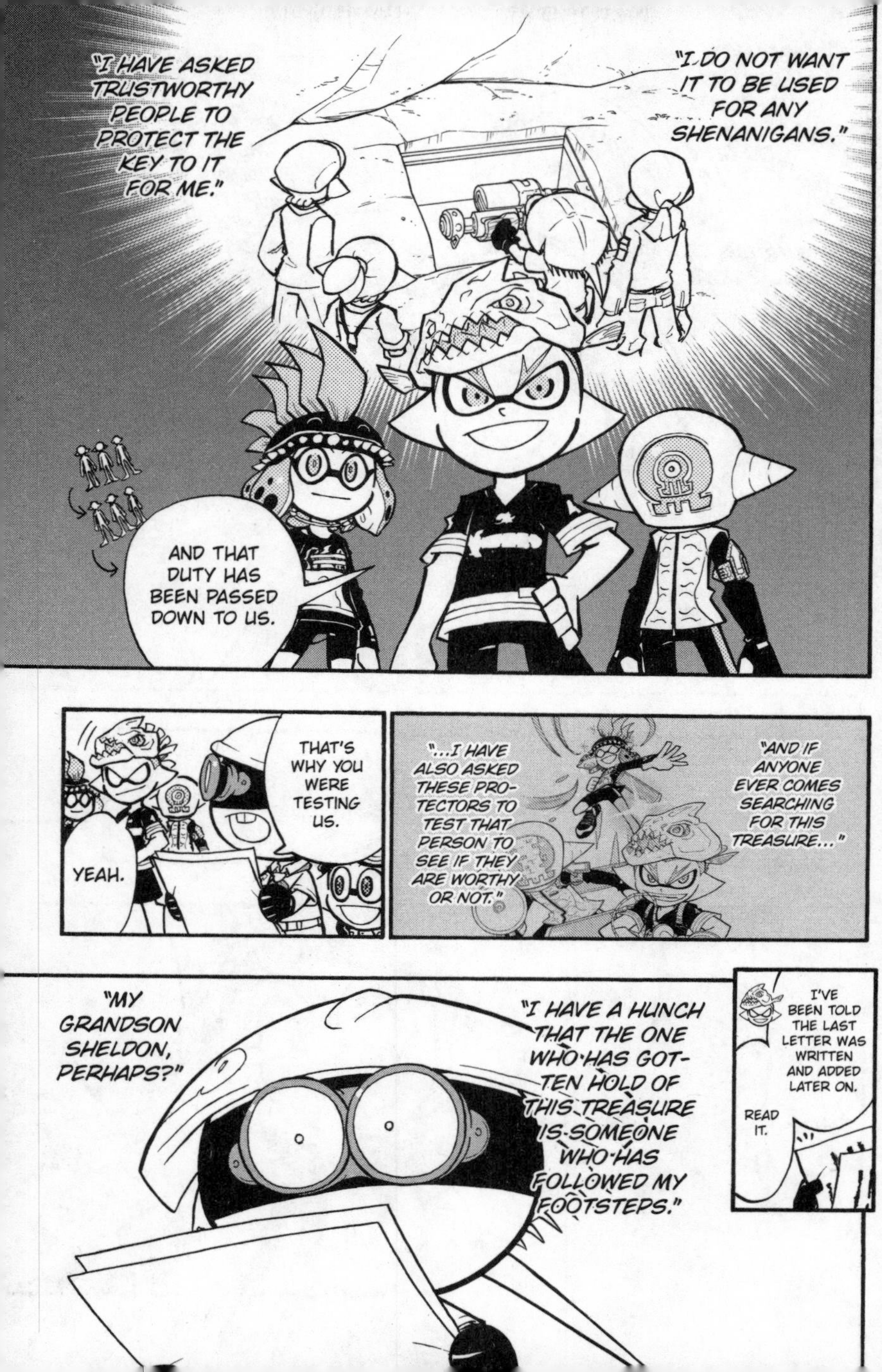
"I DO NOT WANT IT TO BE USED FOR ANY SHENANIGANS."
"I HAVE ASKED TRUSTWORTHY PEOPLE TO PROTECT THE KEY TO IT FOR ME."
AND THAT DUTY HAS BEEN PASSED DOWN TO US.
"AND IF ANYONE EVER COMES SEARCHING FOR THIS TREASURE..."
"...I HAVE ALSO ASKED THESE PRO-TECTORS TO TEST THAT PERSON TO SEE IF THEY ARE WORTHY OR NOT."
THAT'S WHY YOU WERE TESTING US.
YEAH.
I'VE BEEN TOLD THE LAST LETTER WAS WRITTEN AND ADDED LATER ON.
READ IT.
"I HAVE A HUNCH THAT THE ONE WHO HAS GOT-TEN HOLD OF THIS TREASURE IS SOMEONE WHO HAS FOLLOWED MY FOOTSTEPS."
"MY GRANDSON SHELDON, PERHAPS?"

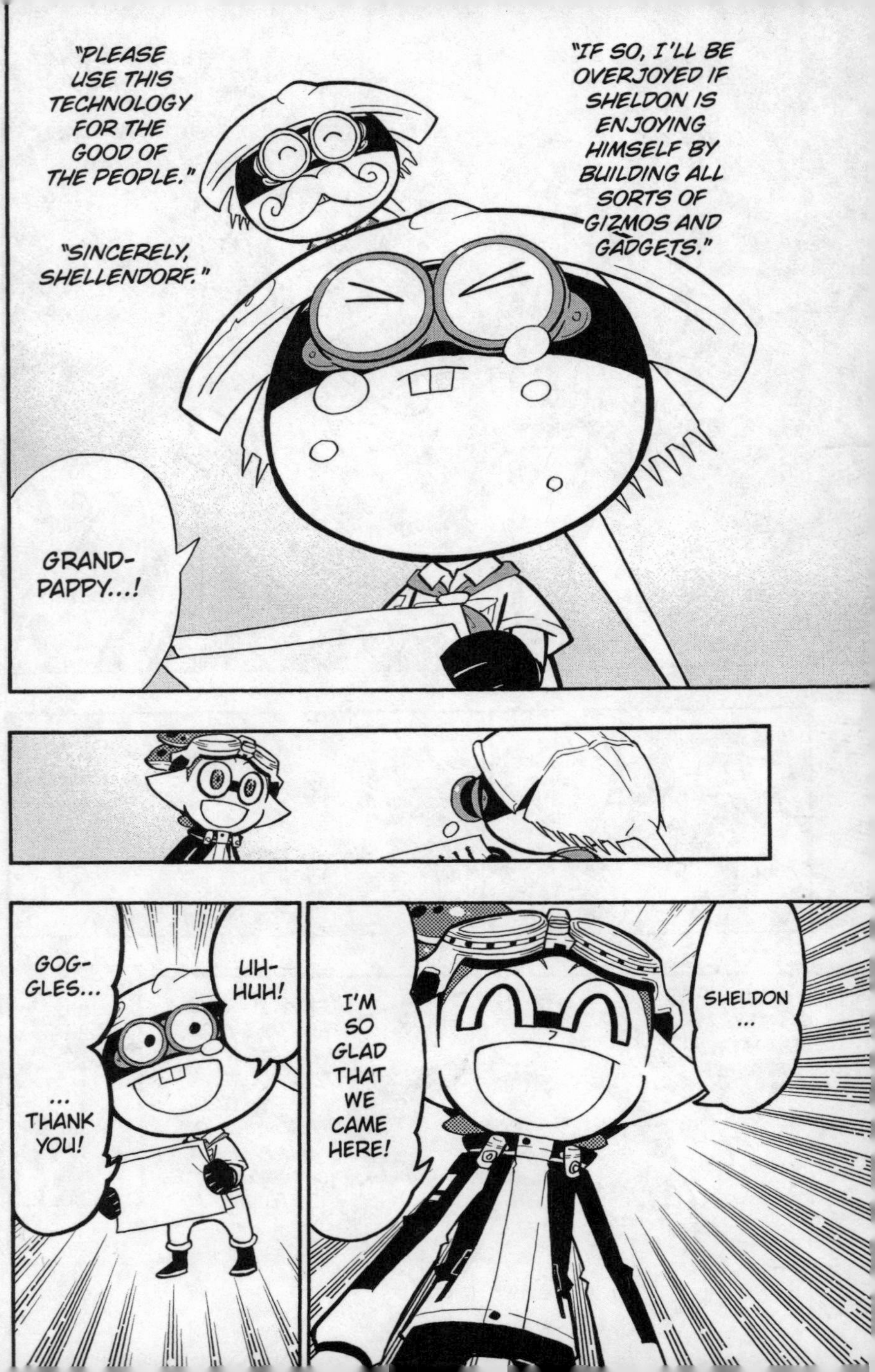
"IF SO, I'LL BE OVERJOYED IF SHELDON IS ENJOYING HIMSELF BY BUILDING ALL SORTS OF GIZMOS AND GADGETS."
"PLEASE USE THIS TECHNOLOGY FOR THE GOOD OF THE PEOPLE."
"SINCERELY, SHELLENDORF."
GRAND-PAPPY...!
SHELDON ...
I'M SO GLAD THAT WE CAME HERE!
UH-HUH!
GOG-GLES...
... THANK YOU!

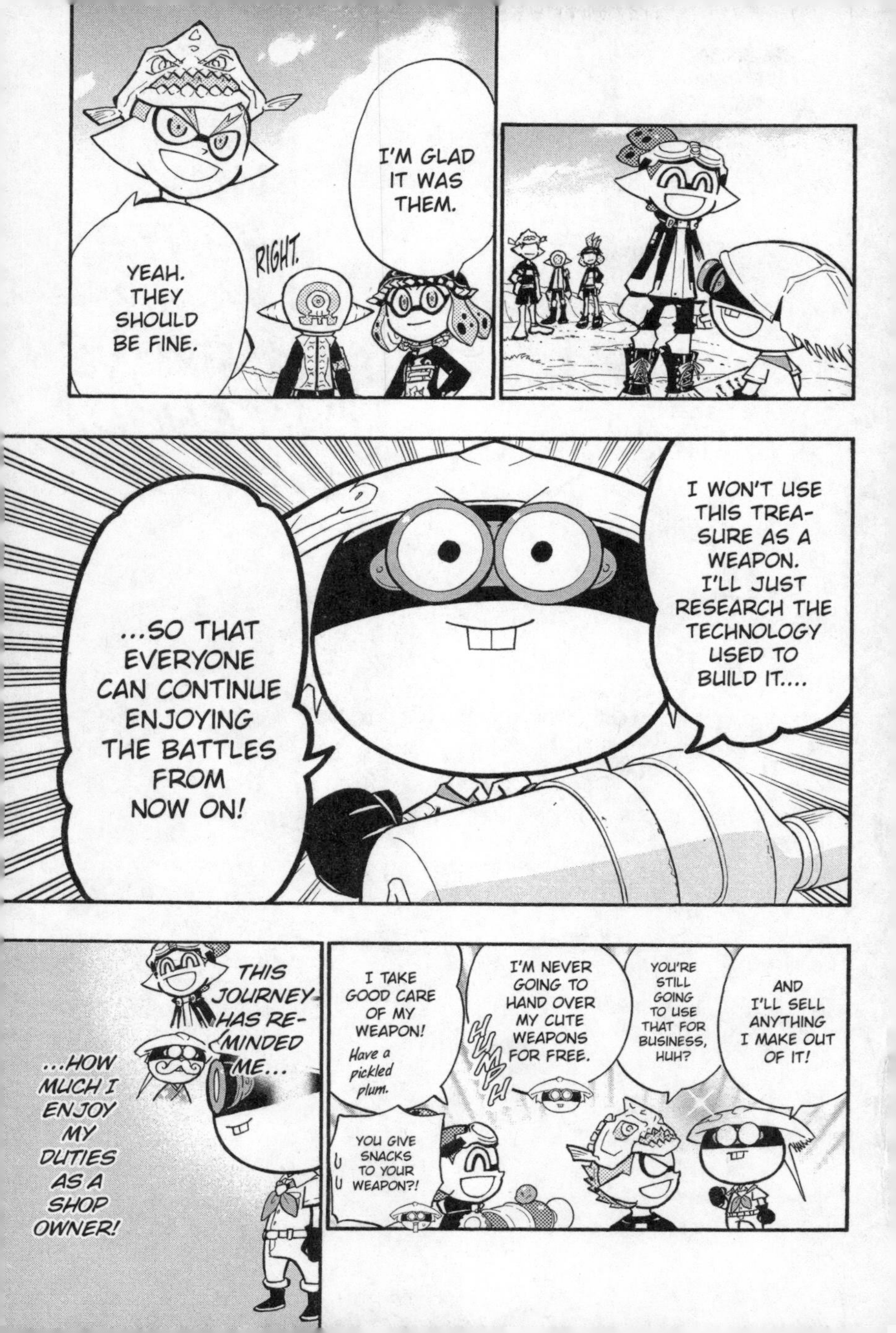
I'M GLAD IT WAS THEM.
RIGHT.
YEAH. THEY SHOULD BE FINE.
I WON'T USE THIS TREASURE AS A WEAPON. I'LL JUST RESEARCH THE TECHNOLOGY USED TO BUILD IT....
...SO THAT EVERYONE CAN CONTINUE ENJOYING THE BATTLES FROM NOW ON!
AND I'LL SELL ANYTHING I MAKE OUT OF IT!
YOU'RE STILL GOING TO USE THAT FOR BUSINESS, HUH?
I'M NEVER GOING TO HAND OVER MY CUTE WEAPONS FOR FREE.
HUMPH
I TAKE GOOD CARE OF MY WEAPON! Have a pickled plum.
YOU GIVE SNACKS TO YOUR WEAPON?!
THIS JOURNEY HAS REMINDED ME...
...HOW MUCH I ENJOY MY DUTIES AS A SHOP OWNER!

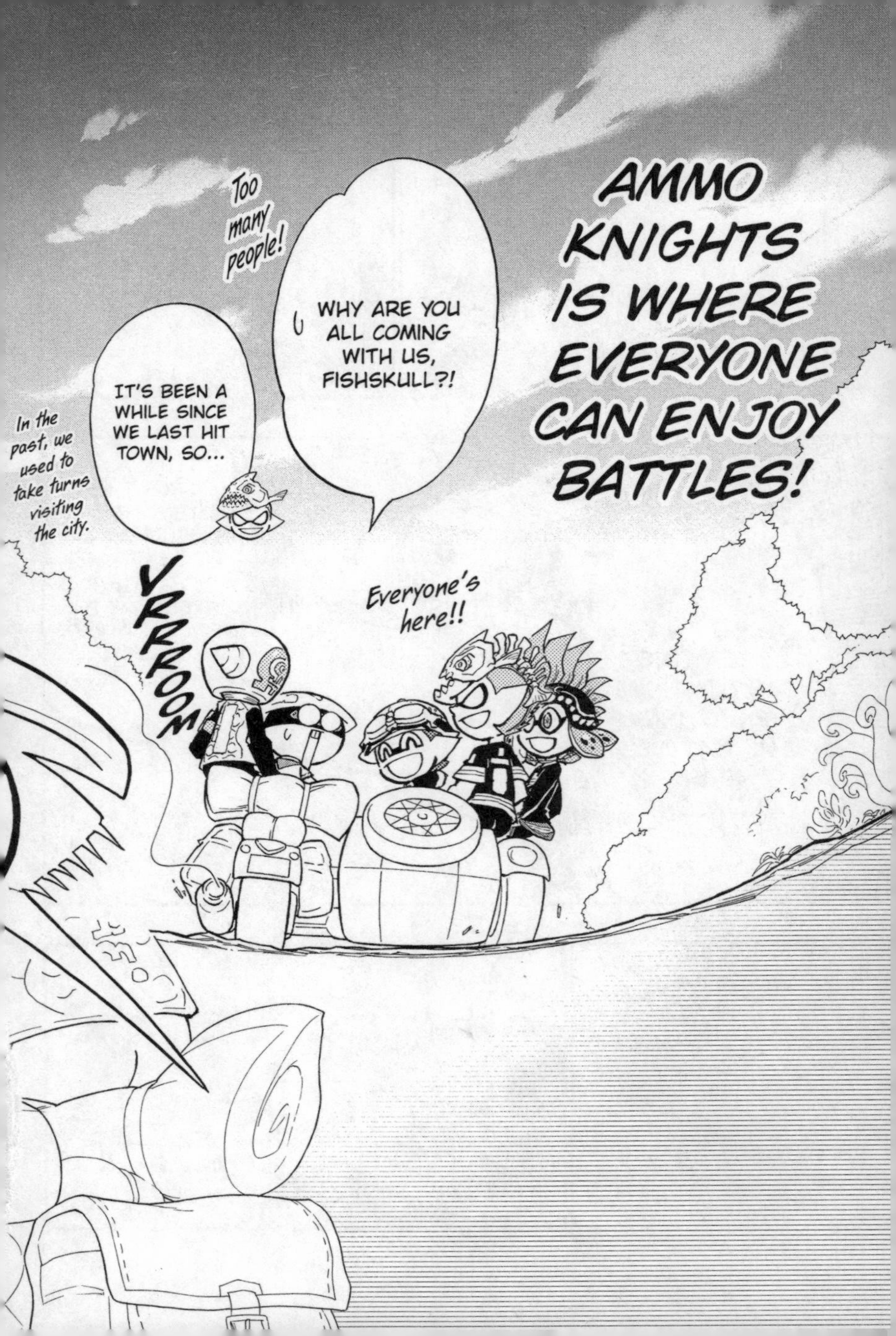
AMMO KNIGHTS IS WHERE EVERYONE CAN ENJOY BATTLES!
WHY ARE YOU ALL COMING WITH US, FISHSKULL?!
Too many people!
IT'S BEEN A WHILE SINCE WE LAST HIT TOWN, SO...
In the past, we used to take turns visiting the city.
Everyone's here!!
VRRROOM

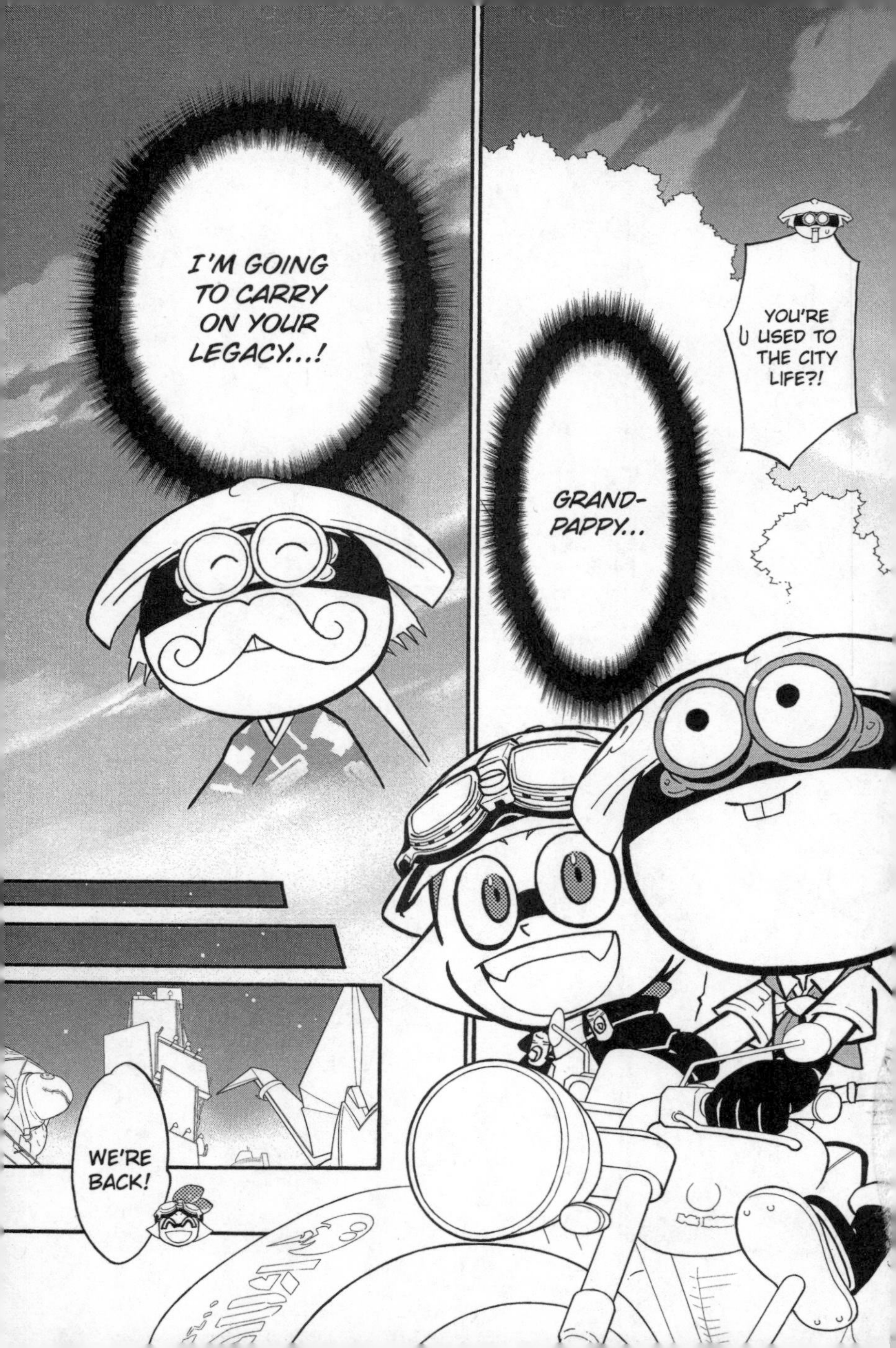
GRAND-PAPPY...
I'M GOING TO CARRY ON YOUR LEGACY...!
WE'RE BACK!
YOU'RE USED TO THE CITY LIFE?!

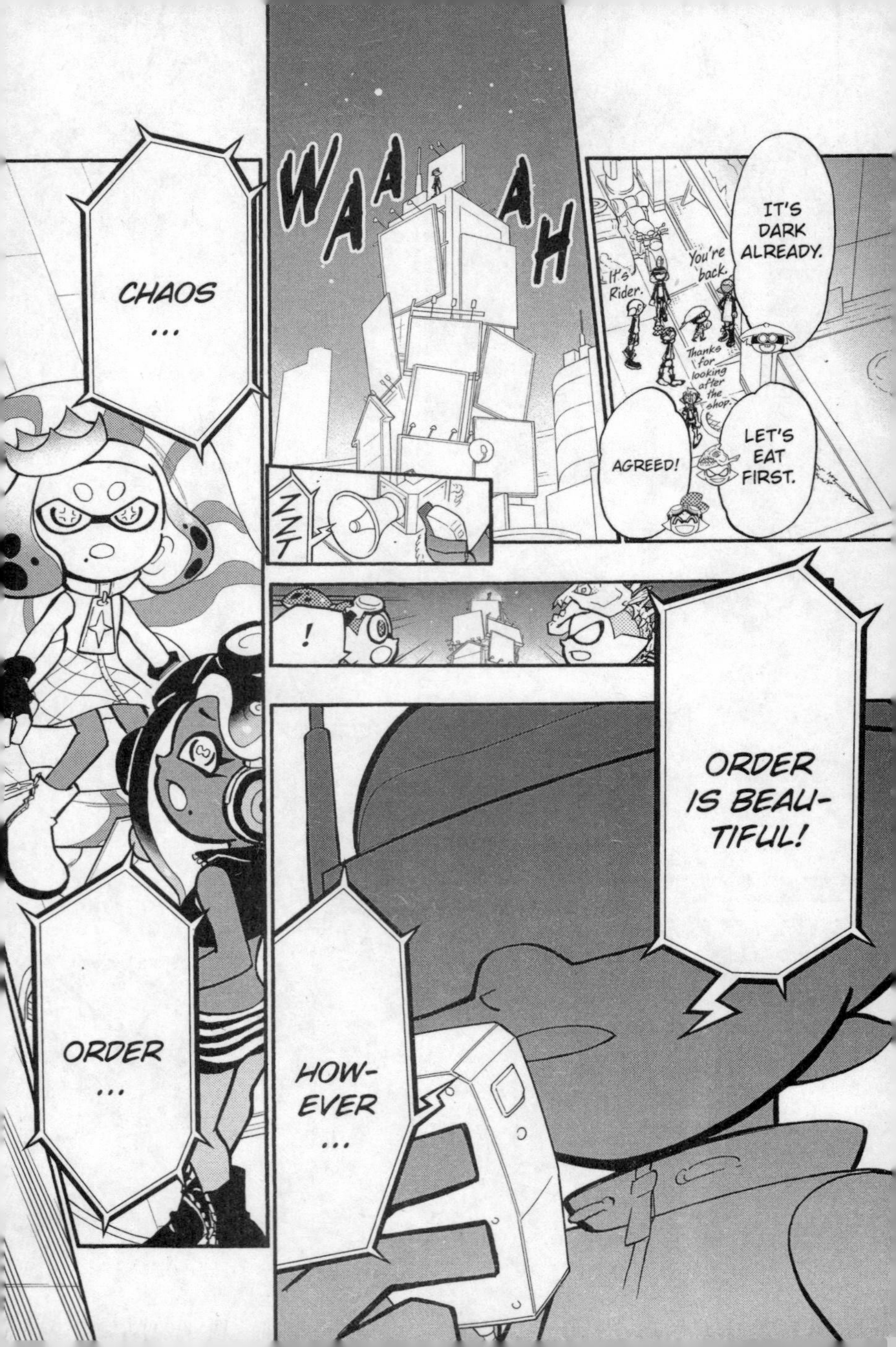
IT'S DARK ALREADY.
You're back.
It's Rider.
Thanks for looking after the shop.
LET'S EAT FIRST.
AGREED!
WAAAAH
ZZZT
!
ORDER IS BEAU-TIFUL!
HOW-EVER ...
CHAOS ...
ORDER ...

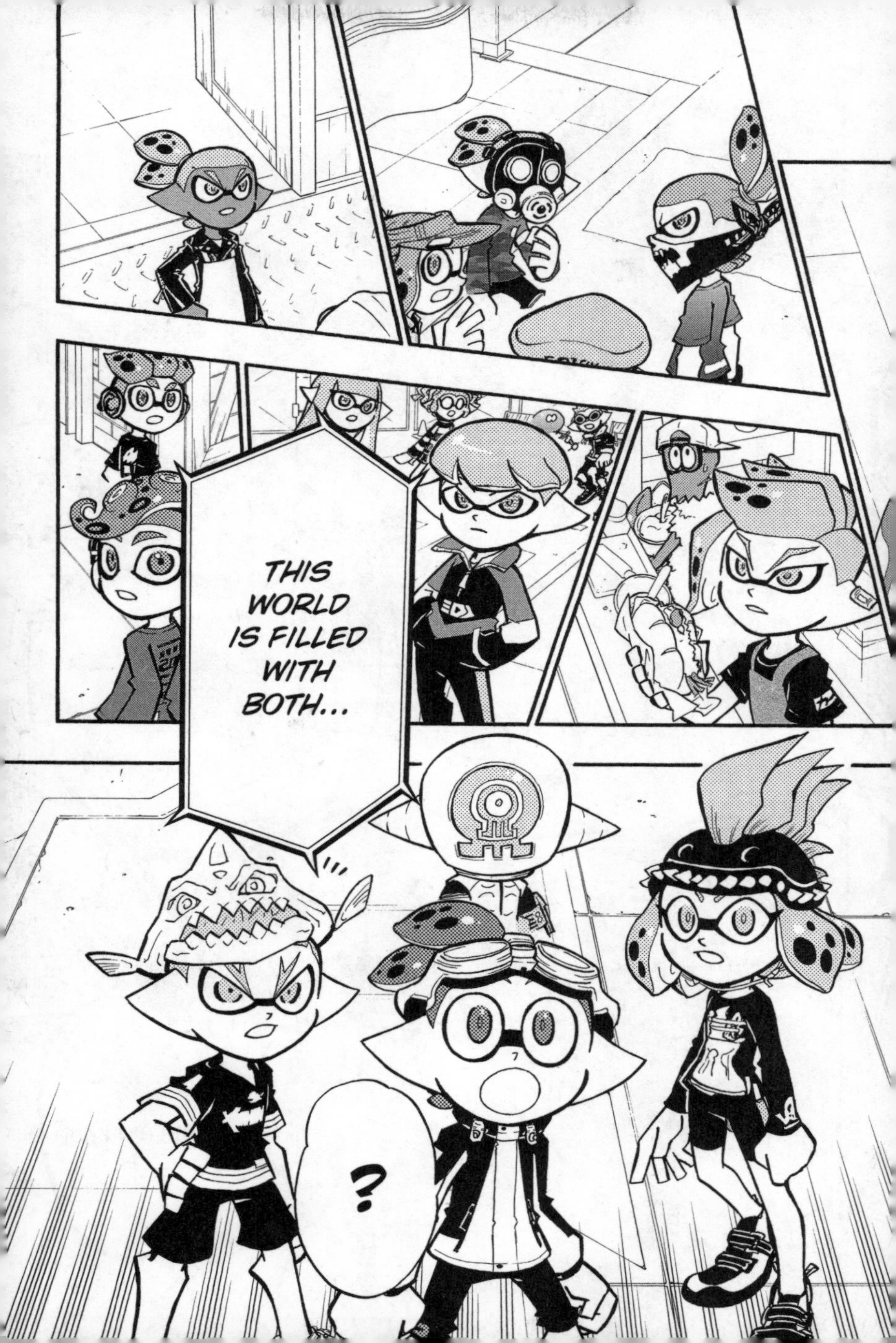
THIS WORLD IS FILLED WITH BOTH...
?

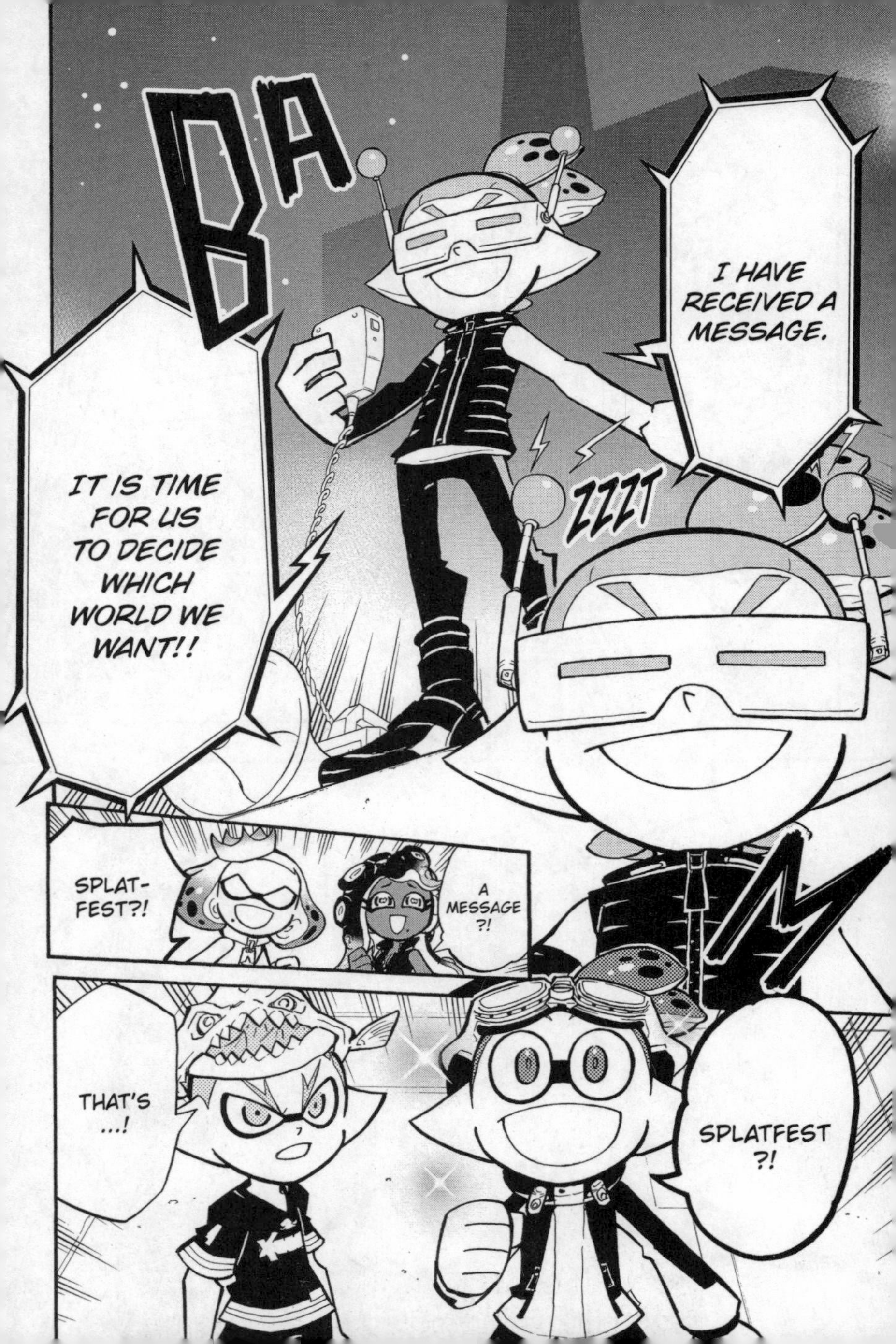
I HAVE RECEIVED A MESSAGE.
BA
ZZZT
IT IS TIME FOR US TO DECIDE WHICH WORLD WE WANT!!
M
A MESSAGE ?!
SPLAT-FEST?!
SPLATFEST ?!
THAT'S ...!

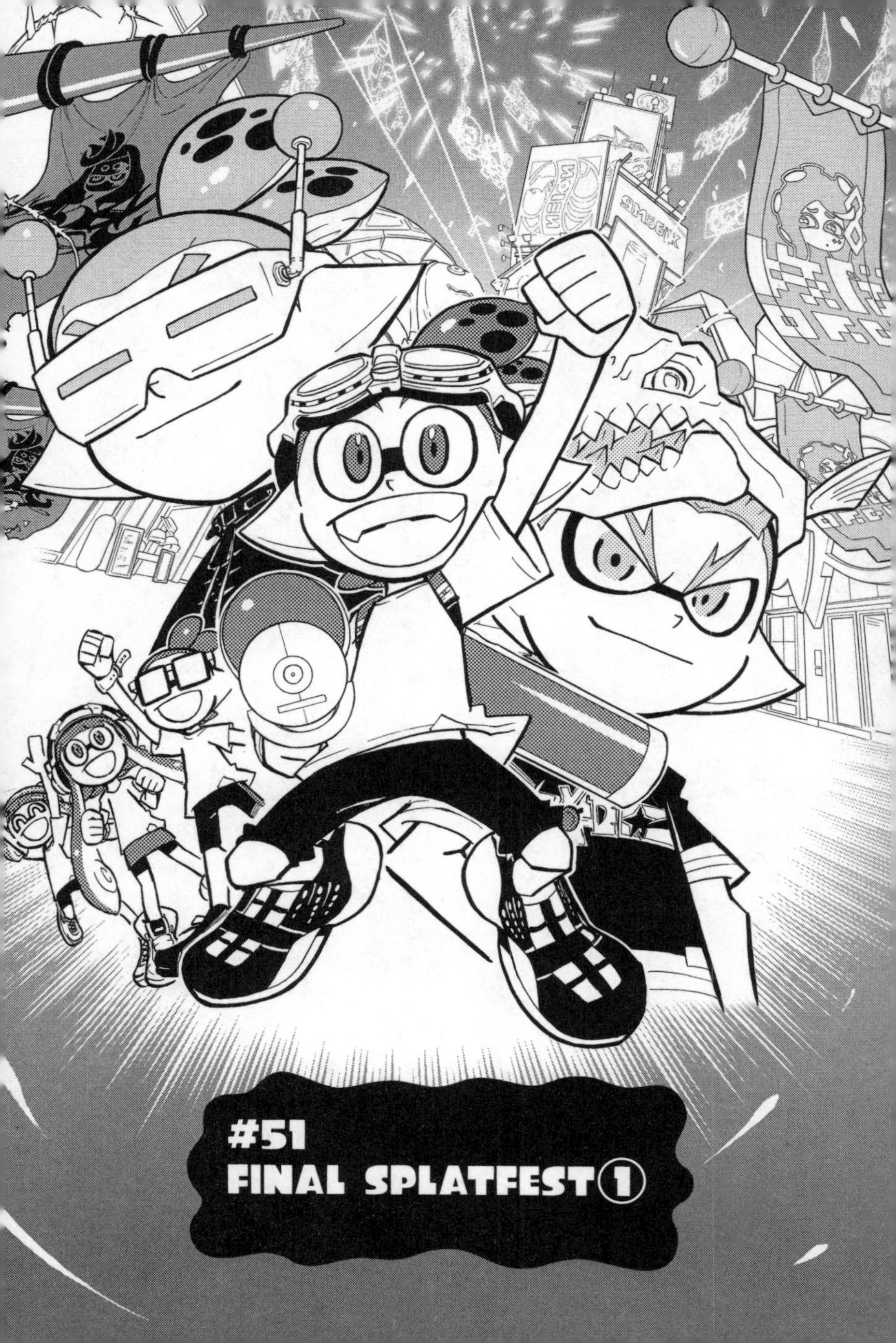
#51
FINAL SPLATFEST ①

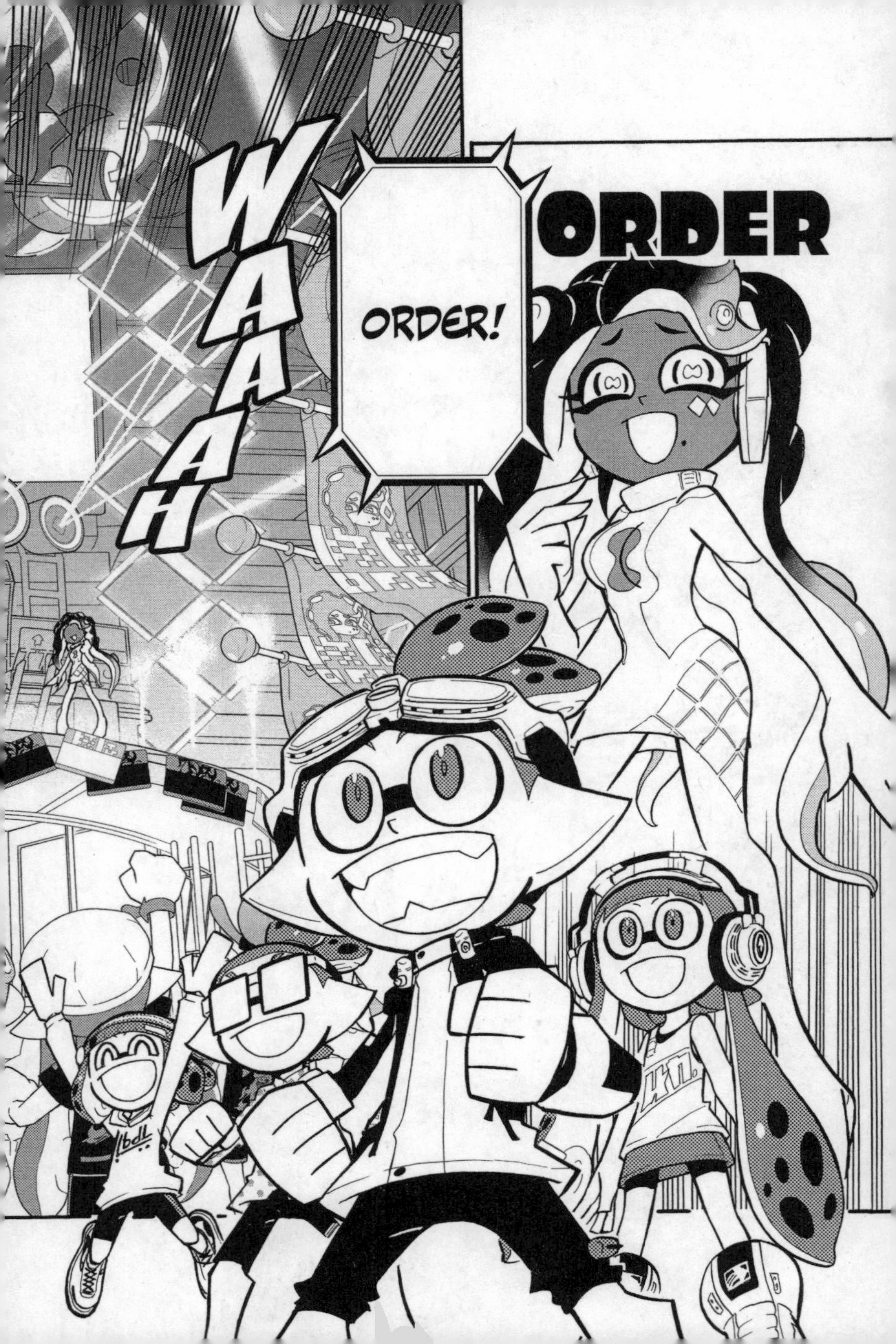
ORDER!
ORDER
WAAAH

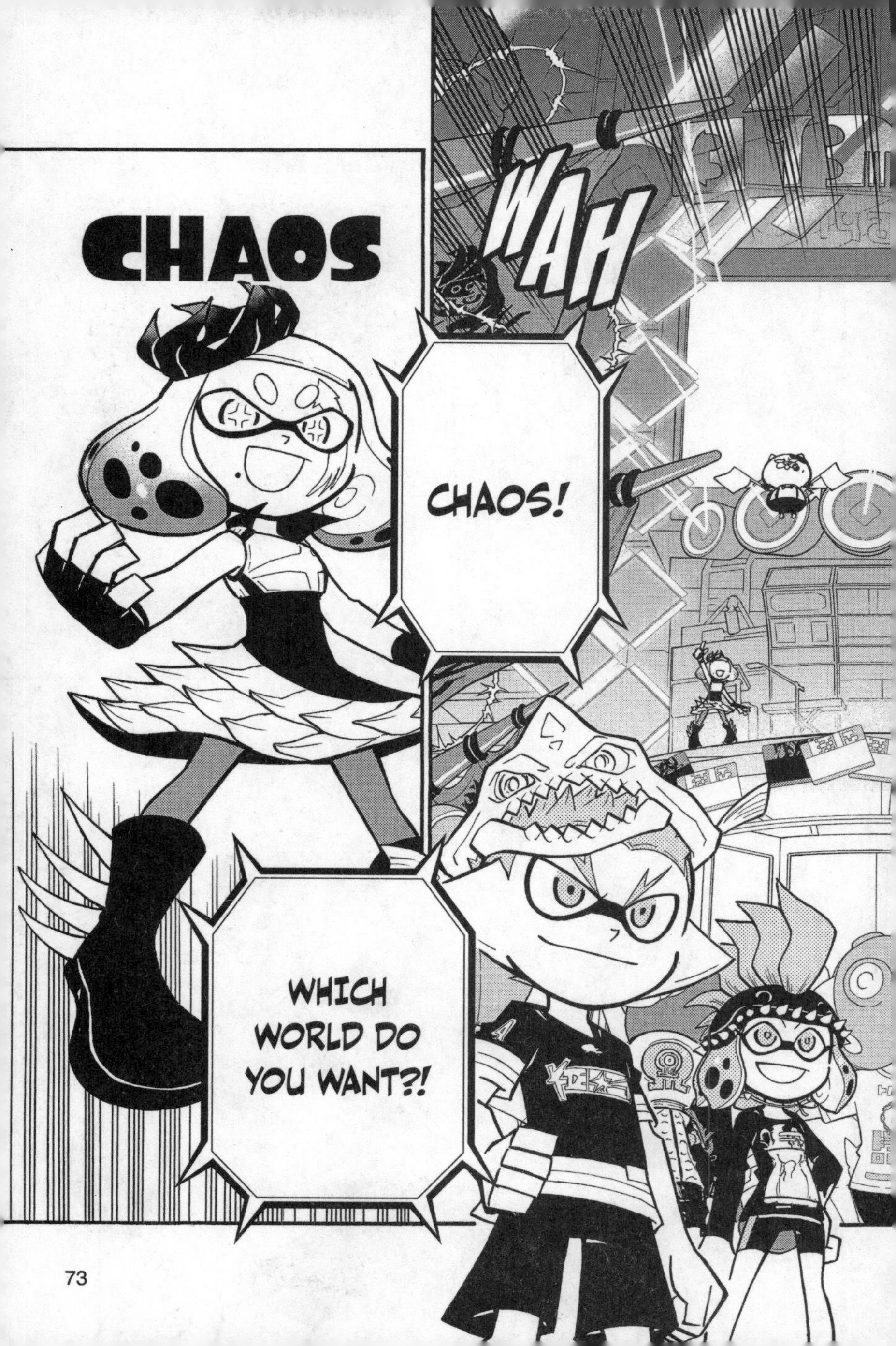
WAH
CHAOS
CHAOS!
WHICH WORLD DO YOU WANT?!

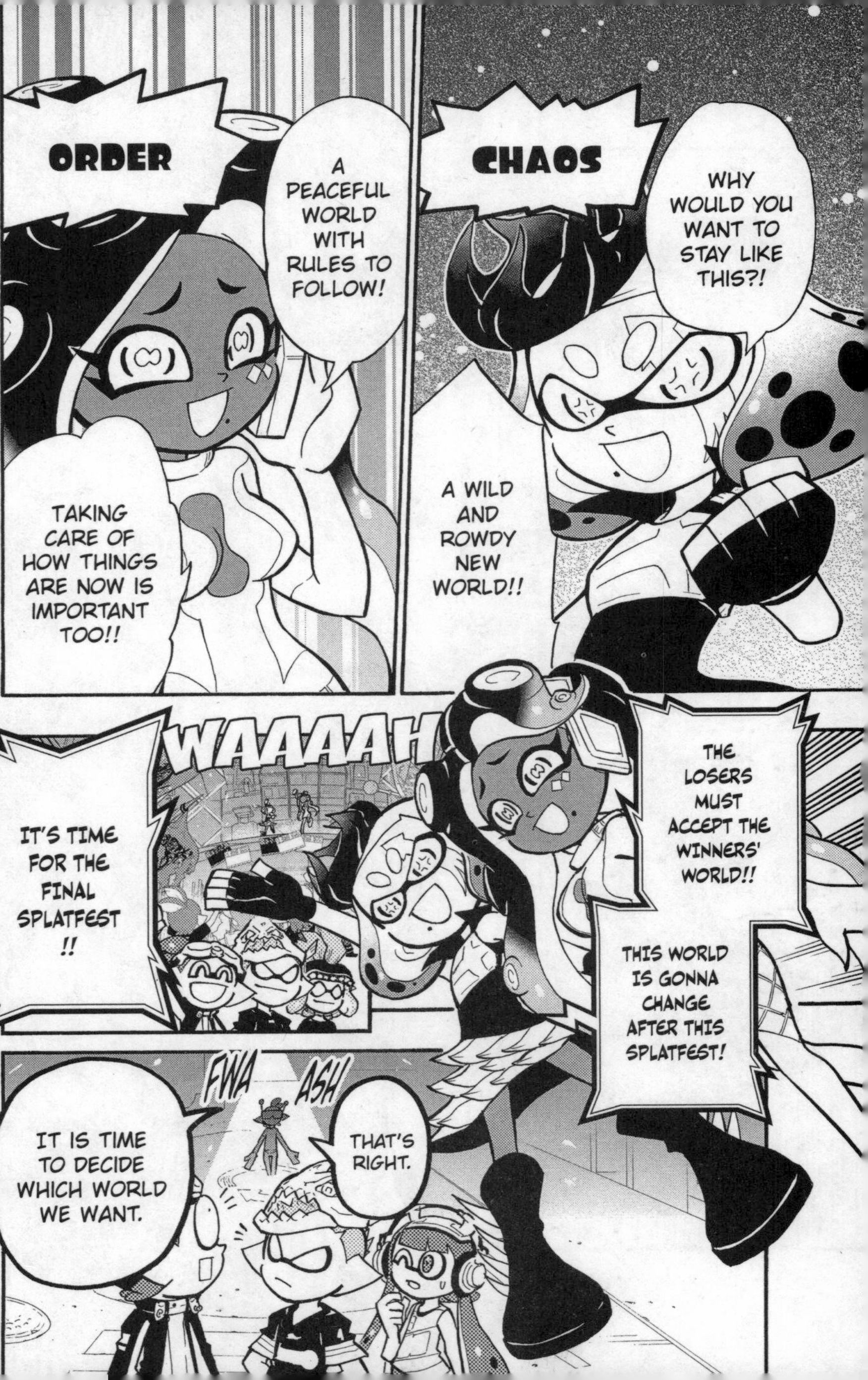

WHY WOULD YOU WANT TO STAY LIKE THIS?!
CHAOS
A WILD AND ROWDY NEW WORLD!!
A PEACEFUL WORLD WITH RULES TO FOLLOW!
ORDER
TAKING CARE OF HOW THINGS ARE NOW IS IMPORTANT TOO!!
THE LOSERS MUST ACCEPT THE WINNERS' WORLD!!
THIS WORLD IS GONNA CHANGE AFTER THIS SPLATFEST!
WAAAAAH
IT'S TIME FOR THE FINAL SPLATFEST !!
FWA ASH
THAT'S RIGHT.
IT IS TIME TO DECIDE WHICH WORLD WE WANT.

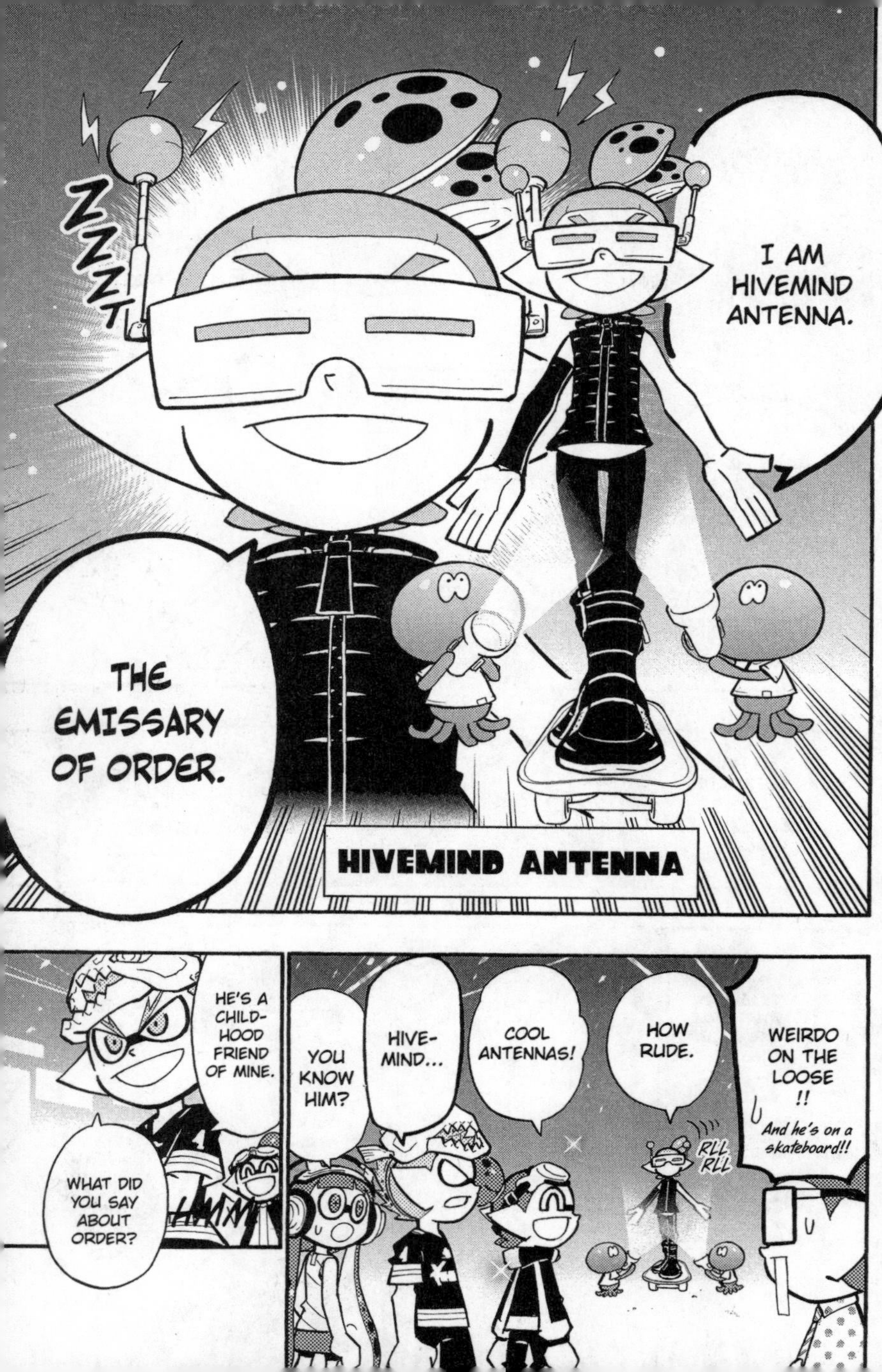
I AM HIVEMIND ANTENNA.
ZZZT
THE EMISSARY OF ORDER.
HIVEMIND ANTENNA
WEIRDO ON THE LOOSE !!
And he's on a skateboard!!
RLL RLL
HOW RUDE.
COOL ANTENNAS!
HIVE-MIND...
YOU KNOW HIM?
HE'S A CHILD-HOOD FRIEND OF MINE.
HMM
WHAT DID YOU SAY ABOUT ORDER?

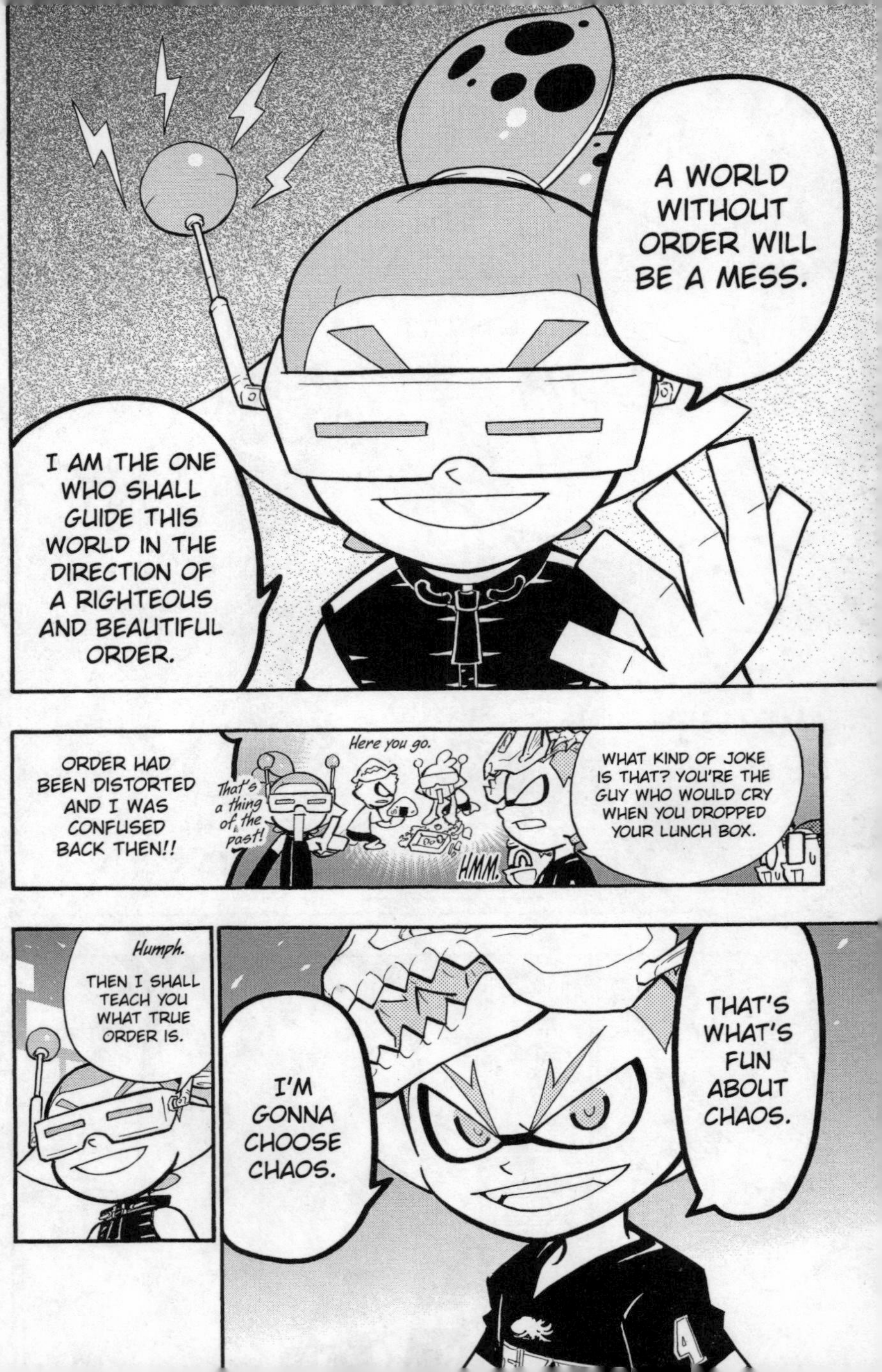
A WORLD WITHOUT ORDER WILL BE A MESS.
I AM THE ONE WHO SHALL GUIDE THIS WORLD IN THE DIRECTION OF A RIGHTEOUS AND BEAUTIFUL ORDER.
WHAT KIND OF JOKE IS THAT? YOU'RE THE GUY WHO WOULD CRY WHEN YOU DROPPED YOUR LUNCH BOX.
HMM.
Here you go.
That's a thing of the past!
ORDER HAD BEEN DISTORTED AND I WAS CONFUSED BACK THEN!!
THAT'S WHAT'S FUN ABOUT CHAOS.
I'M GONNA CHOOSE CHAOS.
Humph.
THEN I SHALL TEACH YOU WHAT TRUE ORDER IS.

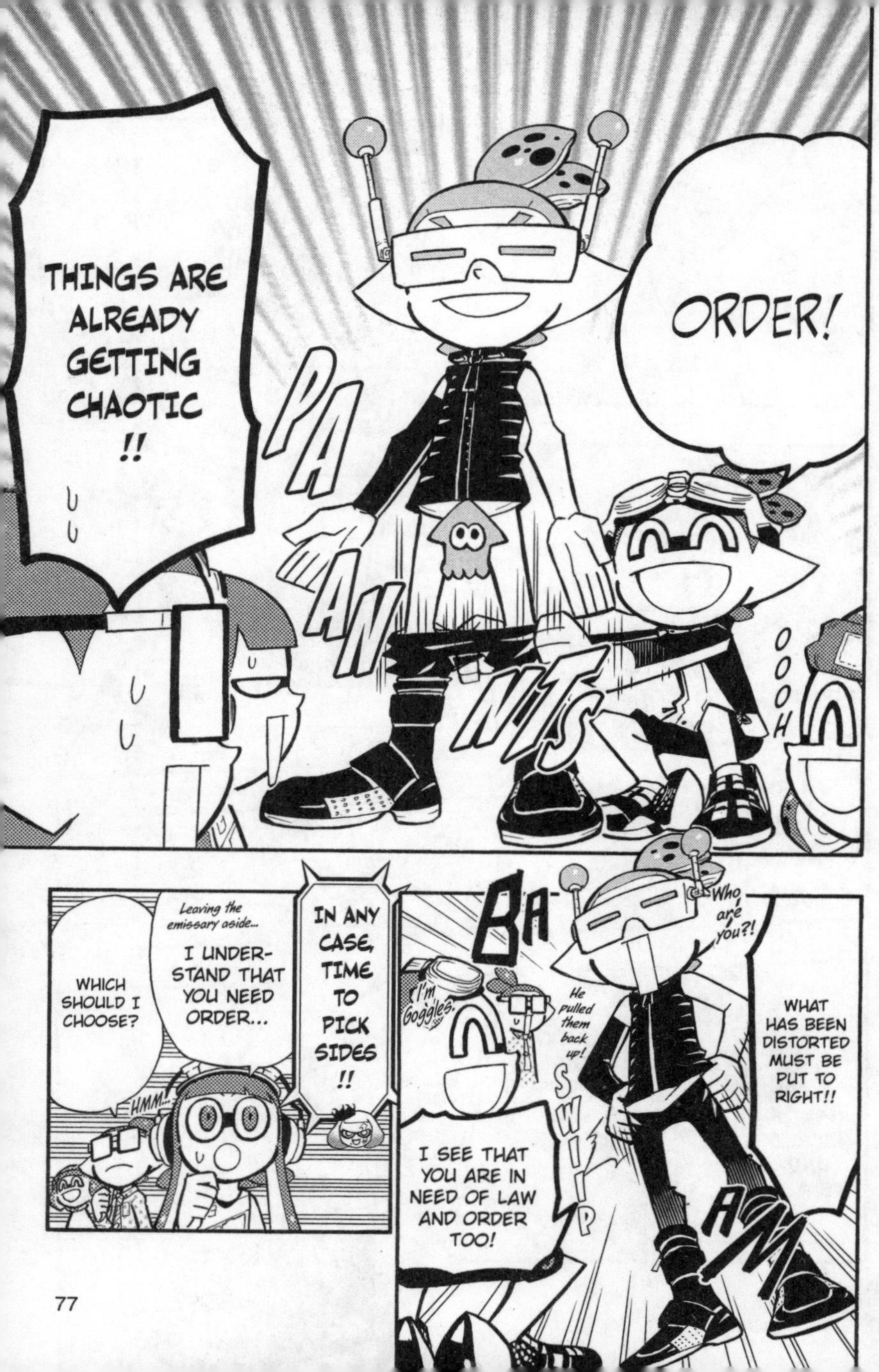
ORDER!
PANTS
OOOOH
THINGS ARE ALREADY GETTING CHAOTIC!!
BA-
Who are you?!
WHAT HAS BEEN DISTORTED MUST BE PUT TO RIGHT!!
He pulled them back up!
I'm Goggles.
SWIP
I SEE THAT YOU ARE IN NEED OF LAW AND ORDER TOO!
AM
IN ANY CASE, TIME TO PICK SIDES!!
Leaving the emissary aside...
I UNDERSTAND THAT YOU NEED ORDER...
WHICH SHOULD I CHOOSE?
HMM...

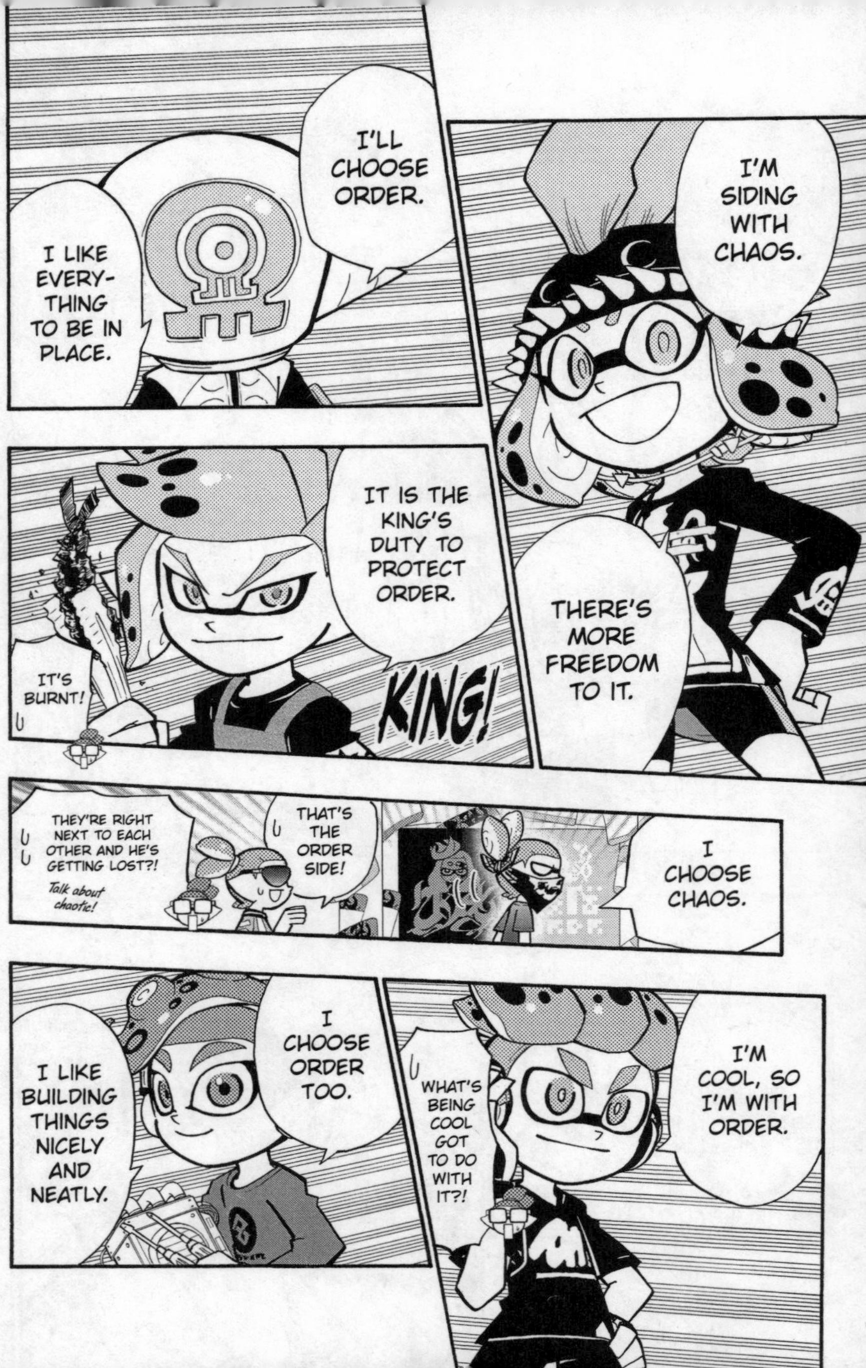

I'M SIDING WITH CHAOS.
THERE'S MORE FREEDOM TO IT.
I'LL CHOOSE ORDER.
I LIKE EVERY-THING TO BE IN PLACE.
IT IS THE KING'S DUTY TO PROTECT ORDER.
KING!
IT'S BURNT!
I CHOOSE CHAOS.
THAT'S THE ORDER SIDE!
THEY'RE RIGHT NEXT TO EACH OTHER AND HE'S GETTING LOST?!
Talk about chaotic!
I'M COOL, SO I'M WITH ORDER.
WHAT'S BEING COOL GOT TO DO WITH IT?!
I CHOOSE ORDER TOO.
I LIKE BUILDING THINGS NICELY AND NEATLY.

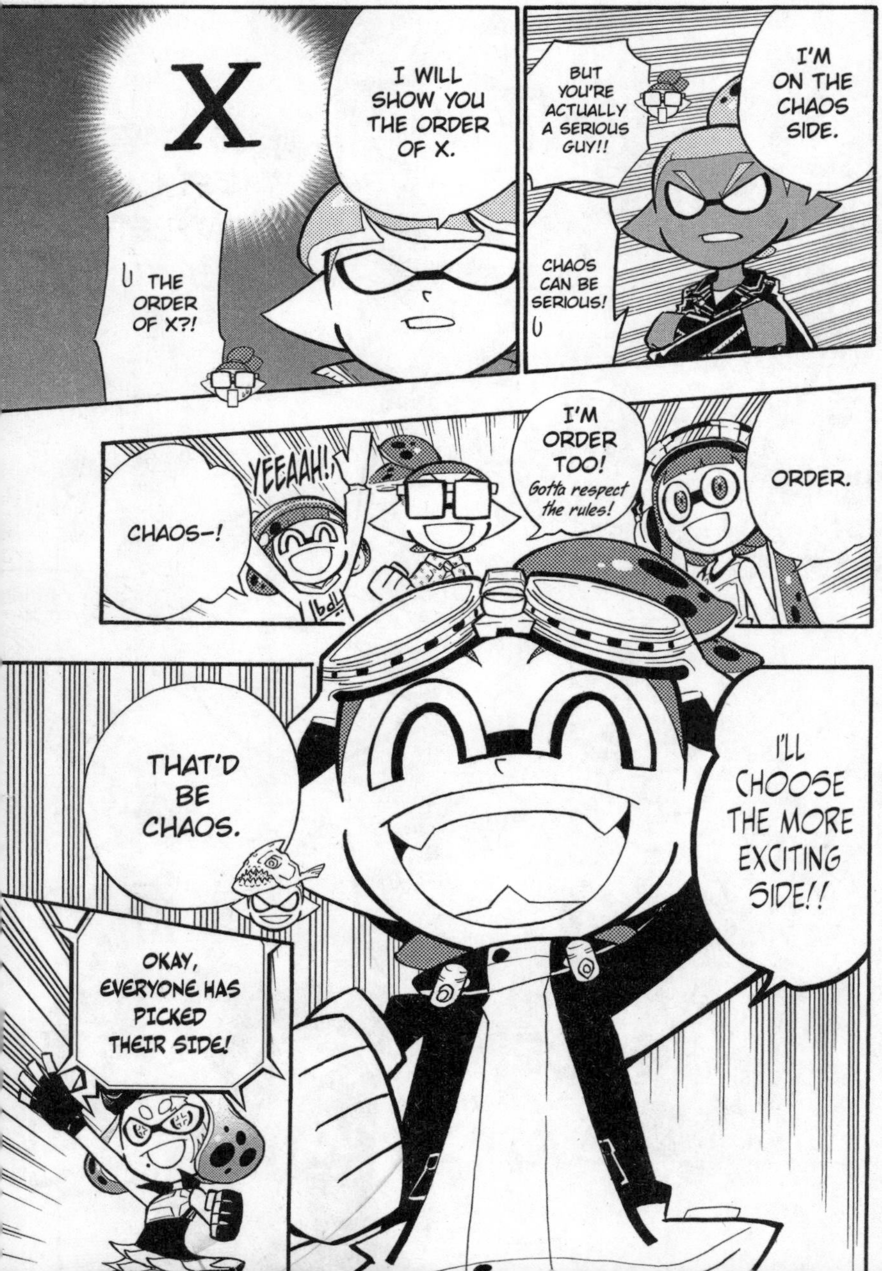
I'M ON THE CHAOS SIDE.
BUT YOU'RE ACTUALLY A SERIOUS GUY!!
CHAOS CAN BE SERIOUS!
X
I WILL SHOW YOU THE ORDER OF X.
THE ORDER OF X?!
ORDER.
I'M ORDER TOO! Gotta respect the rules!
YEEAAH!!
CHAOS-!
I'LL CHOOSE THE MORE EXCITING SIDE!!
THAT'D BE CHAOS.
OKAY, EVERYONE HAS PICKED THEIR SIDE!

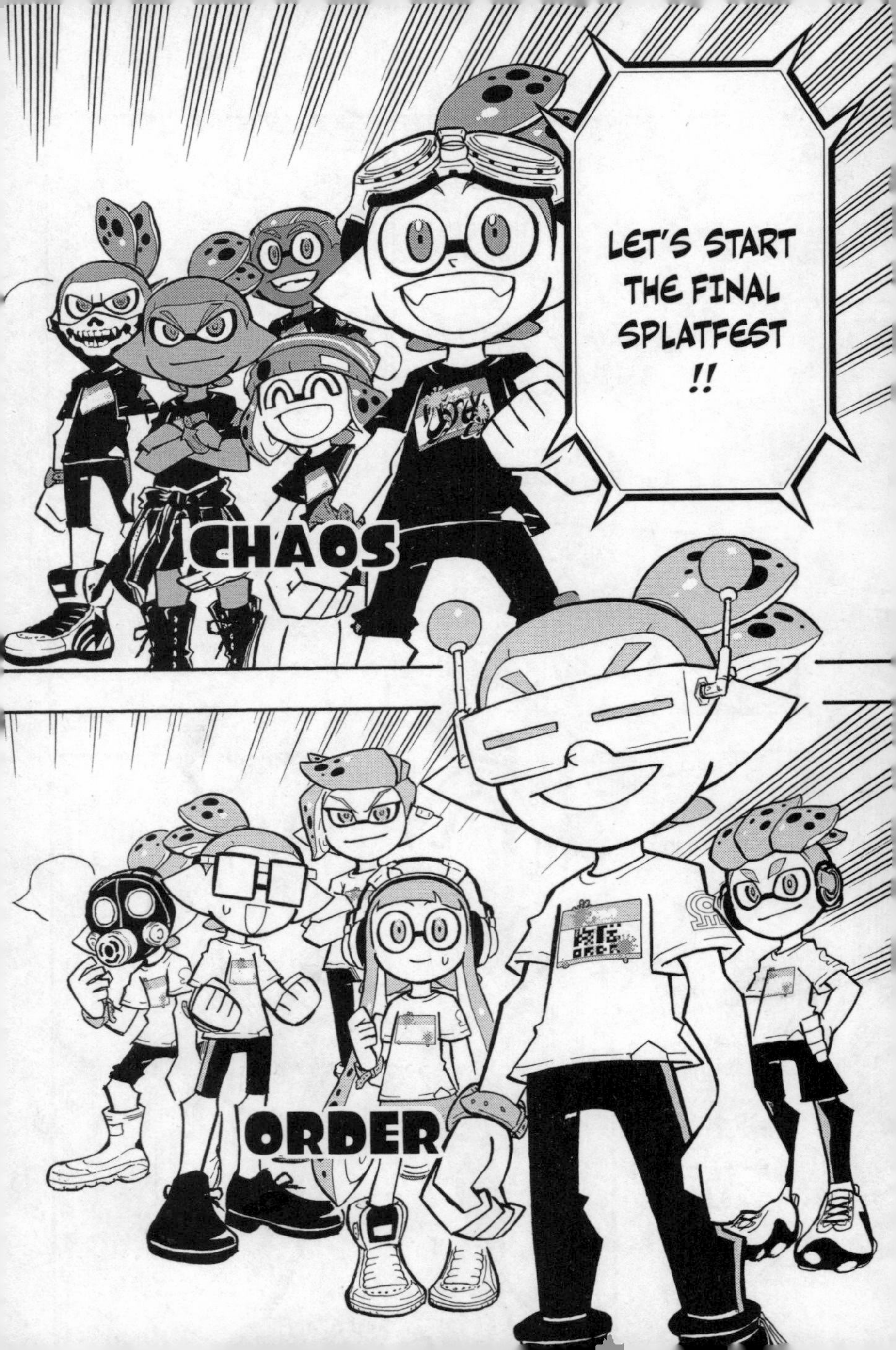
LET'S START THE FINAL SPLATFEST!!
CHAOS
ORDER

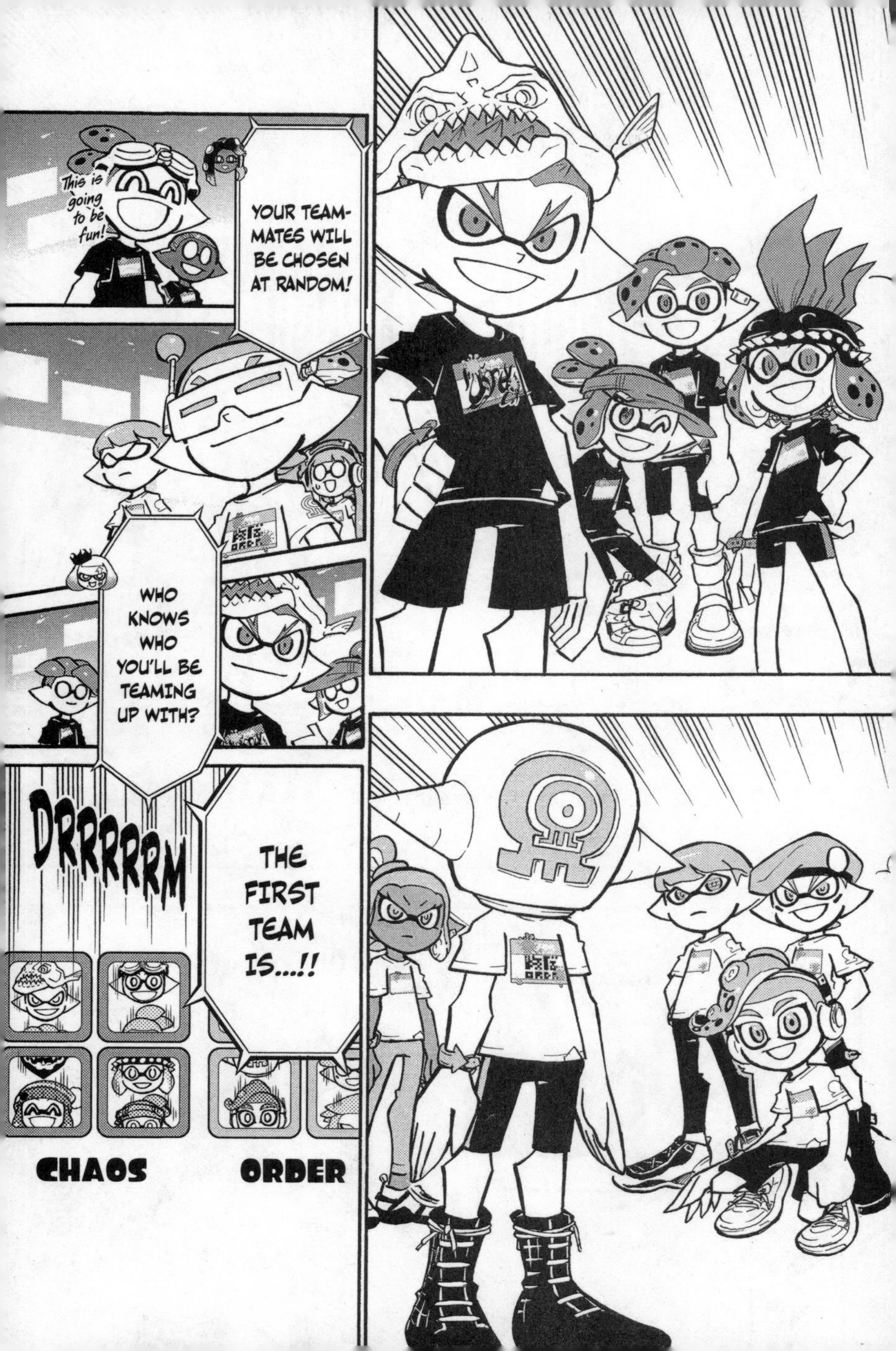
YOUR TEAM-MATES WILL BE CHOSEN AT RANDOM!
This is going to be fun!
WHO KNOWS WHO YOU'LL BE TEAMING UP WITH?
THE FIRST TEAM IS...!!
DRRRRRM
ORDER
CHAOS

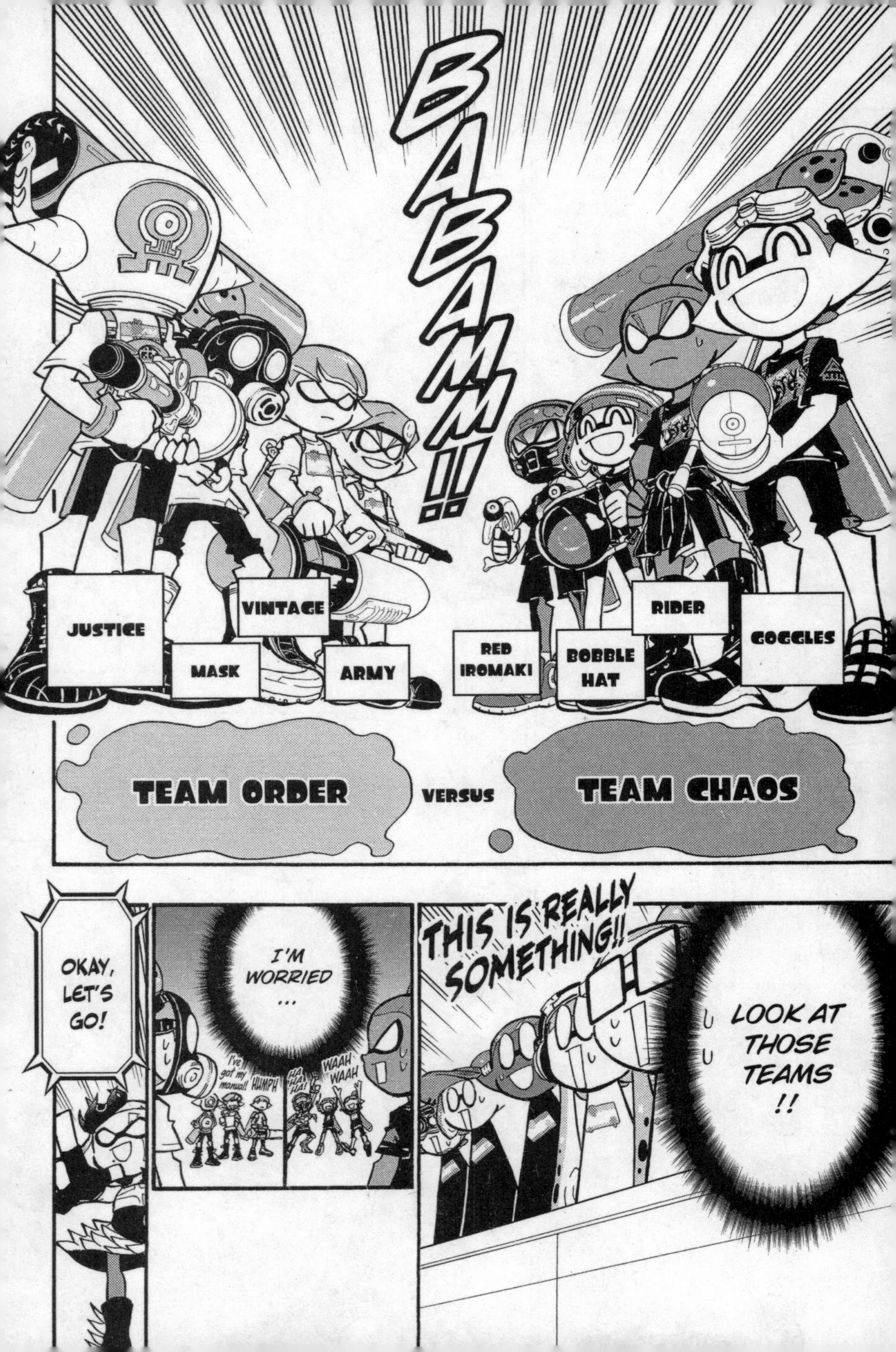

BABAMM!!
GOGGLES
RIDER
BOBBLE HAT
RED IROMAKI
ARMY
VINTAGE
MASK
JUSTICE
TEAM ORDER VERSUS TEAM CHAOS
THIS IS REALLY SOMETHING!!
LOOK AT THOSE TEAMS!!
I'M WORRIED...
WAAH WAAH
HA HA HA!
HUMPH
I've got my manual!
OKAY, LET'S GO!

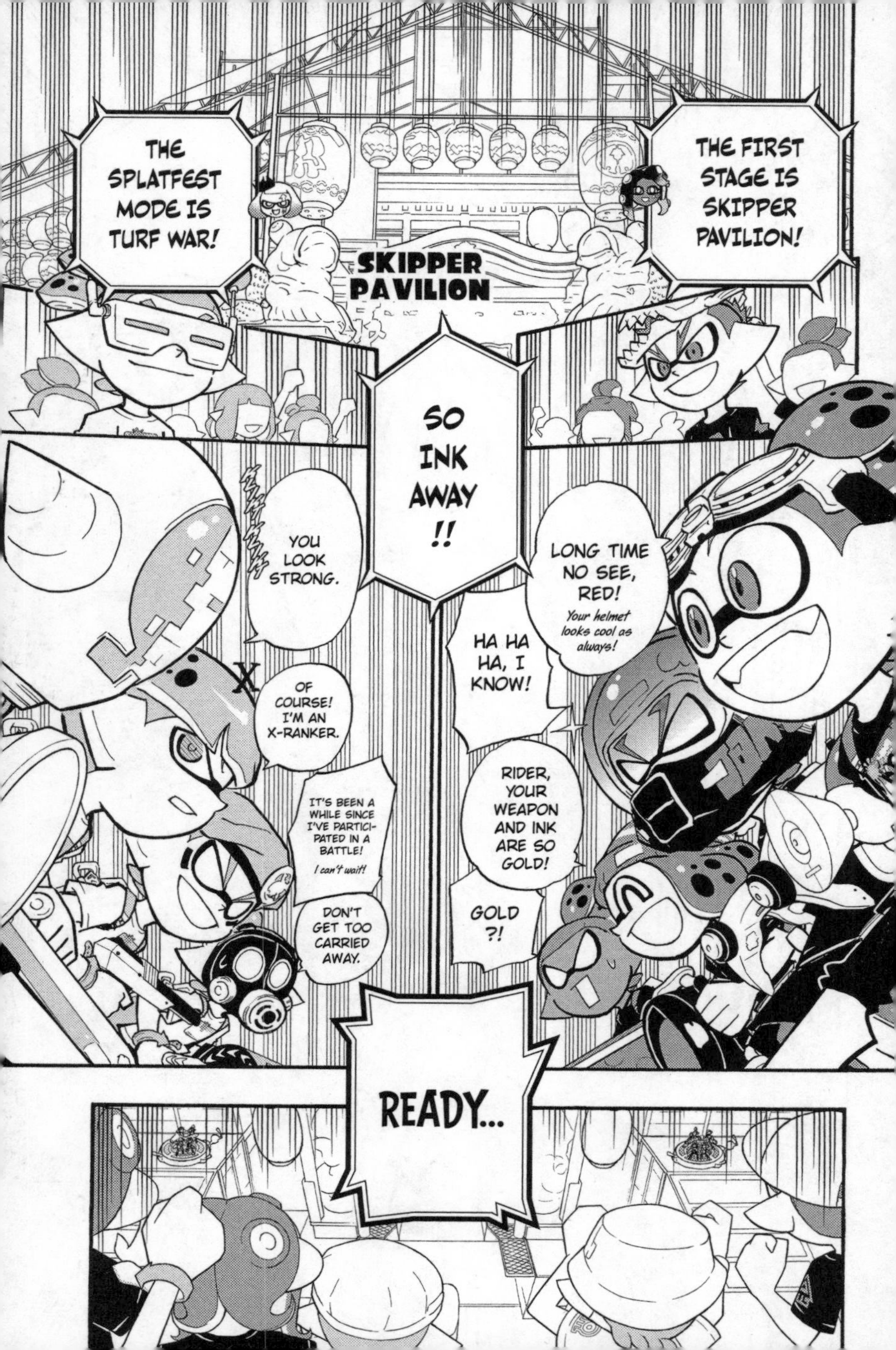
THE FIRST STAGE IS SKIPPER PAVILION!
THE SPLATFEST MODE IS TURF WAR!
SKIPPER PAVILION
SO INK AWAY!!
LONG TIME NO SEE, RED!
Your helmet looks cool as always!
HA HA HA, I KNOW!
RIDER, YOUR WEAPON AND INK ARE SO GOLD!
GOLD?!
YOU LOOK STRONG.
OF COURSE! I'M AN X-RANKER.
IT'S BEEN A WHILE SINCE I'VE PARTICIPATED IN A BATTLE!
I can't wait!
DON'T GET TOO CARRIED AWAY.
READY...

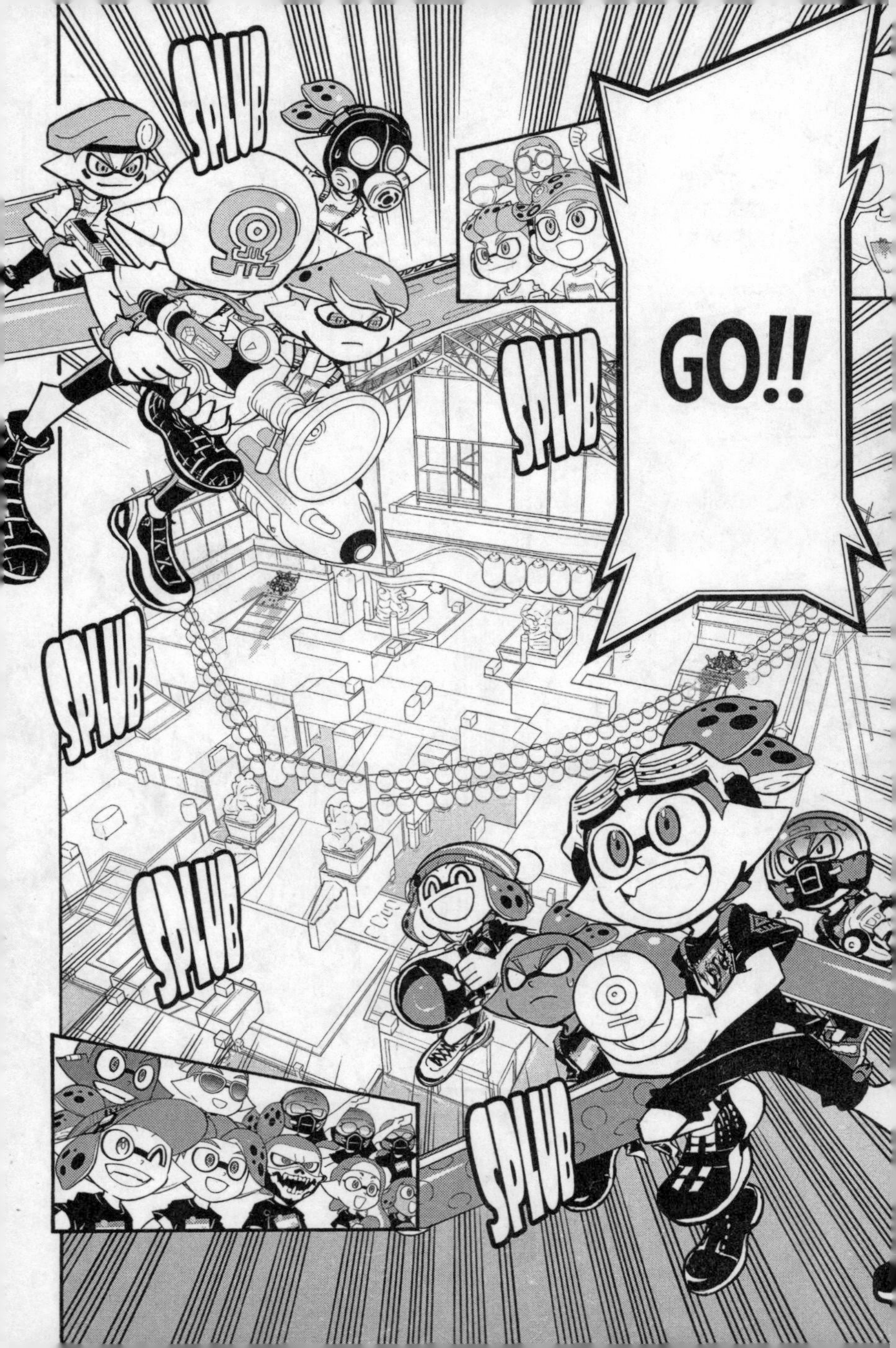
GO!!
SPLUB
SPLUB
SPLUB
SPLUB
SPLUB
SPLUB

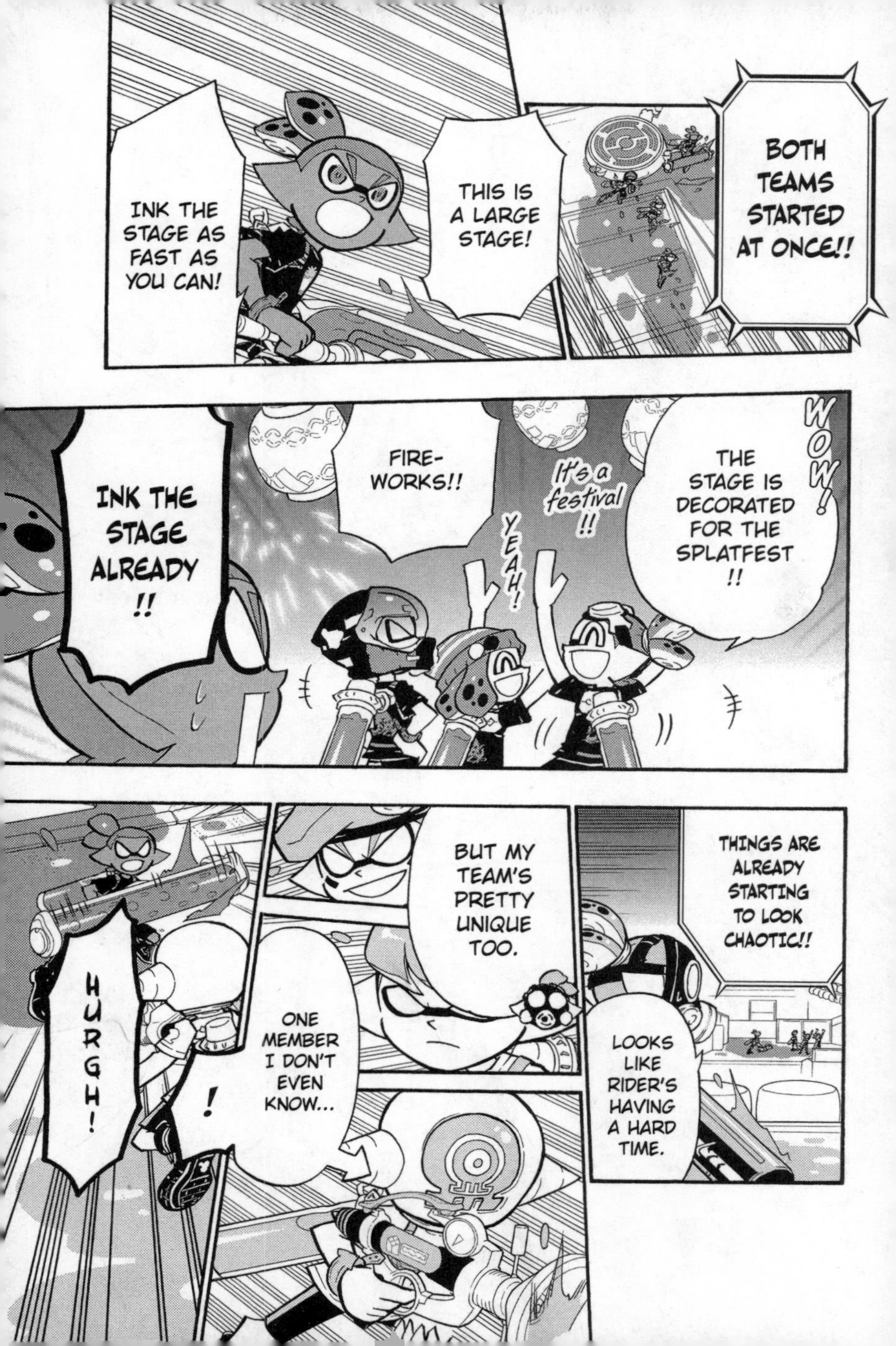
BOTH TEAMS STARTED AT ONCE!!
THIS IS A LARGE STAGE!
INK THE STAGE AS FAST AS YOU CAN!
WOW!
THE STAGE IS DECORATED FOR THE SPLATFEST!!
It's a festival!!
YEAH!
FIRE-WORKS!!
INK THE STAGE ALREADY!!
THINGS ARE ALREADY STARTING TO LOOK CHAOTIC!!
LOOKS LIKE RIDER'S HAVING A HARD TIME.
BUT MY TEAM'S PRETTY UNIQUE TOO.
ONE MEMBER I DON'T EVEN KNOW...
HURGH!
!

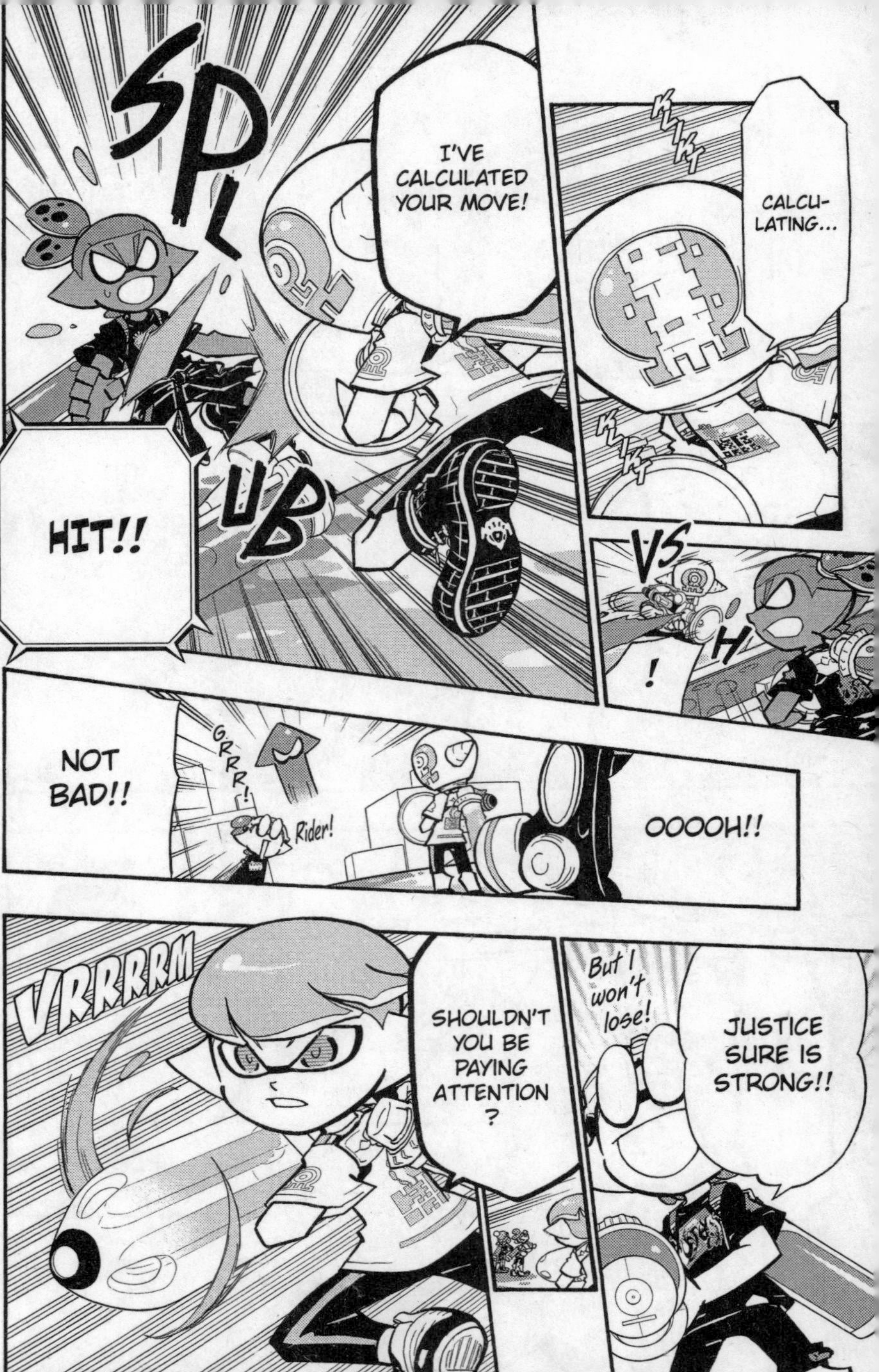
KLIK
CALCU-LATING...
KLIK
VS
H
!
I'VE CALCULATED YOUR MOVE!
SPL
UB
HIT!!
OOOOH!!
GRRR!
Rider!
NOT BAD!!
JUSTICE SURE IS STRONG!!
But I won't lose!
SHOULDN'T YOU BE PAYING ATTENTION ?
VRRRRM

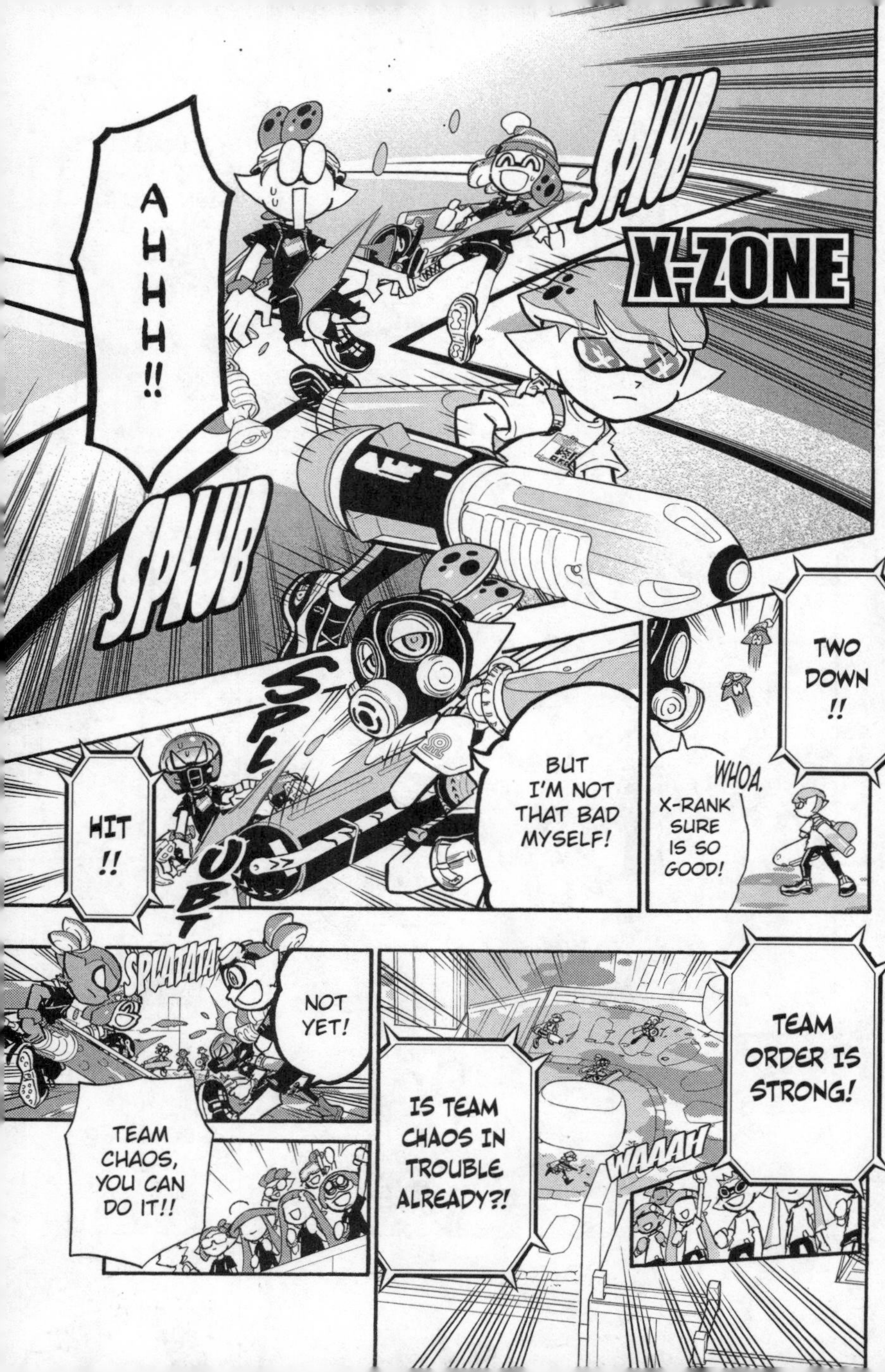
SPLUB
X-ZONE
AHHH!!
SPLUB
TWO DOWN!!
WHOA.
X-RANK SURE IS SO GOOD!
BUT I'M NOT THAT BAD MYSELF!
SPLUBT
HIT!!
TEAM ORDER IS STRONG!
WAAAH
IS TEAM CHAOS IN TROUBLE ALREADY?!
NOT YET!
SPLATATA
TEAM CHAOS, YOU CAN DO IT!!

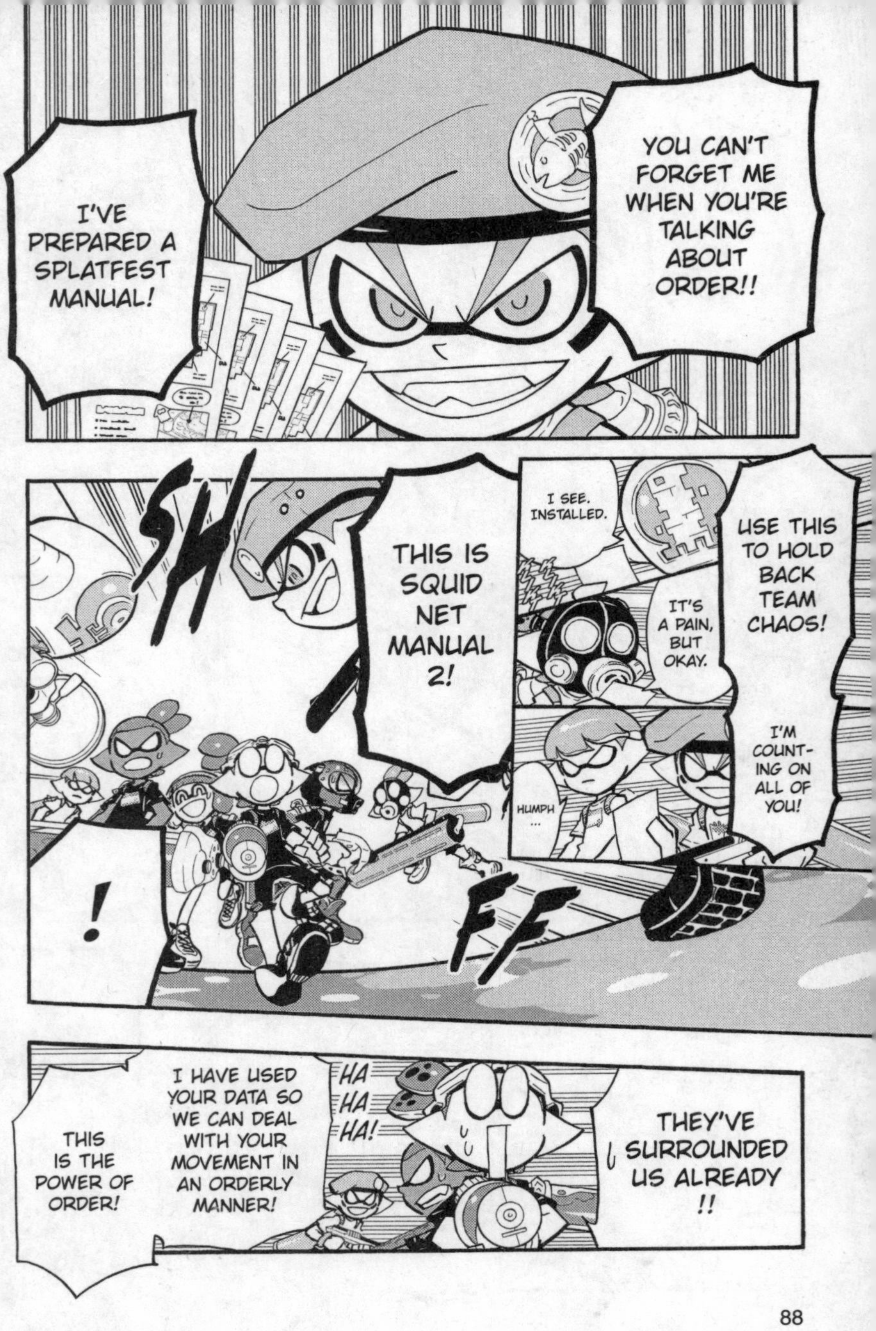
YOU CAN'T FORGET ME WHEN YOU'RE TALKING ABOUT ORDER!!
I'VE PREPARED A SPLATFEST MANUAL!
USE THIS TO HOLD BACK TEAM CHAOS!
I SEE. INSTALLED.
IT'S A PAIN, BUT OKAY.
I'M COUNTING ON ALL OF YOU!
HUMPH ...
SH
THIS IS SQUID NET MANUAL 2!
FF
!
THEY'VE SURROUNDED US ALREADY !!
HA HA HA!
I HAVE USED YOUR DATA SO WE CAN DEAL WITH YOUR MOVEMENT IN AN ORDERLY MANNER!
THIS IS THE POWER OF ORDER!

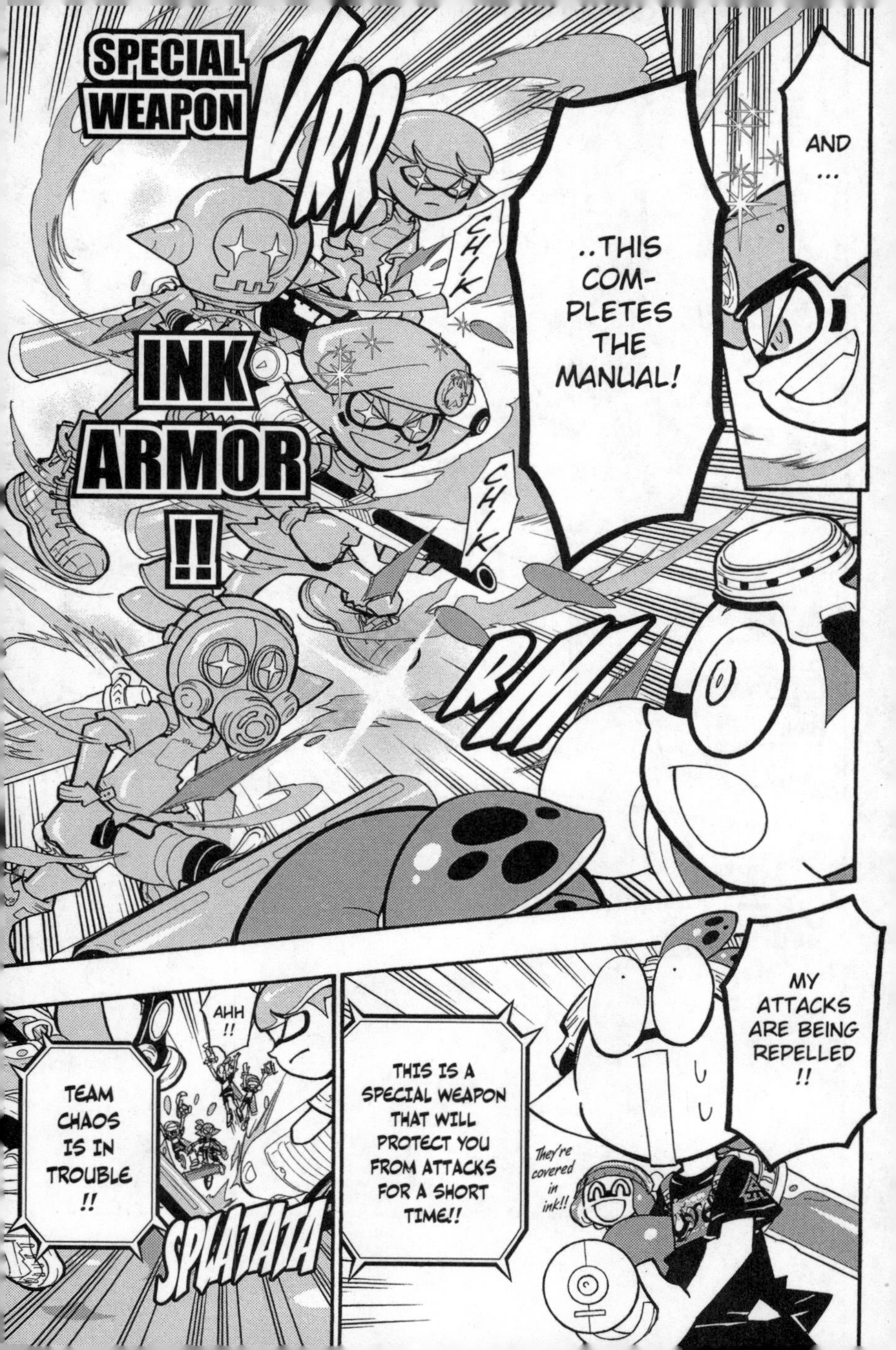
AND ...
..THIS COMPLETES THE MANUAL!
VRR
SPECIAL WEAPON
CHIK
INK ARMOR !!
CHIK
RM
MY ATTACKS ARE BEING REPELLED !!
They're covered in ink!!
THIS IS A SPECIAL WEAPON THAT WILL PROTECT YOU FROM ATTACKS FOR A SHORT TIME!!
AHH !!
TEAM CHAOS IS IN TROUBLE !!
SPLATATA

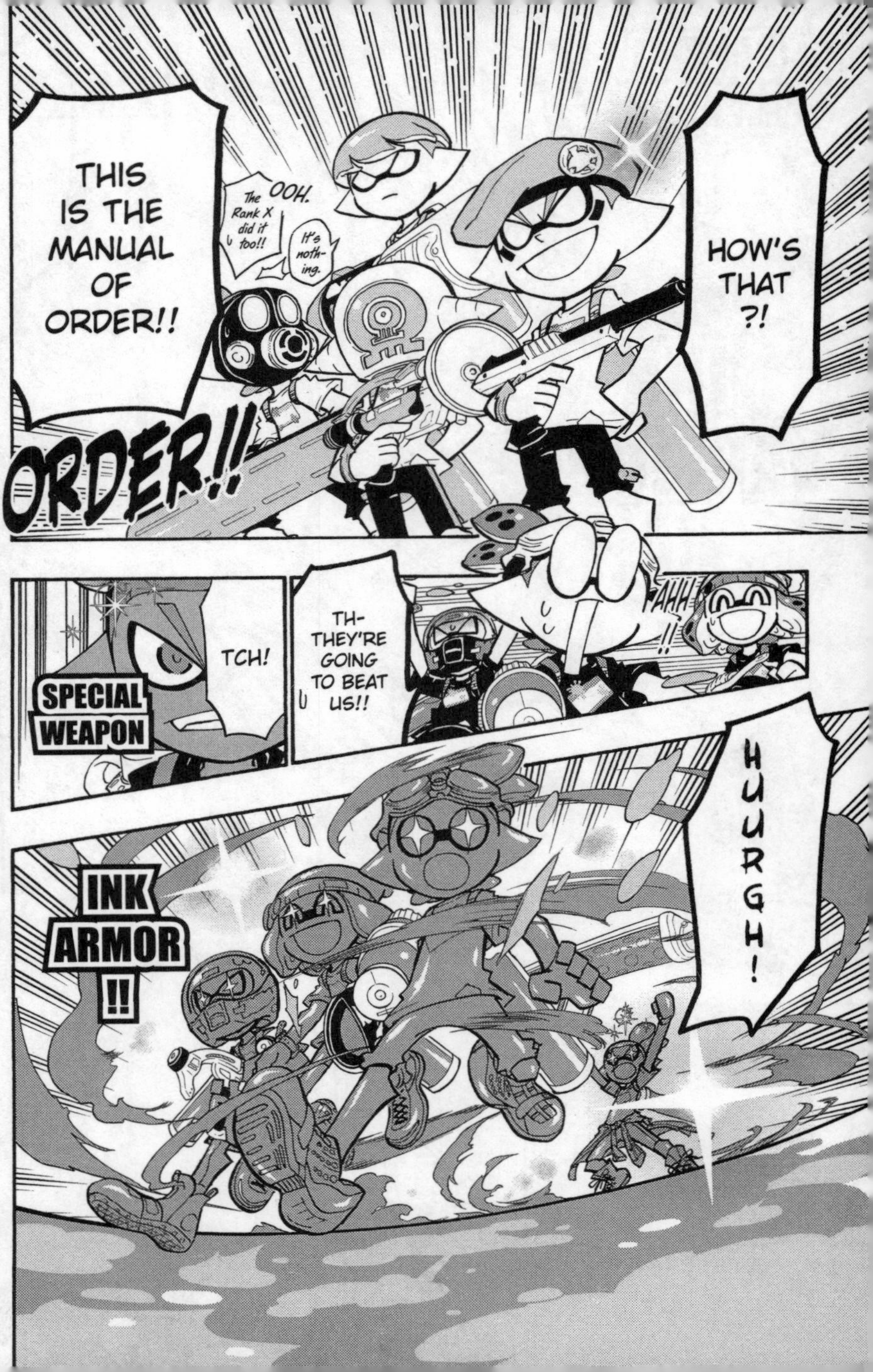

HOW'S THAT ?!
OOH.
The Rank X did it too!!
It's nothing.
THIS IS THE MANUAL OF ORDER!!
ORDER!!
TH- THEY'RE GOING TO BEAT US!!
AHH !!
TCH!
SPECIAL WEAPON
HUURGH!
INK ARMOR !!

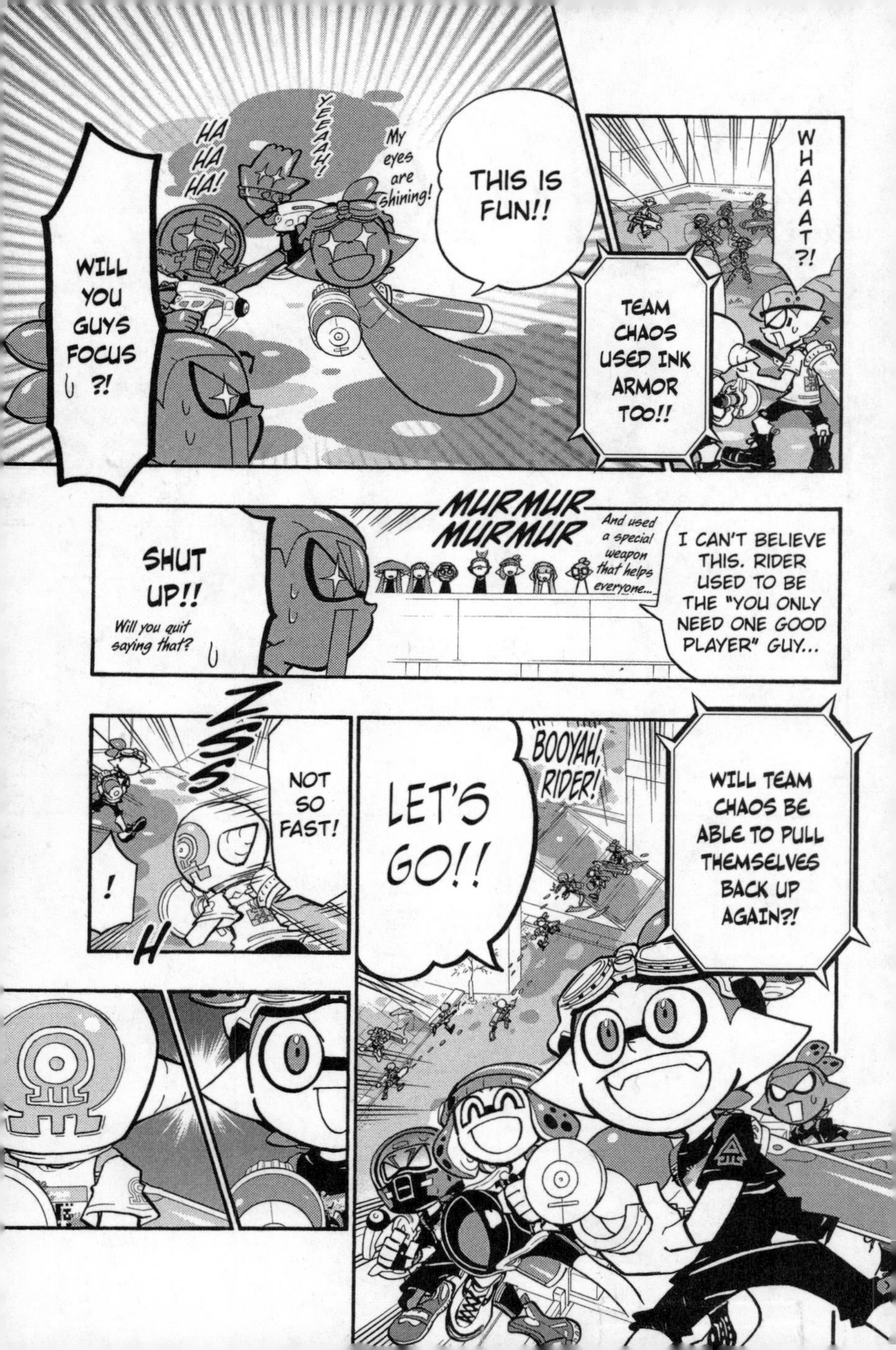
WHAAAAT?!
TEAM CHAOS USED INK ARMOR TOO!!
THIS IS FUN!!
My eyes are shining!
YEEAAH!
HA HA HA!
WILL YOU GUYS FOCUS?!
I CAN'T BELIEVE THIS. RIDER USED TO BE THE "YOU ONLY NEED ONE GOOD PLAYER" GUY...
And used a special weapon that helps everyone...
MURMUR MURMUR
SHUT UP!!
Will you quit saying that?
WILL TEAM CHAOS BE ABLE TO PULL THEMSELVES BACK UP AGAIN?!
BOOYAH, RIDER!
LET'S GO!!
NOT SO FAST!
ZSSH
!

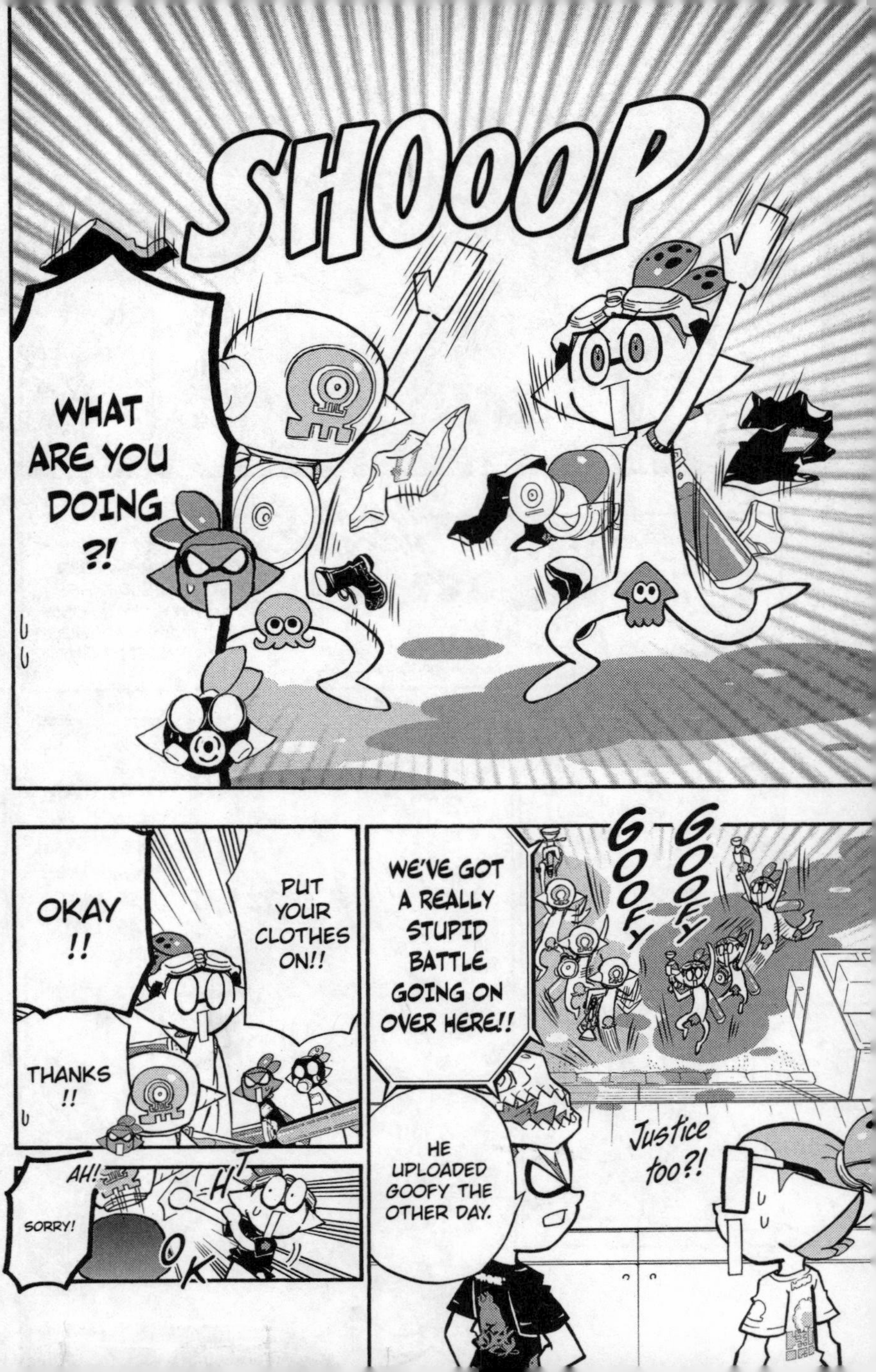
SHOOOP
WHAT ARE YOU DOING ?!
GOOFY GOOFY
WE'VE GOT A REALLY STUPID BATTLE GOING ON OVER HERE!!
Justice too?!
HE UPLOADED GOOFY THE OTHER DAY.
PUT YOUR CLOTHES ON!!
OKAY !!
THANKS !!
HIT
AH!
SORRY!

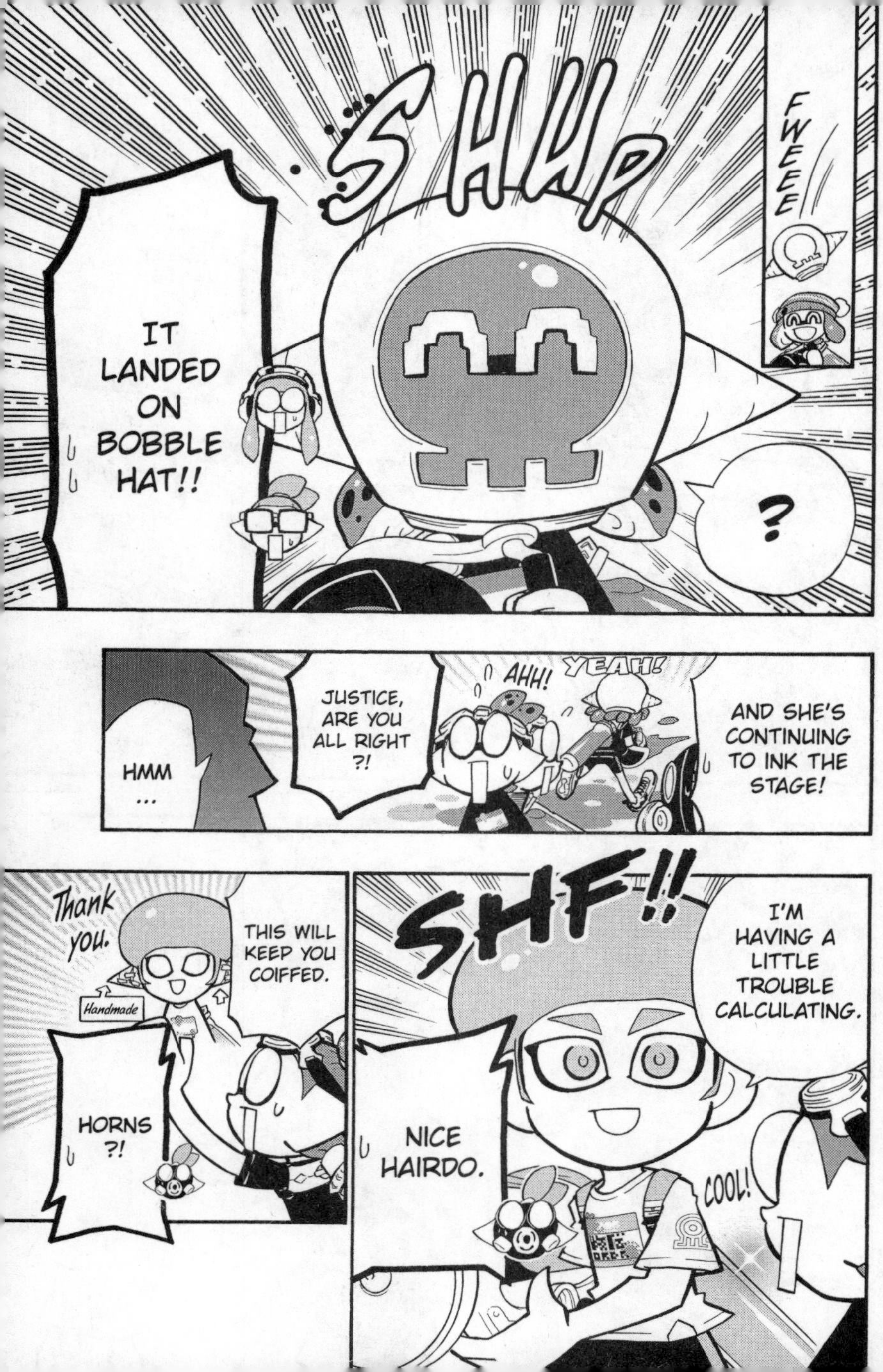
FWEEE
SHUP
?
IT LANDED ON BOBBLE HAT!!
AND SHE'S CONTINUING TO INK THE STAGE!
YEAH!
AHH!
JUSTICE, ARE YOU ALL RIGHT?!
HMM...
I'M HAVING A LITTLE TROUBLE CALCULATING.
SHF!!
COOL!
NICE HAIRDO.
THIS WILL KEEP YOU COIFFED.
Thank you.
Handmade
HORNS?!

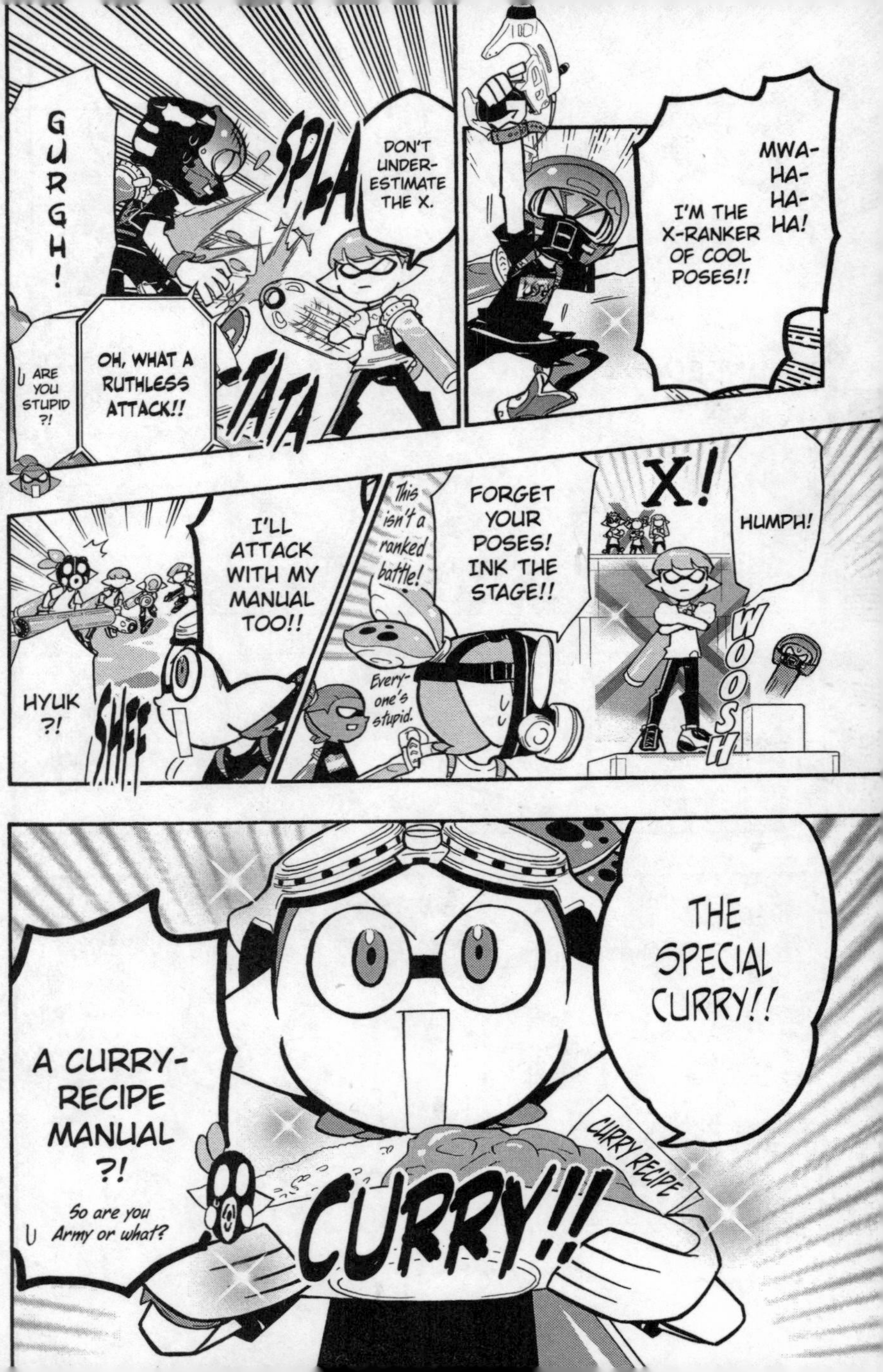
MWA-HA-HA-HA!
I'M THE X-RANKER OF COOL POSES!!
DON'T UNDER-ESTIMATE THE X.
SPLA
TATA
GURGH!
OH, WHAT A RUTHLESS ATTACK!!
ARE YOU STUPID?!
X!
HUMPH!
WOOSH
FORGET YOUR POSES! INK THE STAGE!!
This isn't a ranked battle!
Every-one's stupid.
I'LL ATTACK WITH MY MANUAL TOO!!
SHFF
HYUK?!
THE SPECIAL CURRY!!
CURRY RECIPE
CURRY!!
A CURRY-RECIPE MANUAL?!
So are you Army or what?

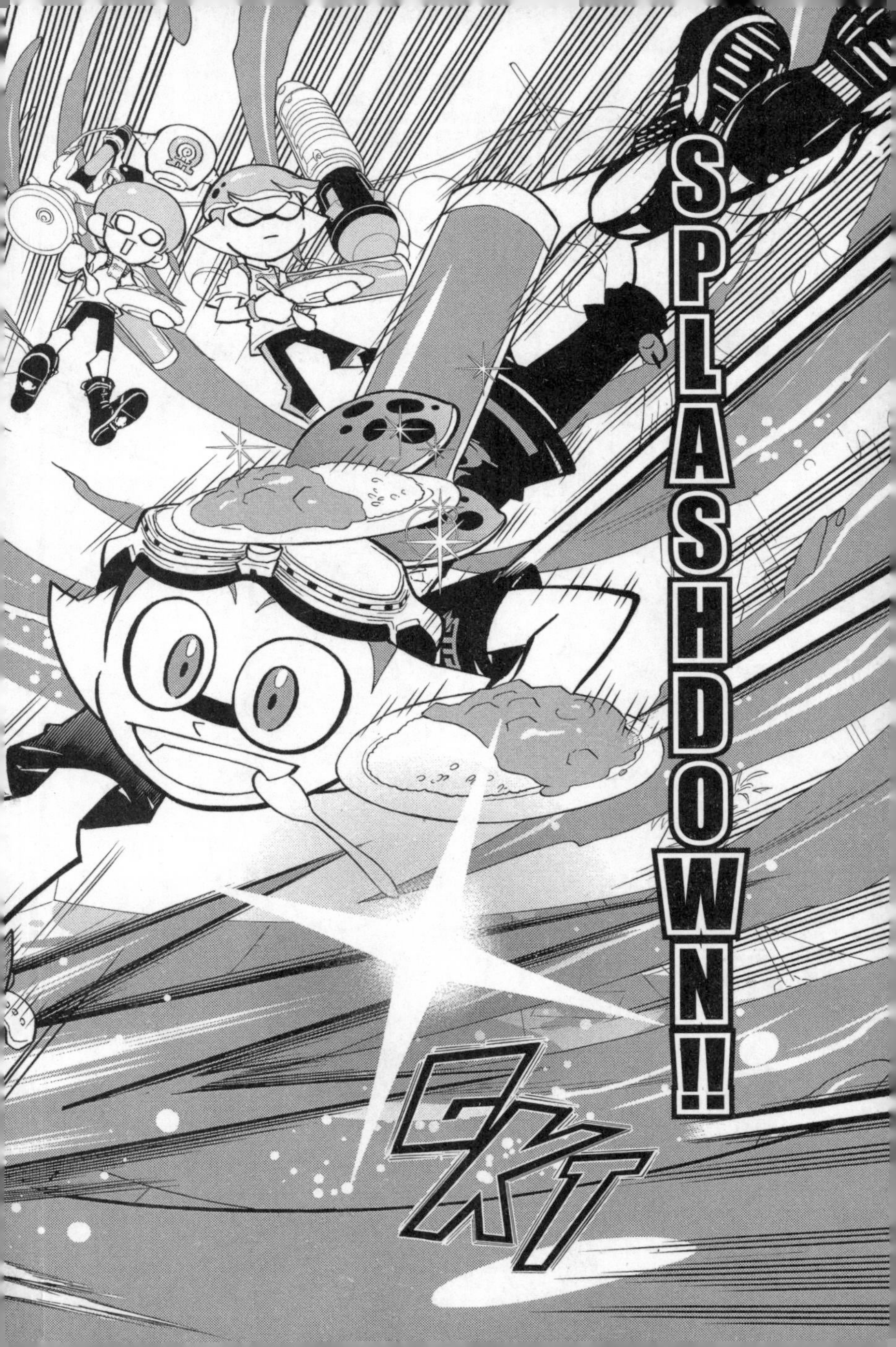
SPLASHDOWN!!

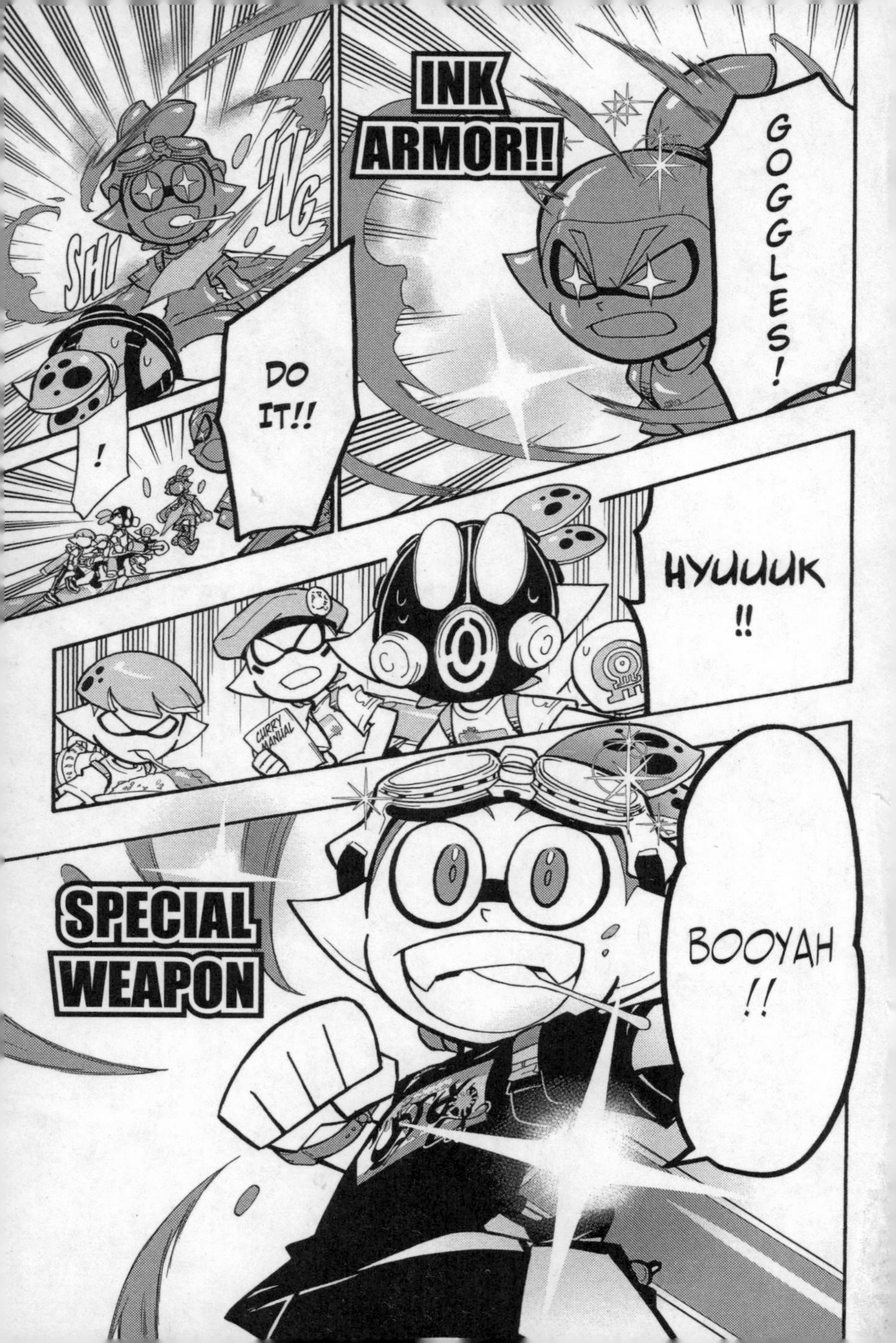
GOGGLES!
INK ARMOR!!
DO IT!!
SHI-ING
!
HYUUUK !!
CURRY MANUAL
BOOYAH !!
SPECIAL WEAPON

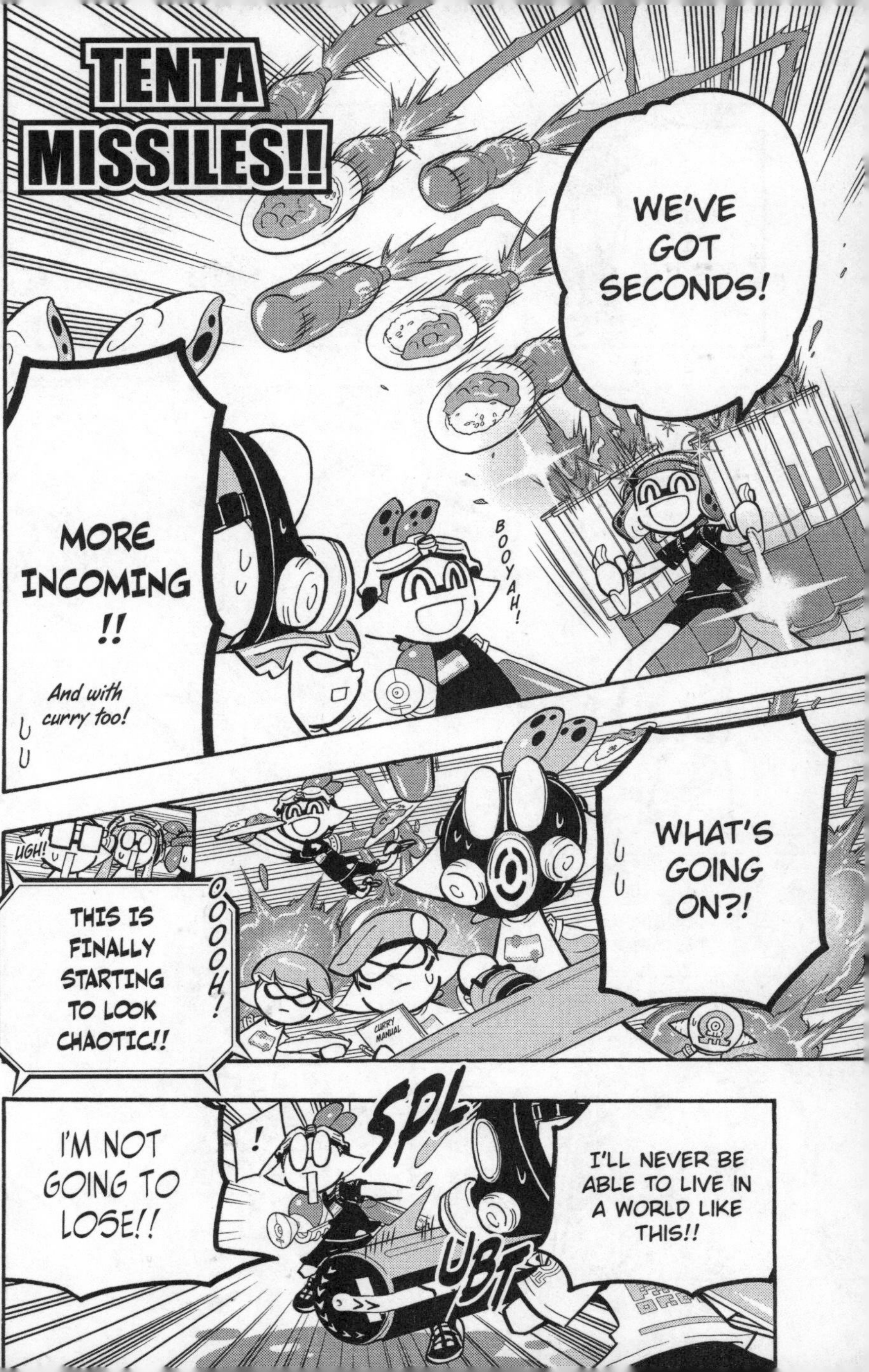
WE'VE GOT SECONDS!
TENTA MISSILES!!
BOOYAH!
MORE INCOMING!!
And with curry too!
WHAT'S GOING ON?!
OOOOOH!
THIS IS FINALLY STARTING TO LOOK CHAOTIC!!
UGH!
CURRY MANUAL
I'LL NEVER BE ABLE TO LIVE IN A WORLD LIKE THIS!!
SPL
UBT
!
I'M NOT GOING TO LOSE!!

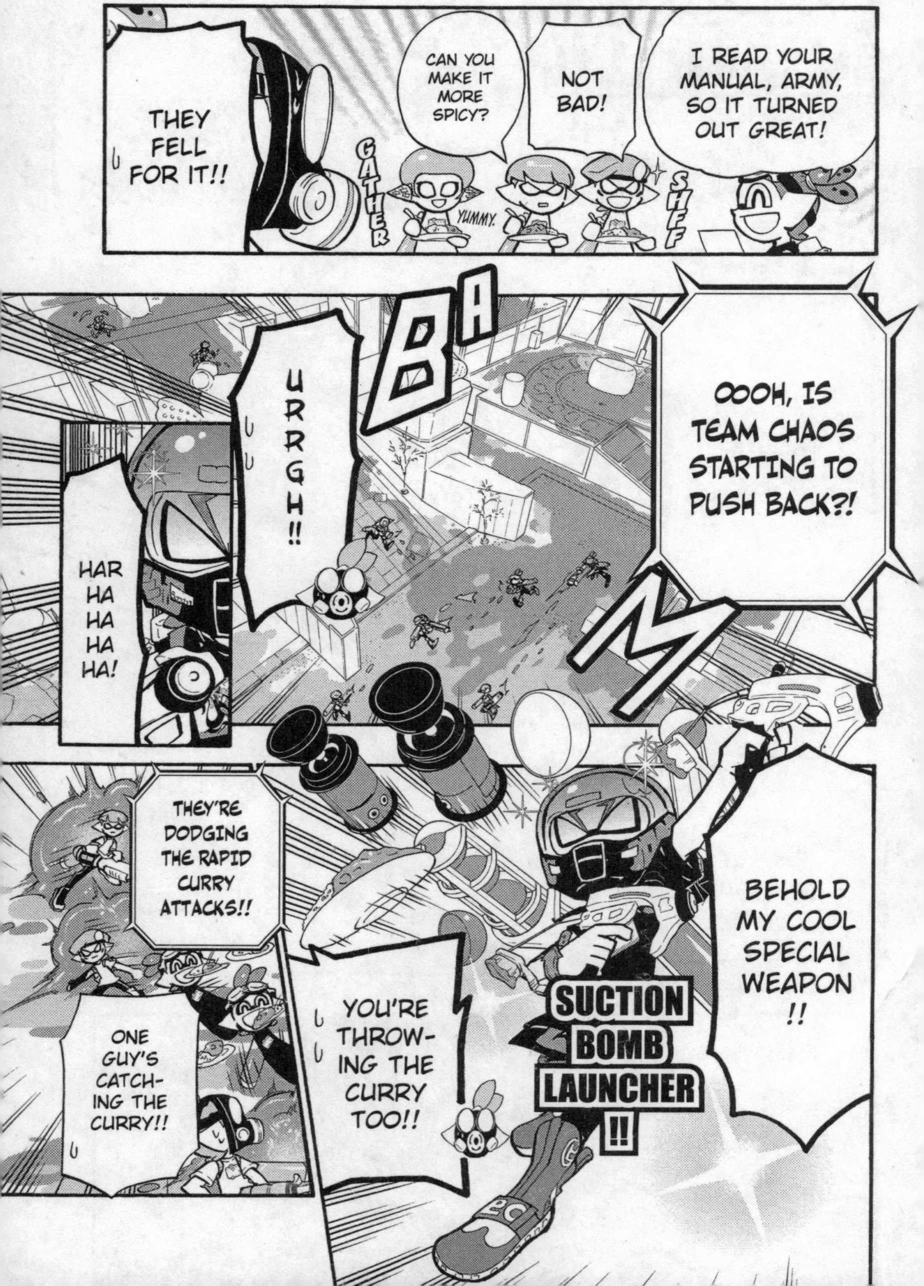
I READ YOUR MANUAL, ARMY, SO IT TURNED OUT GREAT!
SHFF
NOT BAD!
CAN YOU MAKE IT MORE SPICY?
YUMMY.
GATHER
THEY FELL FOR IT!!
OOOH, IS TEAM CHAOS STARTING TO PUSH BACK?!
BAM
URRGH!!
HAR HA HA HA HA!
BEHOLD MY COOL SPECIAL WEAPON!!
SUCTION BOMB LAUNCHER!!
THEY'RE DODGING THE RAPID CURRY ATTACKS!!
YOU'RE THROW-ING THE CURRY TOO!!
ONE GUY'S CATCH-ING THE CURRY!!

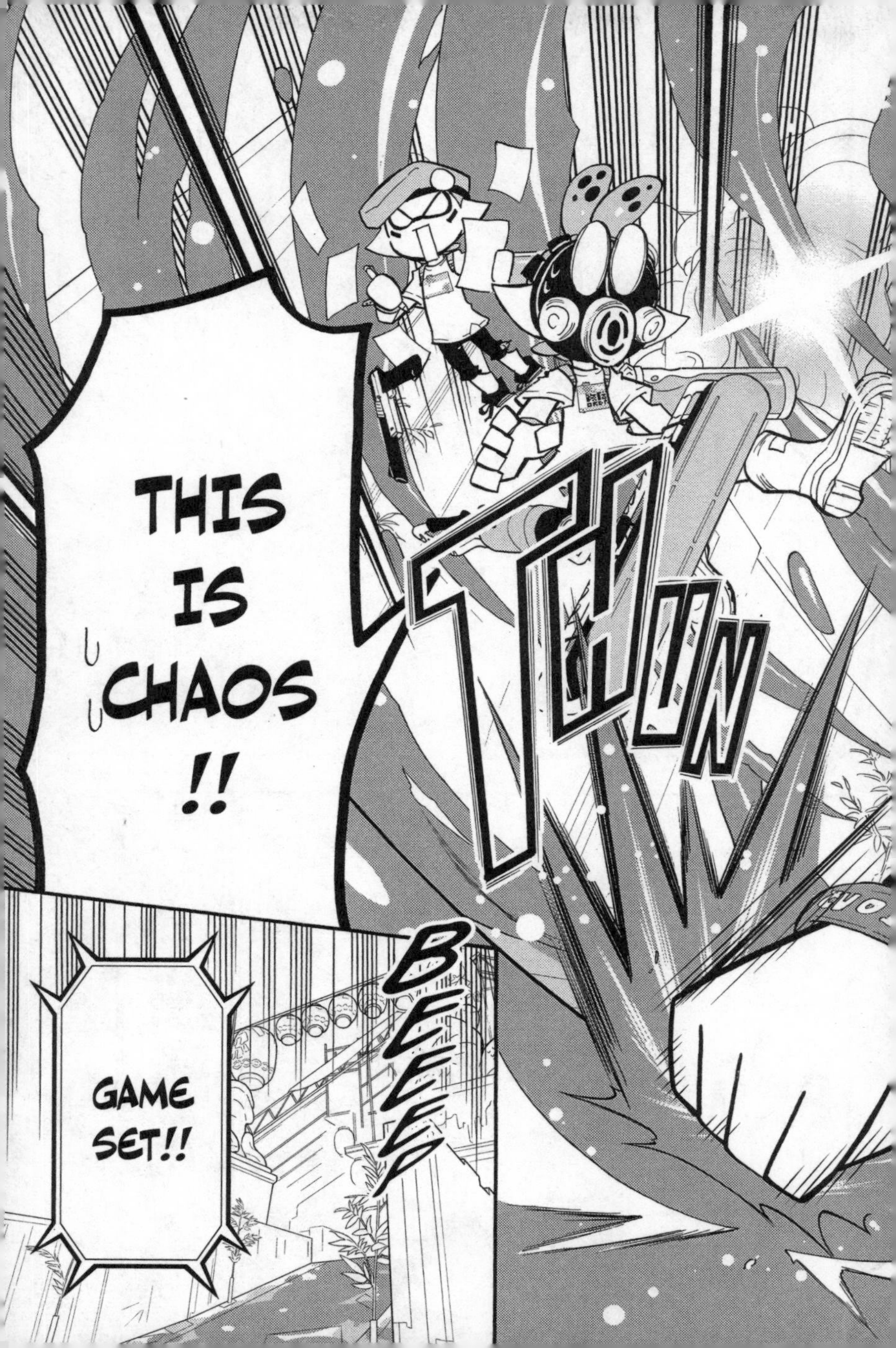
THUN
THIS IS CHAOS!!
BEEEEP
GAME SET!!

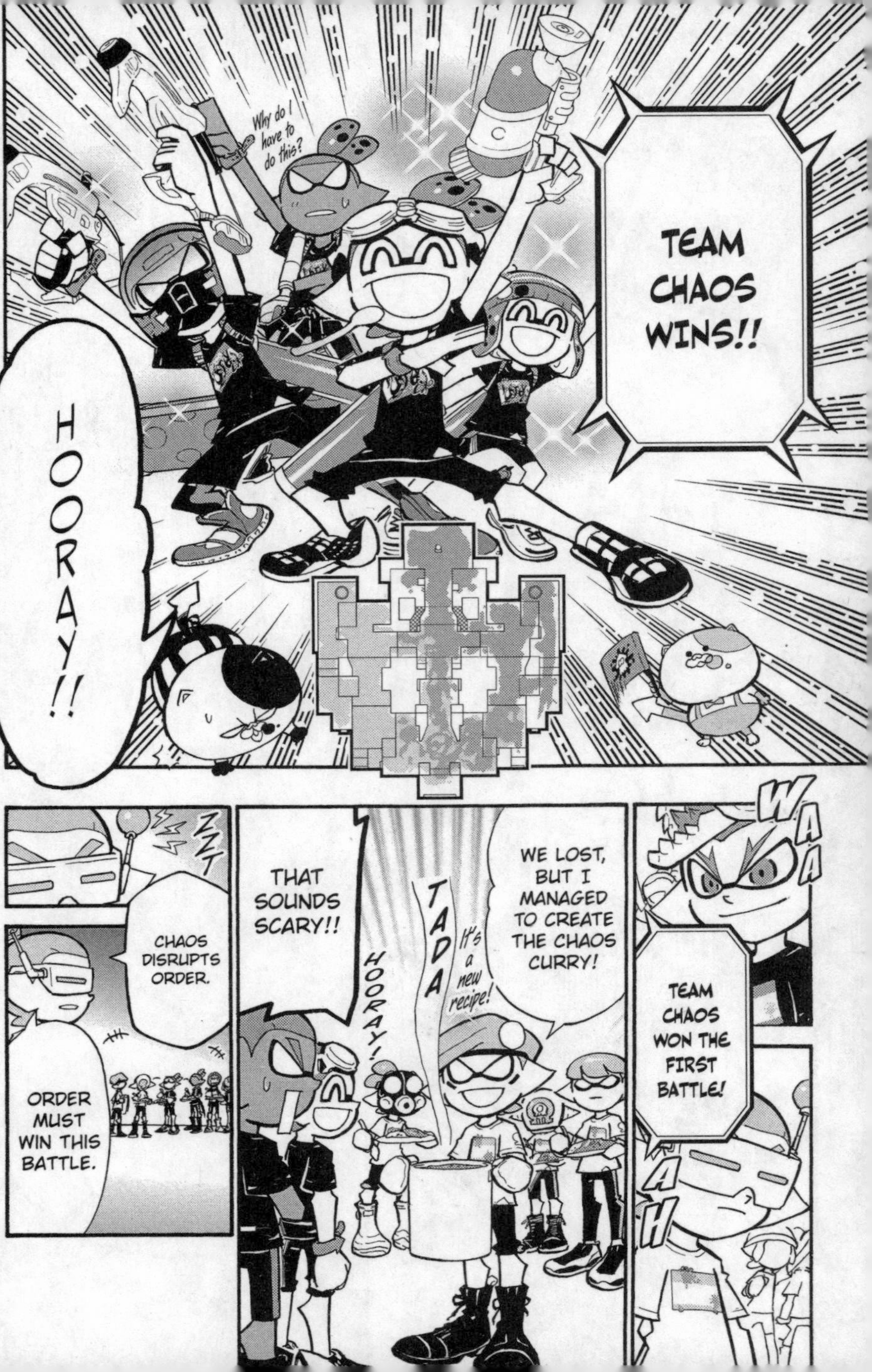
TEAM CHAOS WINS!!
Why do I have to do this?
HOORAY!!
WAAA
TEAM CHAOS WON THE FIRST BATTLE!
AAH
WE LOST, BUT I MANAGED TO CREATE THE CHAOS CURRY!
It's a new recipe!
TADA
THAT SOUNDS SCARY!!
HOORAY!
ZZZT
CHAOS DISRUPTS ORDER.
ORDER MUST WIN THIS BATTLE.

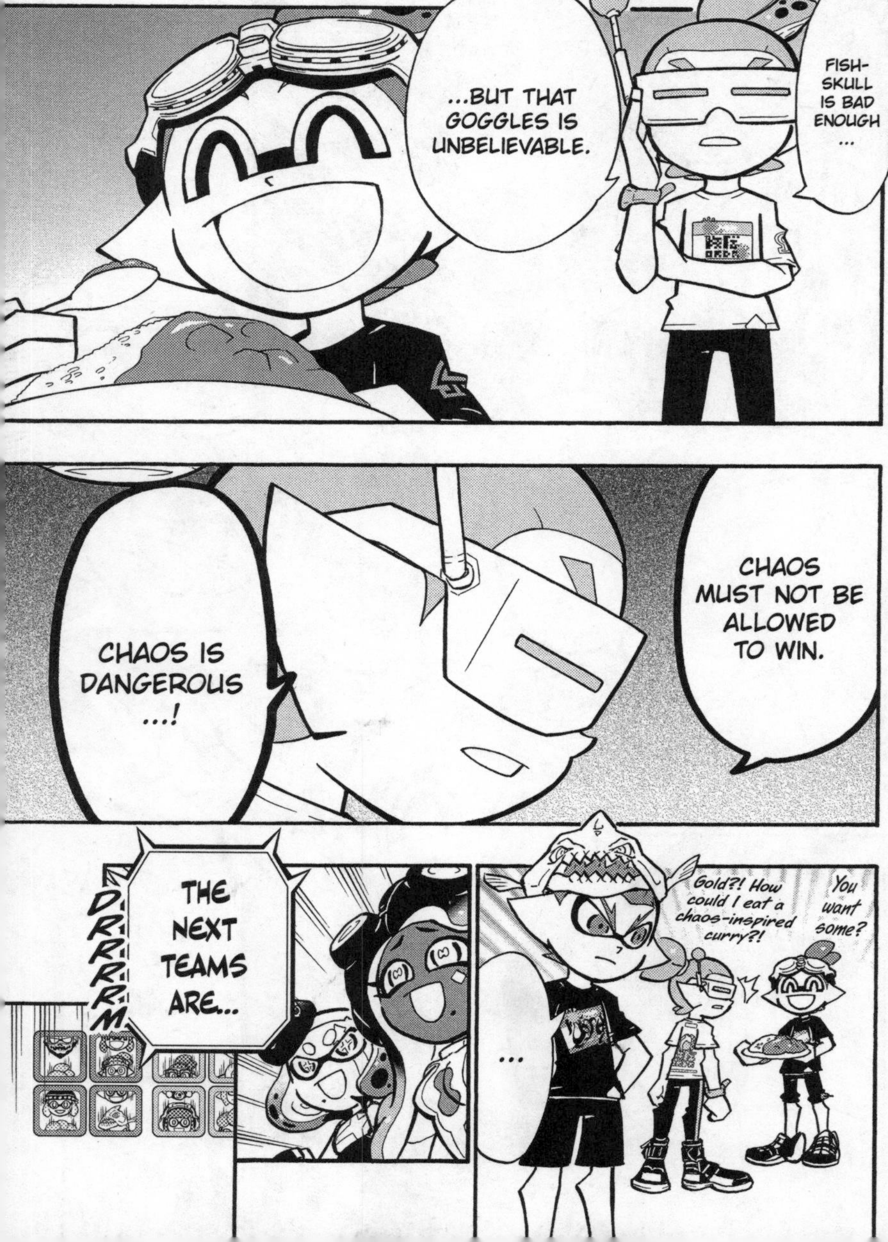
FISH-SKULL IS BAD ENOUGH...
...BUT THAT GOGGLES IS UNBELIEVABLE.
CHAOS MUST NOT BE ALLOWED TO WIN.
CHAOS IS DANGEROUS...!
You want some?
Gold?! How could I eat a chaos-inspired curry?!
...
THE NEXT TEAMS ARE...
DRRRRRM.

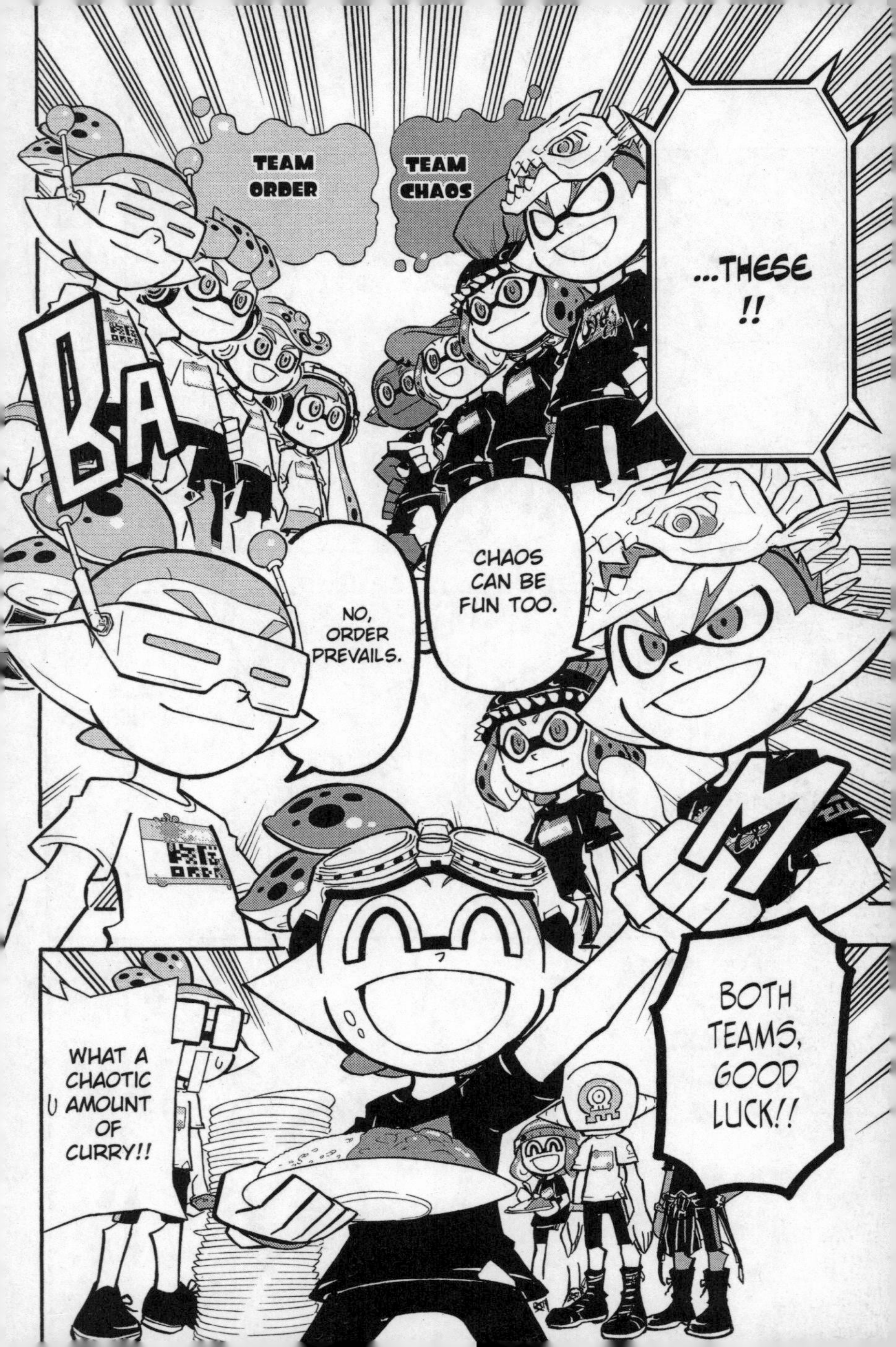
...THESE !!
TEAM CHAOS
TEAM ORDER
CHAOS CAN BE FUN TOO.
NO, ORDER PREVAILS.
M
BA
BOTH TEAMS, GOOD LUCK!!
WHAT A CHAOTIC AMOUNT OF CURRY!!

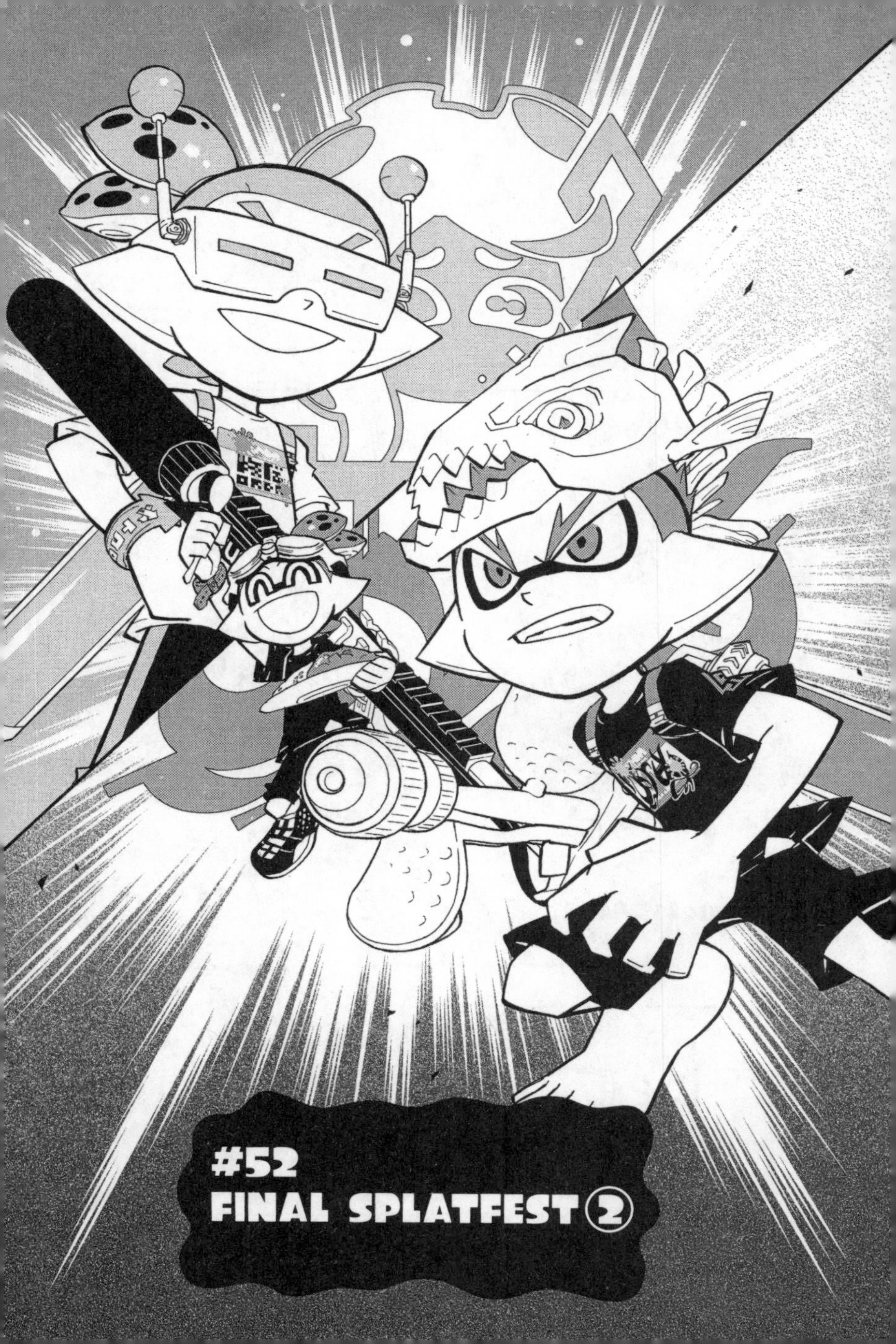
#52
FINAL SPLATFEST ②

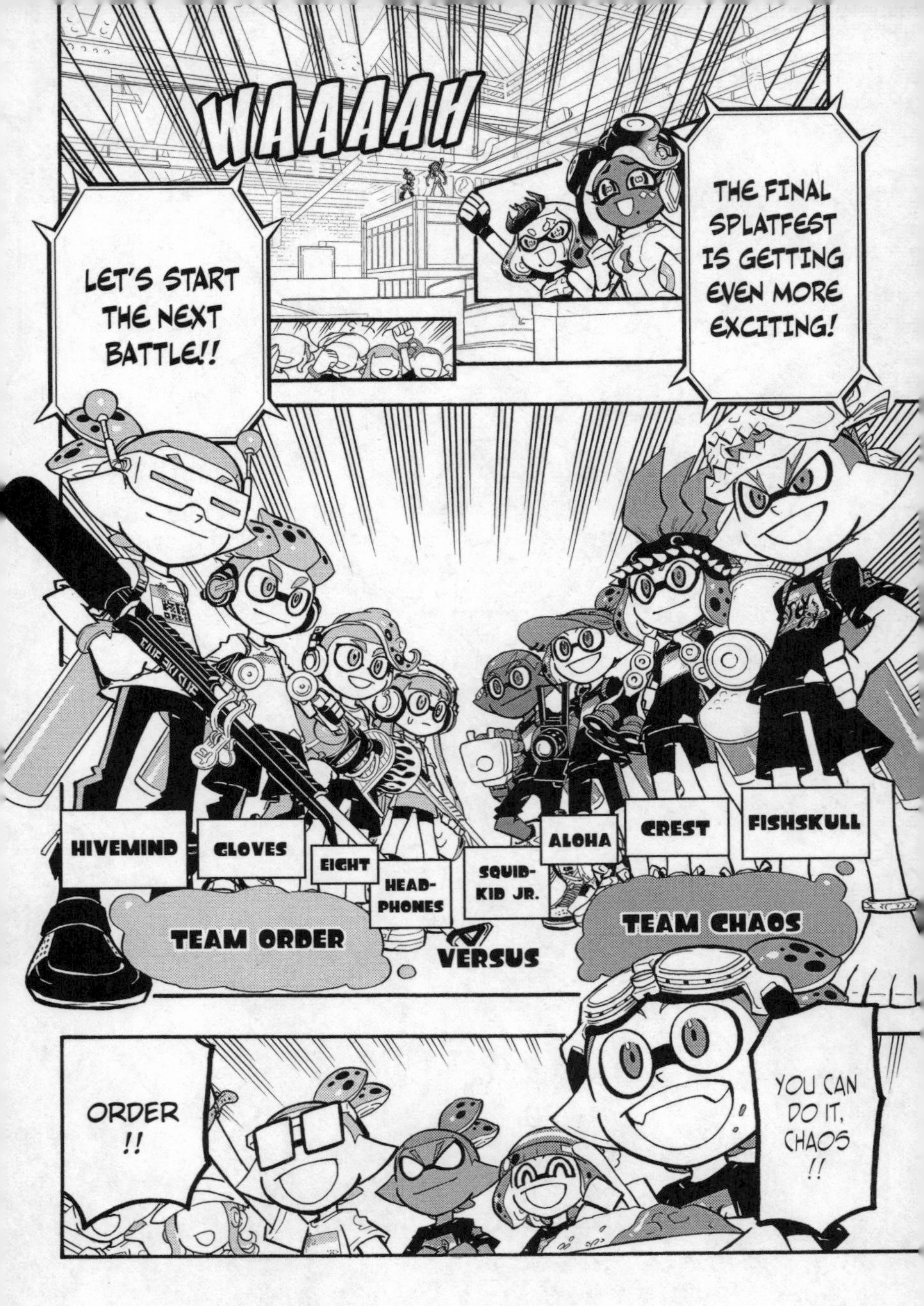
WAAAAAH
THE FINAL SPLATFEST IS GETTING EVEN MORE EXCITING!
LET'S START THE NEXT BATTLE!!
FISHSKULL
CREST
ALOHA
SQUID-KID JR.
HEAD-PHONES
EIGHT
GLOVES
HIVEMIND
TEAM CHAOS
VERSUS
TEAM ORDER
YOU CAN DO IT, CHAOS!!
ORDER!!

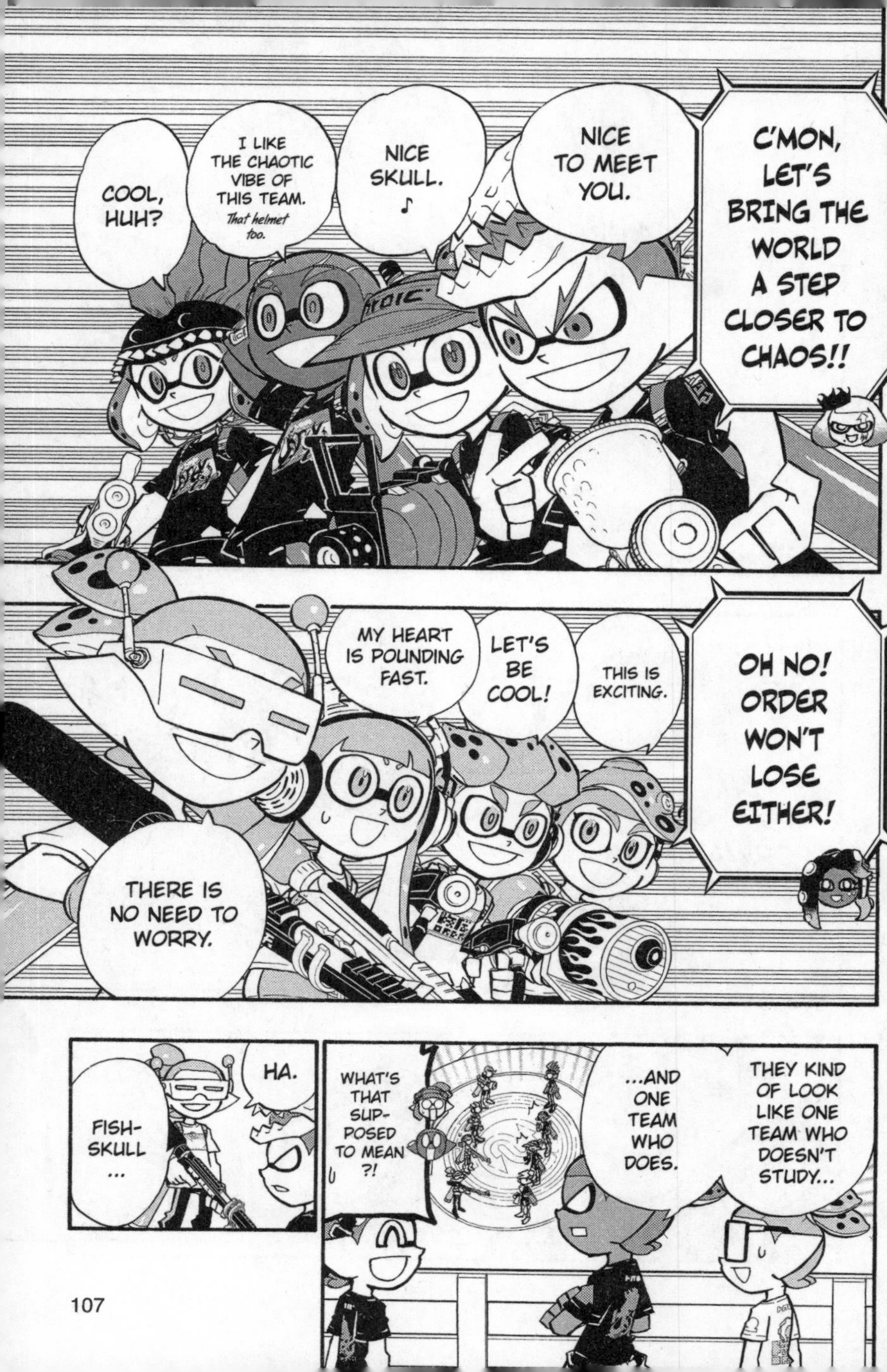
C'MON, LET'S BRING THE WORLD A STEP CLOSER TO CHAOS!!
NICE TO MEET YOU.
NICE SKULL. ♪
I LIKE THE CHAOTIC VIBE OF THIS TEAM. *That helmet too.*
COOL, HUH?
OH NO! ORDER WON'T LOSE EITHER!
THIS IS EXCITING.
LET'S BE COOL!
MY HEART IS POUNDING FAST.
THERE IS NO NEED TO WORRY.
THEY KIND OF LOOK LIKE ONE TEAM WHO DOESN'T STUDY...
...AND ONE TEAM WHO DOES.
WHAT'S THAT SUPPOSED TO MEAN?!
HA.
FISH-SKULL...

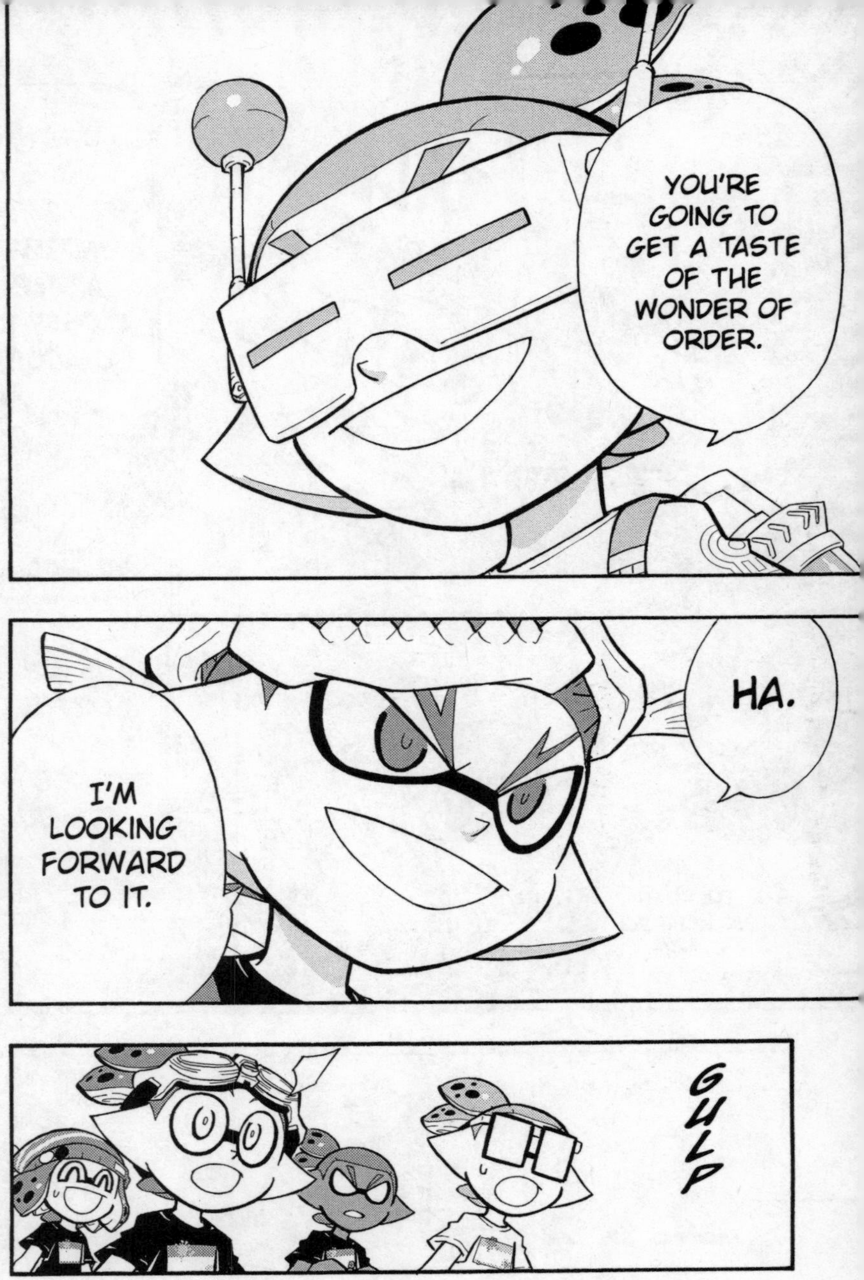
YOU'RE GOING TO GET A TASTE OF THE WONDER OF ORDER.
HA.
I'M LOOKING FORWARD TO IT.
GULP

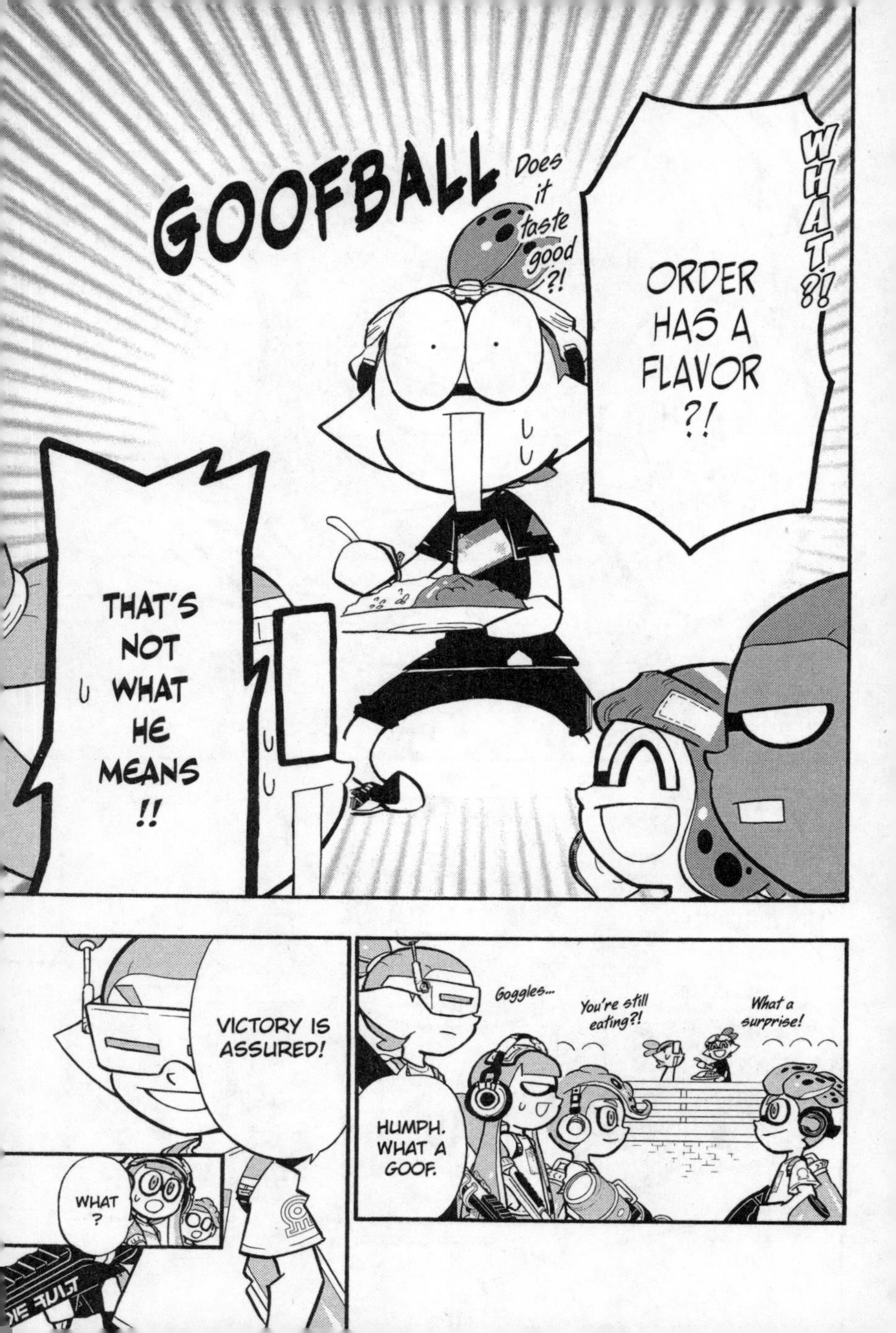
WHAT?!
ORDER HAS A FLAVOR?!
Does it taste good?!
GOOFBALL
THAT'S NOT WHAT HE MEANS!!
What a surprise!
You're still eating?!
Goggles...
HUMPH. WHAT A GOOF.
VICTORY IS ASSURED!
WHAT?

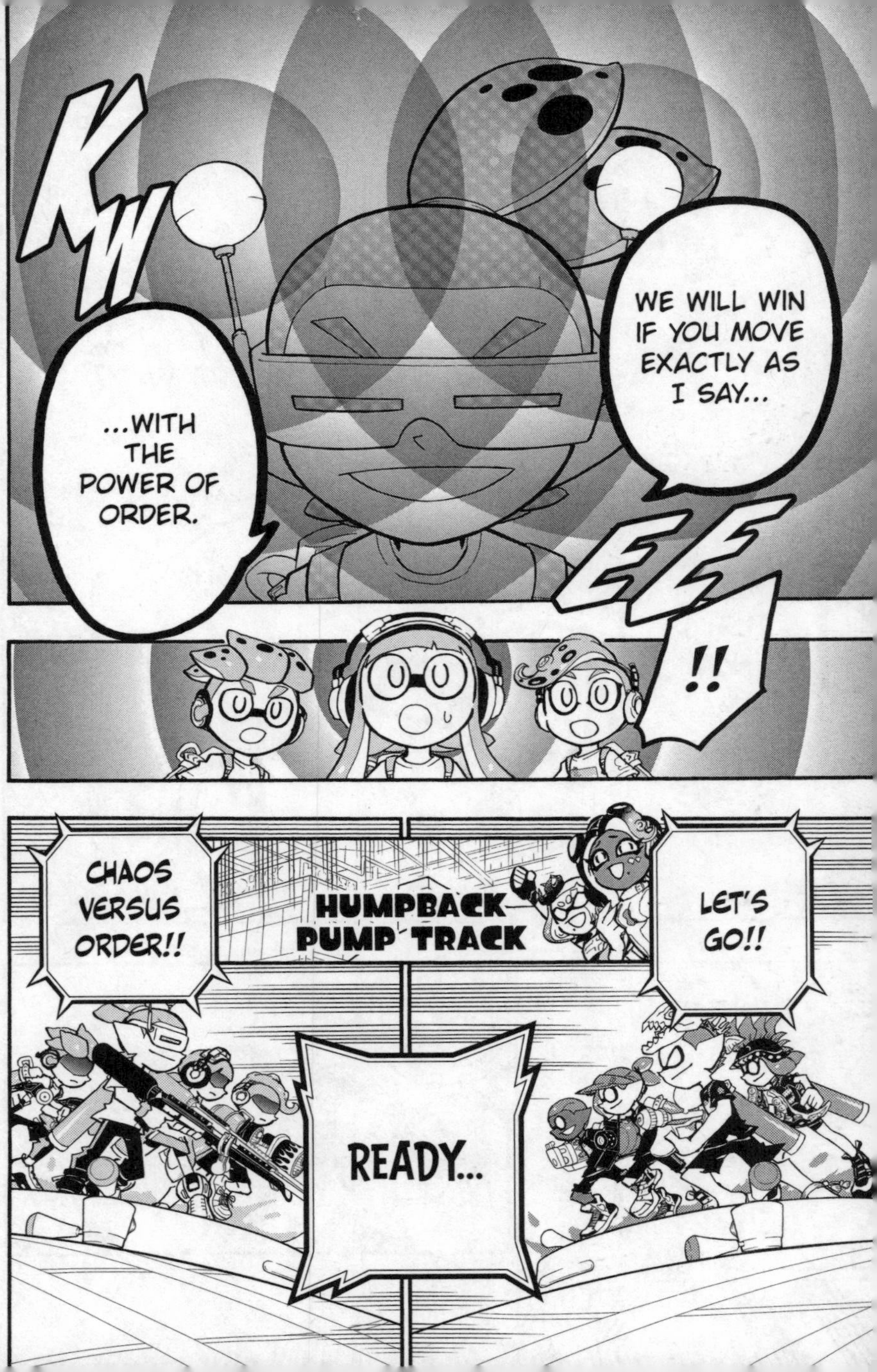
WE WILL WIN IF YOU MOVE EXACTLY AS I SAY...
KWEE
...WITH THE POWER OF ORDER.
!!
LET'S GO!!
HUMPBACK PUMP TRACK
CHAOS VERSUS ORDER!!
READY...

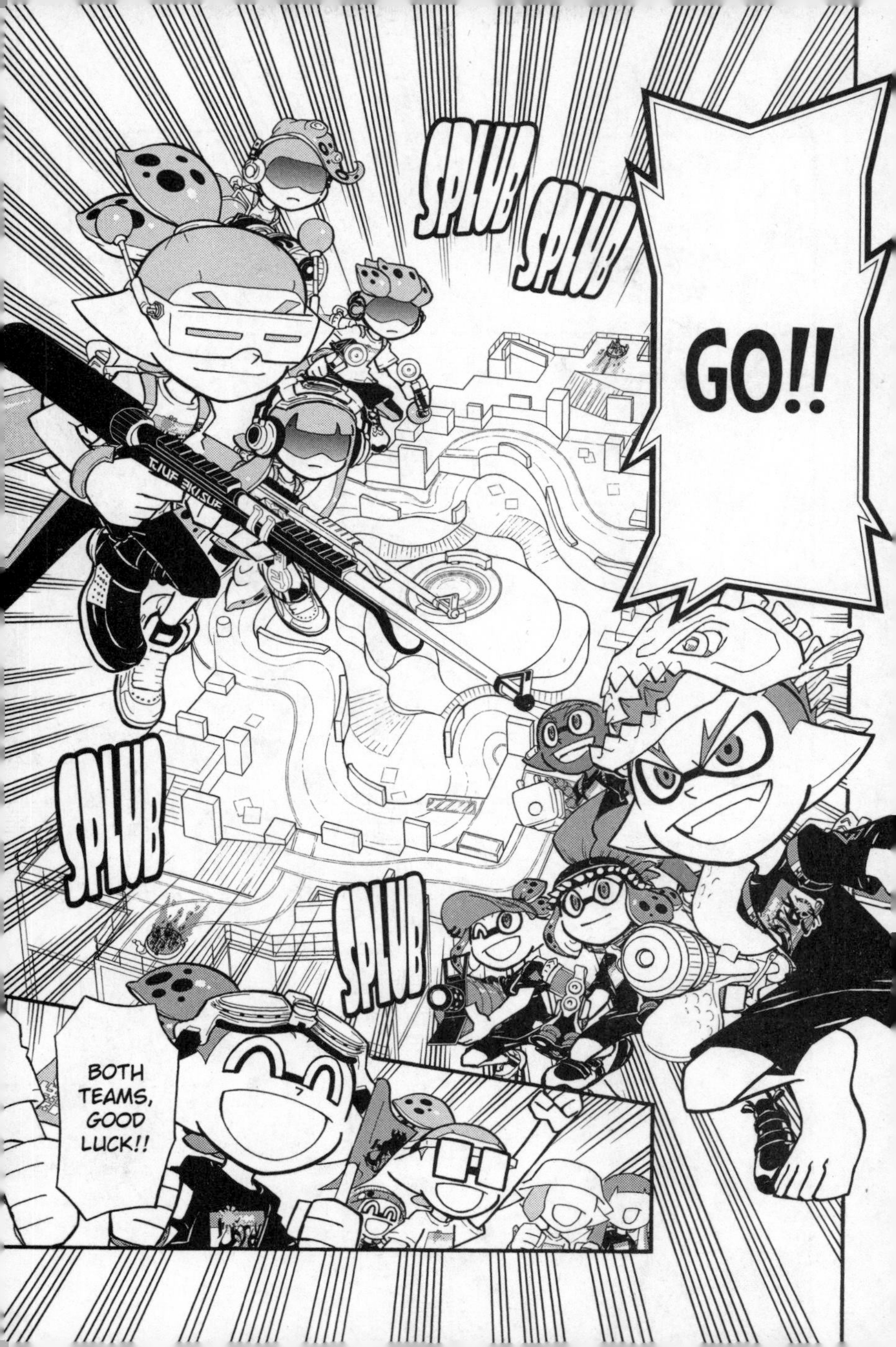
GO!!
SPLUB
SPLUB
SPLUB
SPLUB
BOTH TEAMS, GOOD LUCK!!

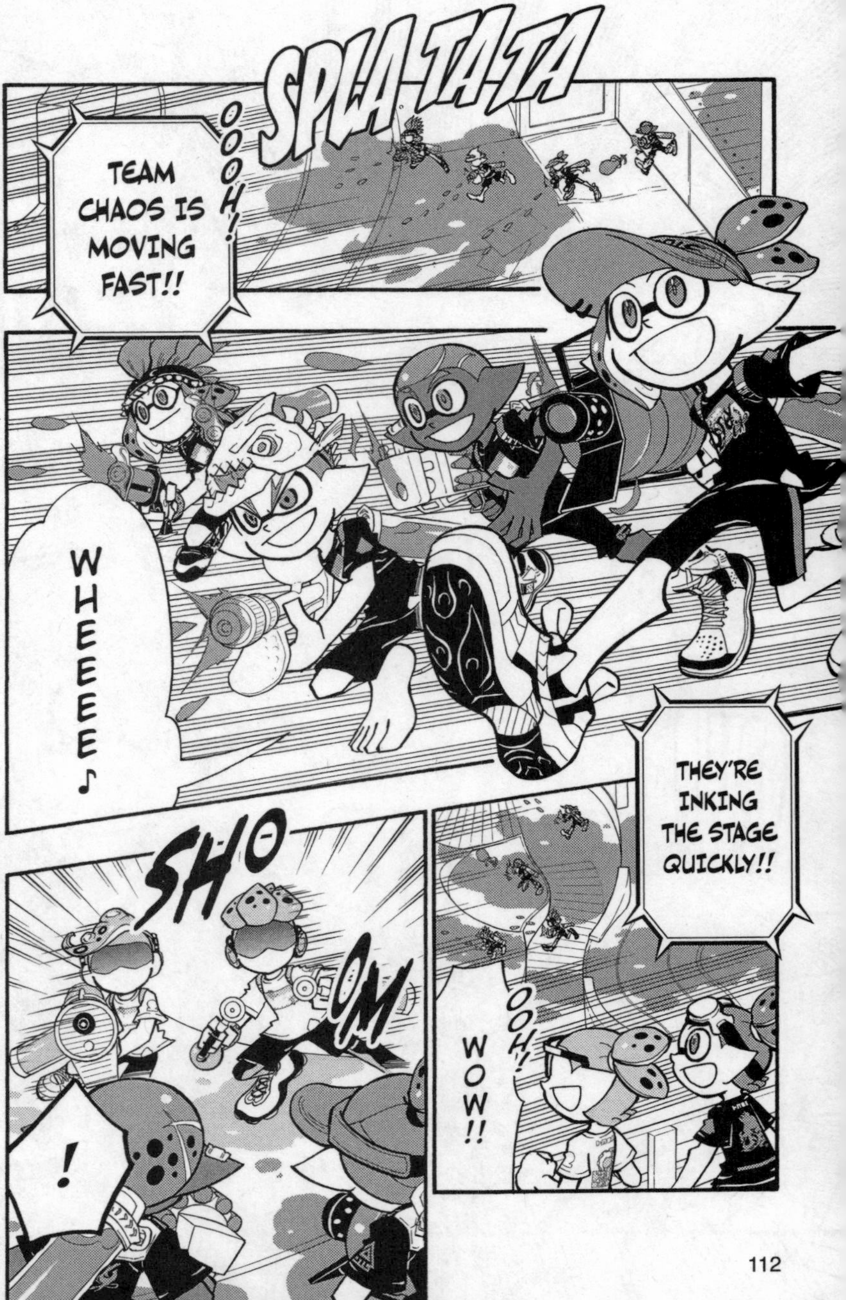
SPLA-TA-TA
OOOOH!
TEAM CHAOS IS MOVING FAST!!
WHEEEEE♪
THEY'RE INKING THE STAGE QUICKLY!!
OOOH!!
WOW!!
SHO-
OM
!

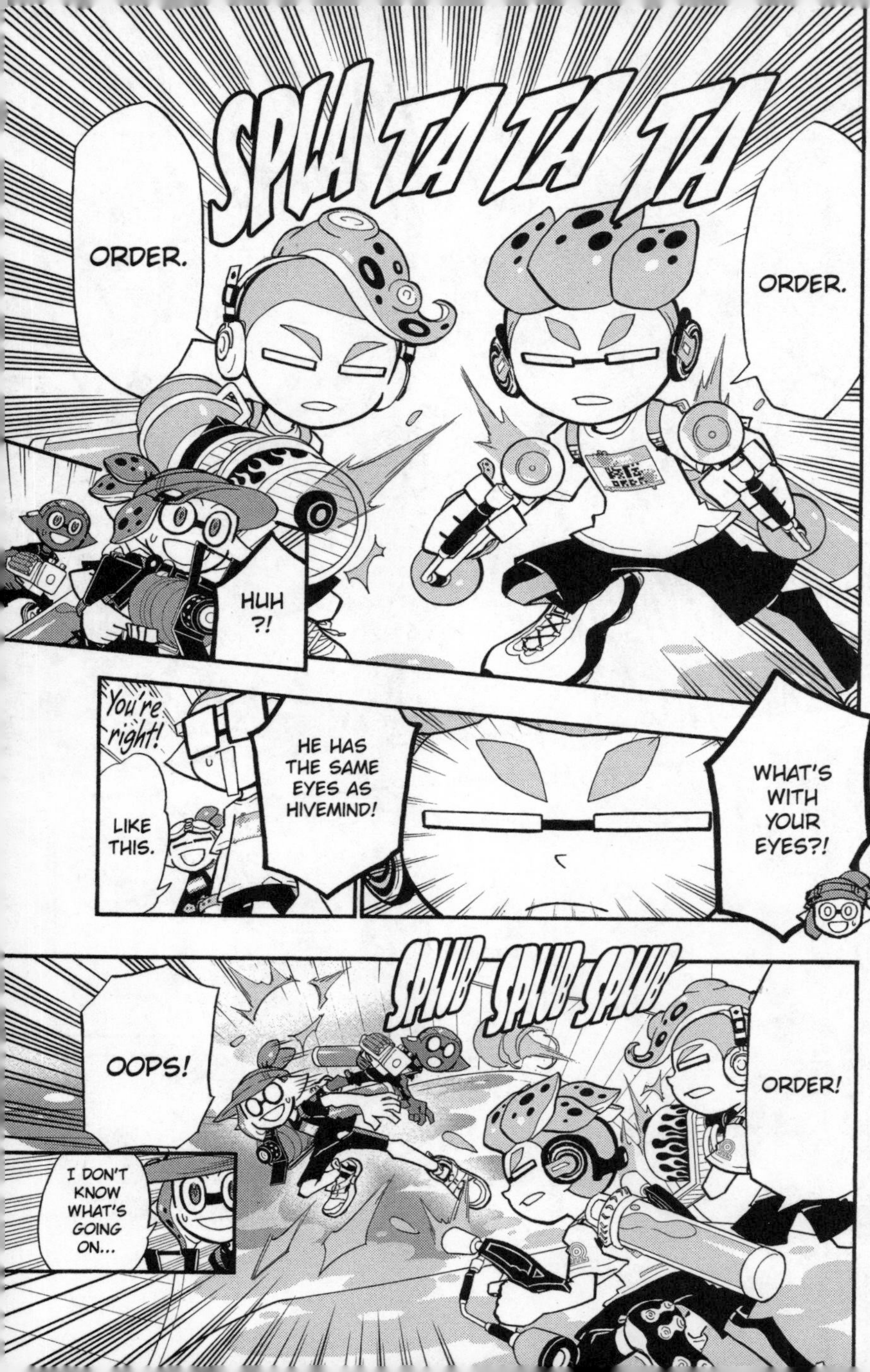
SPLA TA TA TA
ORDER.
ORDER.
HUH ?!
WHAT'S WITH YOUR EYES?!
HE HAS THE SAME EYES AS HIVEMIND!
You're right!
LIKE THIS.
SPLUB SPLUB SPLUB
ORDER!
OOPS!
I DON'T KNOW WHAT'S GOING ON...

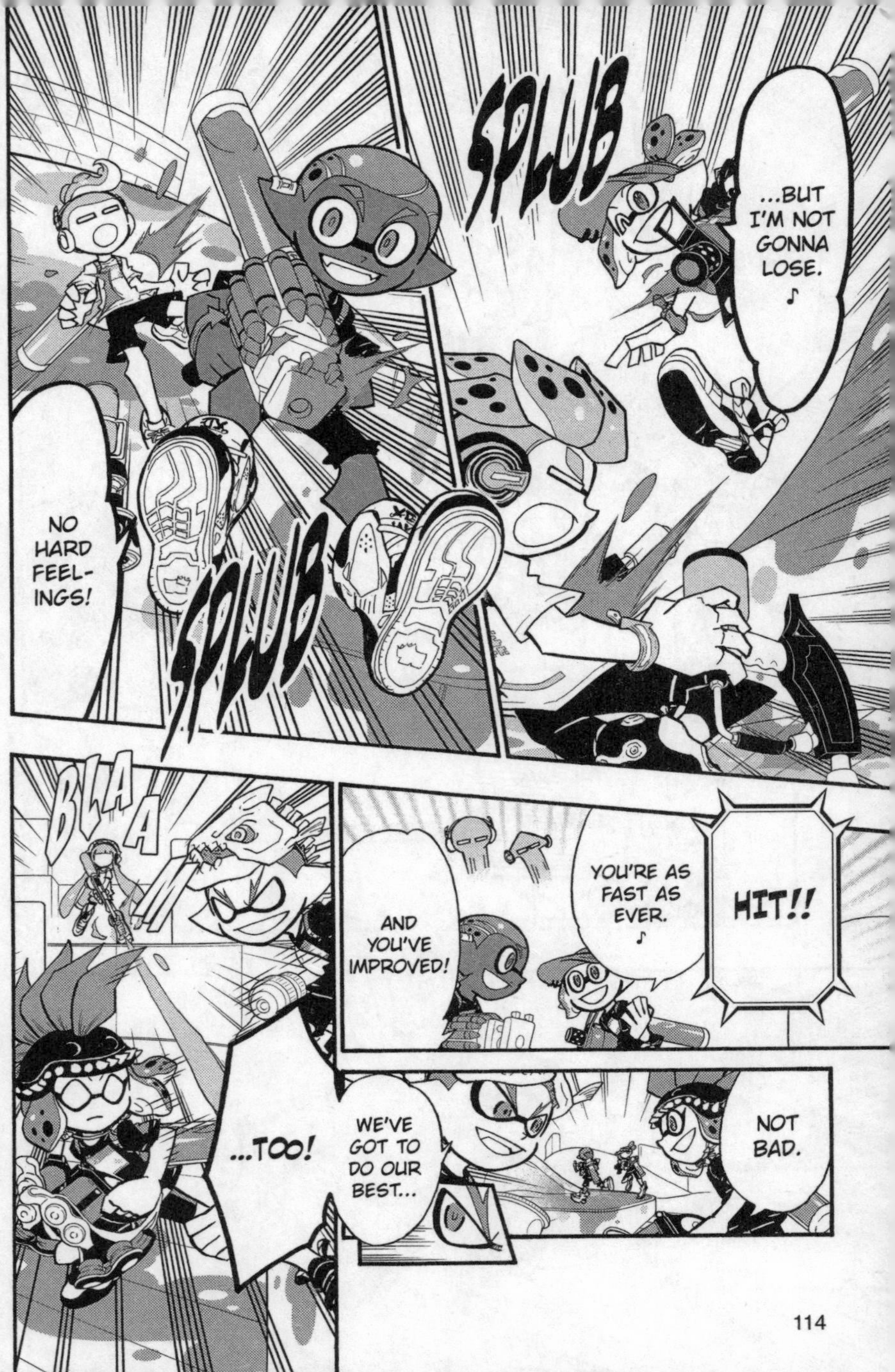
...BUT I'M NOT GONNA LOSE. ♪
SPLUB
SPLUB
NO HARD FEEL-INGS!
HIT!!
YOU'RE AS FAST AS EVER. ♪
AND YOU'VE IMPROVED!
NOT BAD.
WE'VE GOT TO DO OUR BEST...
BLAA
...TOO!

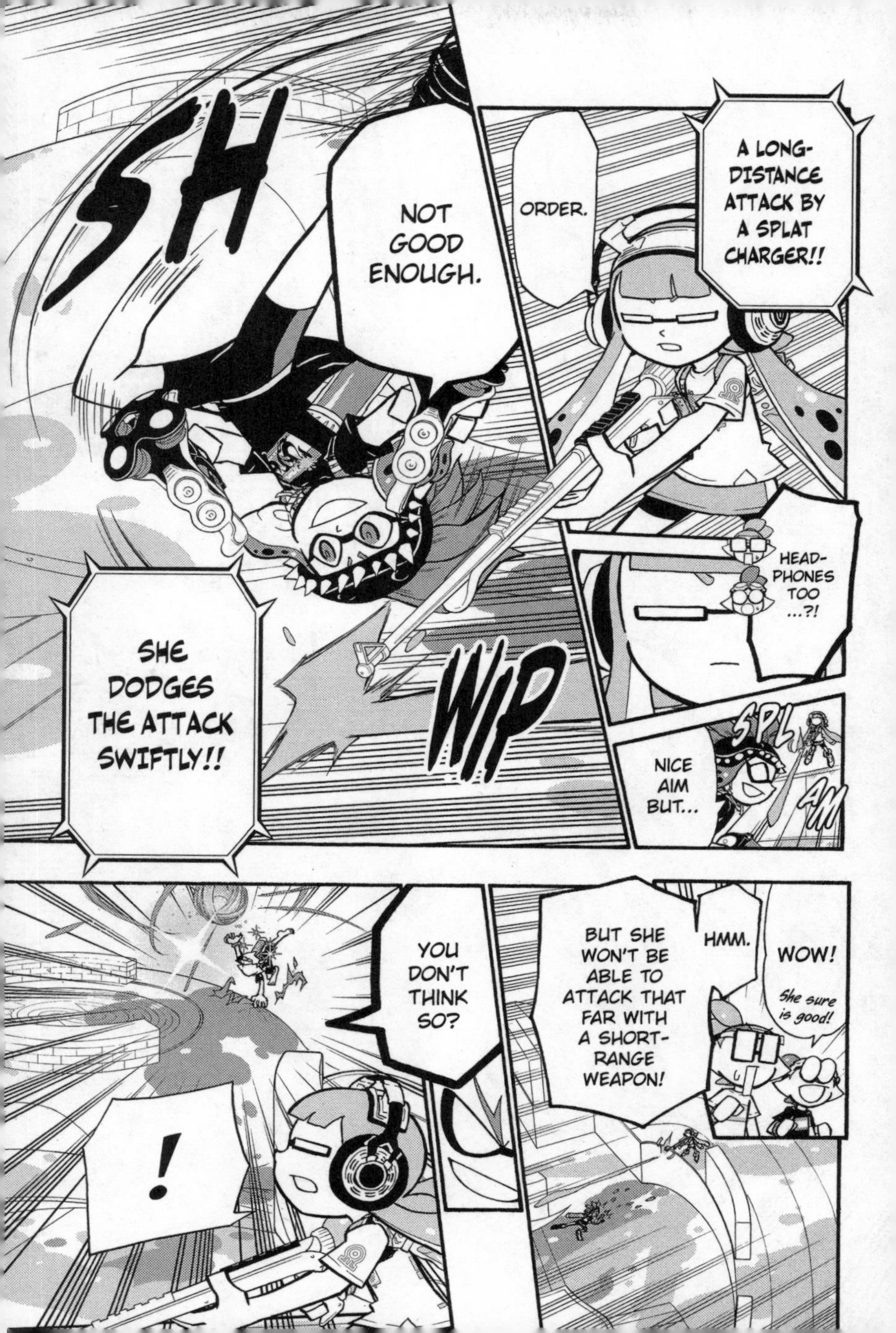
A LONG-DISTANCE ATTACK BY A SPLAT CHARGER!!
ORDER.
HEAD-PHONES TOO ...?!
SPL
AM
NICE AIM BUT...
NOT GOOD ENOUGH.
SH
WIP
SHE DODGES THE ATTACK SWIFTLY!!
WOW!
She sure is good!
HMM.
BUT SHE WON'T BE ABLE TO ATTACK THAT FAR WITH A SHORT-RANGE WEAPON!
YOU DON'T THINK SO?
!

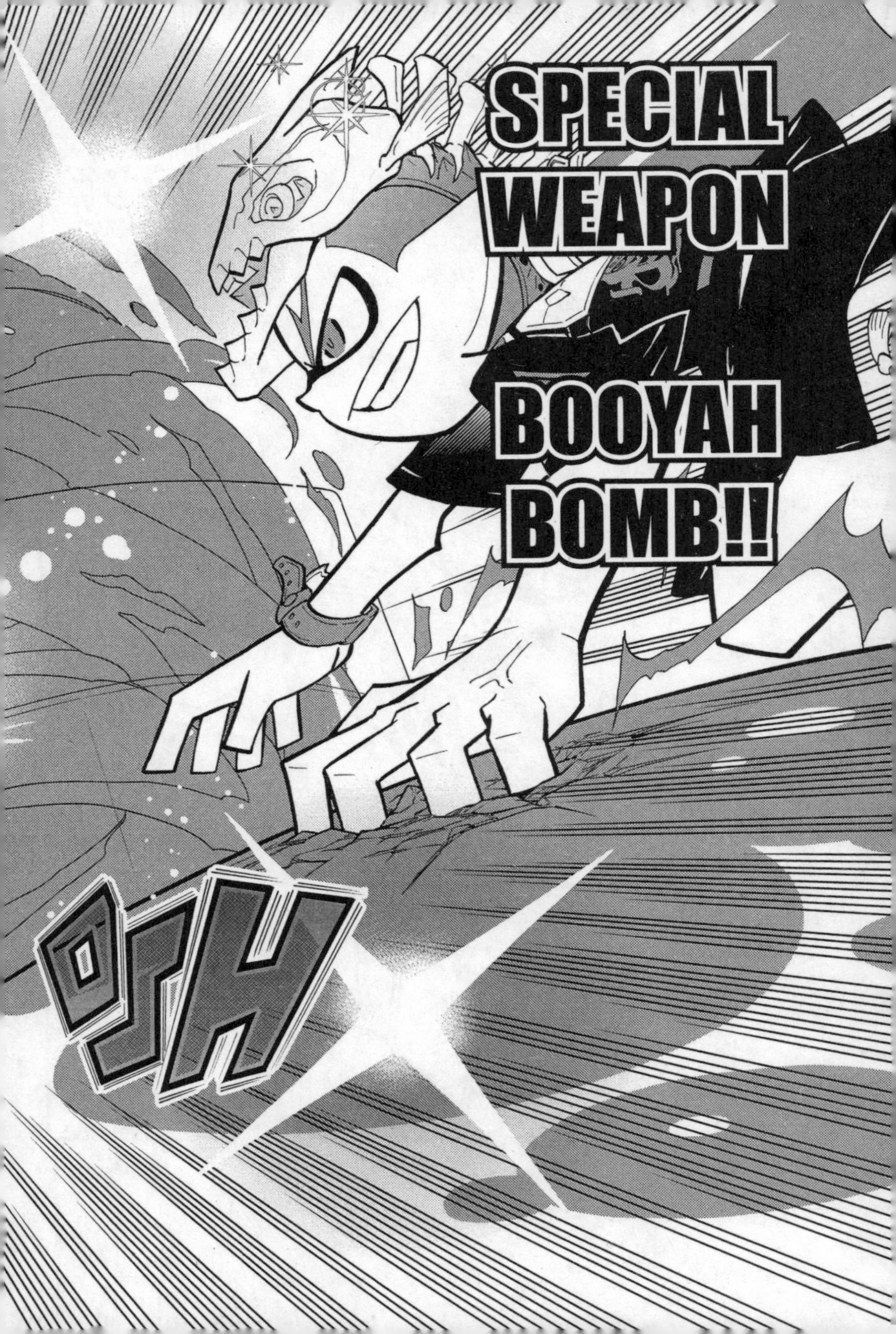
SPECIAL WEAPON
BOOYAH BOMB!!
DSH

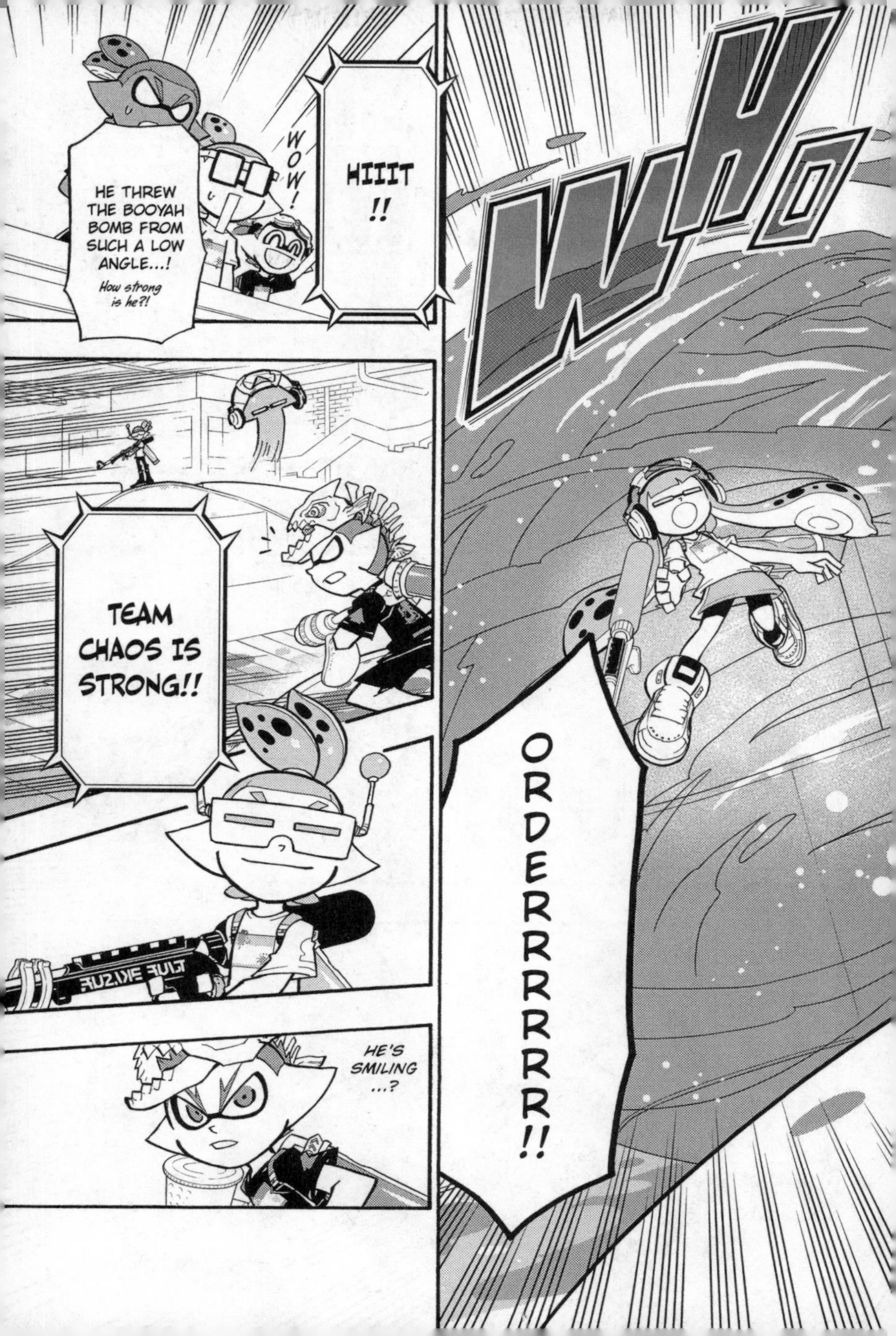
WHO
ORDERRRRRR!!
HIIIT!!
WOW!
HE THREW THE BOOYAH BOMB FROM SUCH A LOW ANGLE...!
How strong is he?!
TEAM CHAOS IS STRONG!!
HE'S SMILING ...?

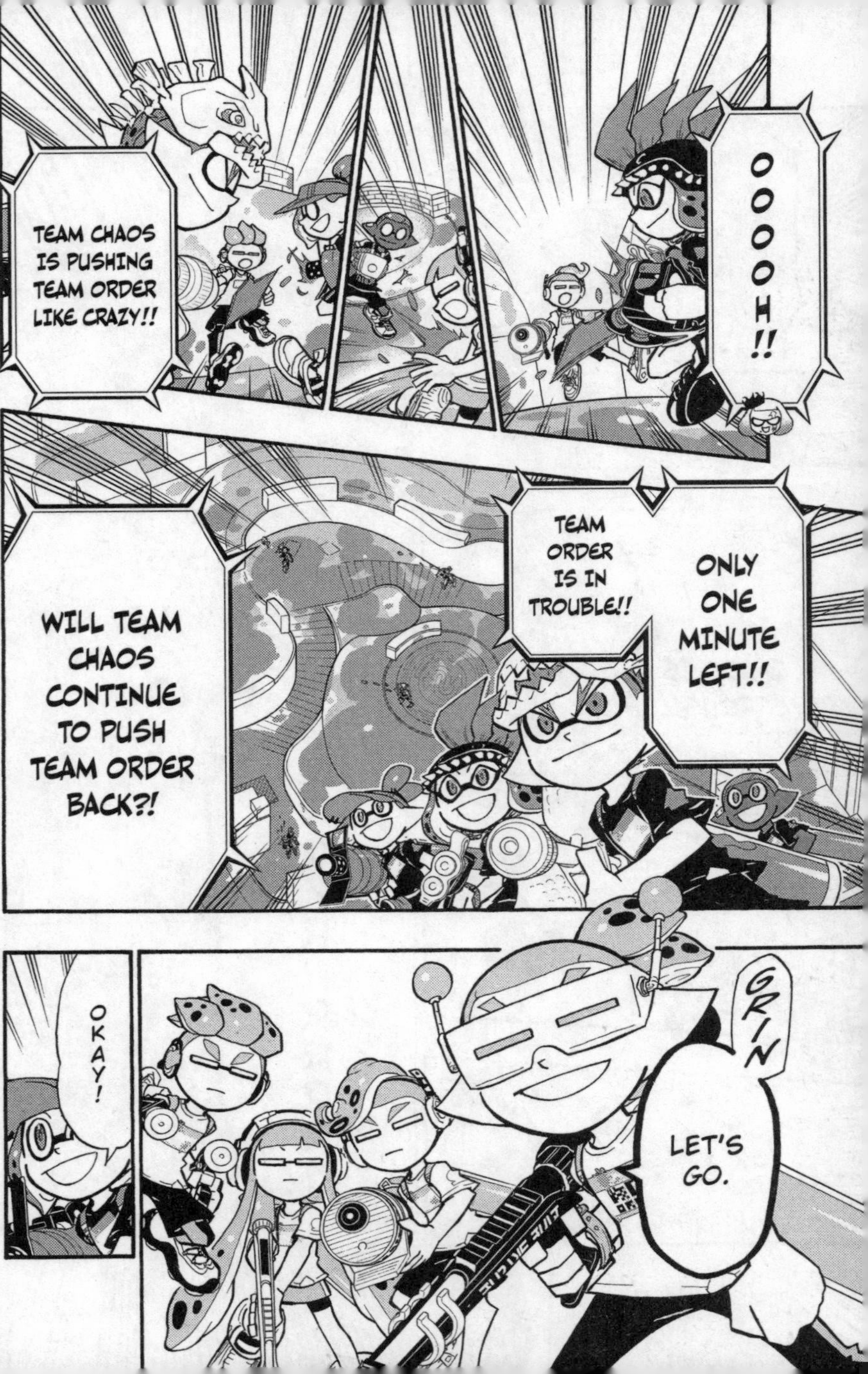
OOOOH!!
TEAM CHAOS IS PUSHING TEAM ORDER LIKE CRAZY!!
ONLY ONE MINUTE LEFT!!
TEAM ORDER IS IN TROUBLE!!
WILL TEAM CHAOS CONTINUE TO PUSH TEAM ORDER BACK?!
GRIN
LET'S GO.
OKAY!

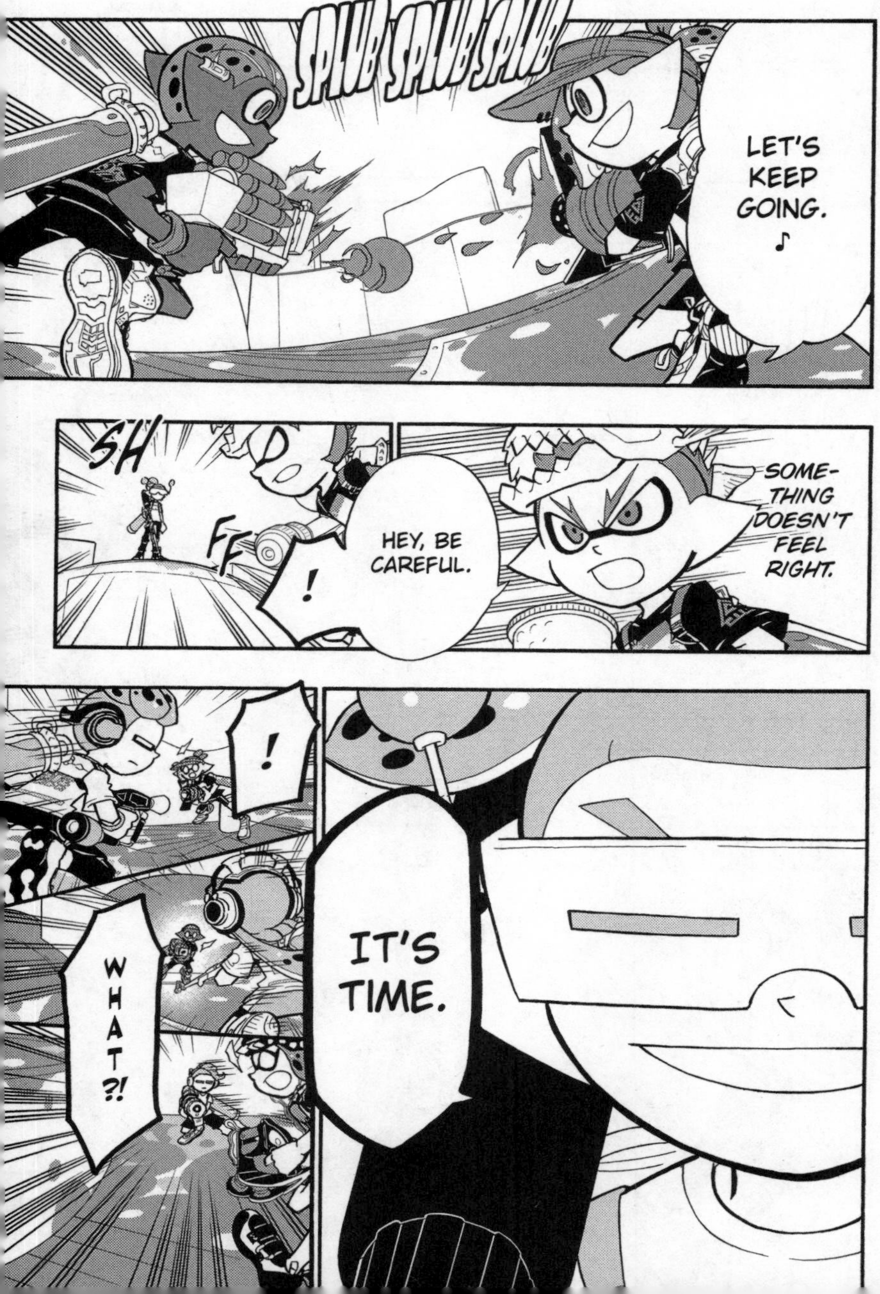
SPLUB SPLUB SPLUB
LET'S KEEP GOING. ♪
SOME-THING DOESN'T FEEL RIGHT.
HEY, BE CAREFUL.
SHFF
!
IT'S TIME.
!
WHAT?!

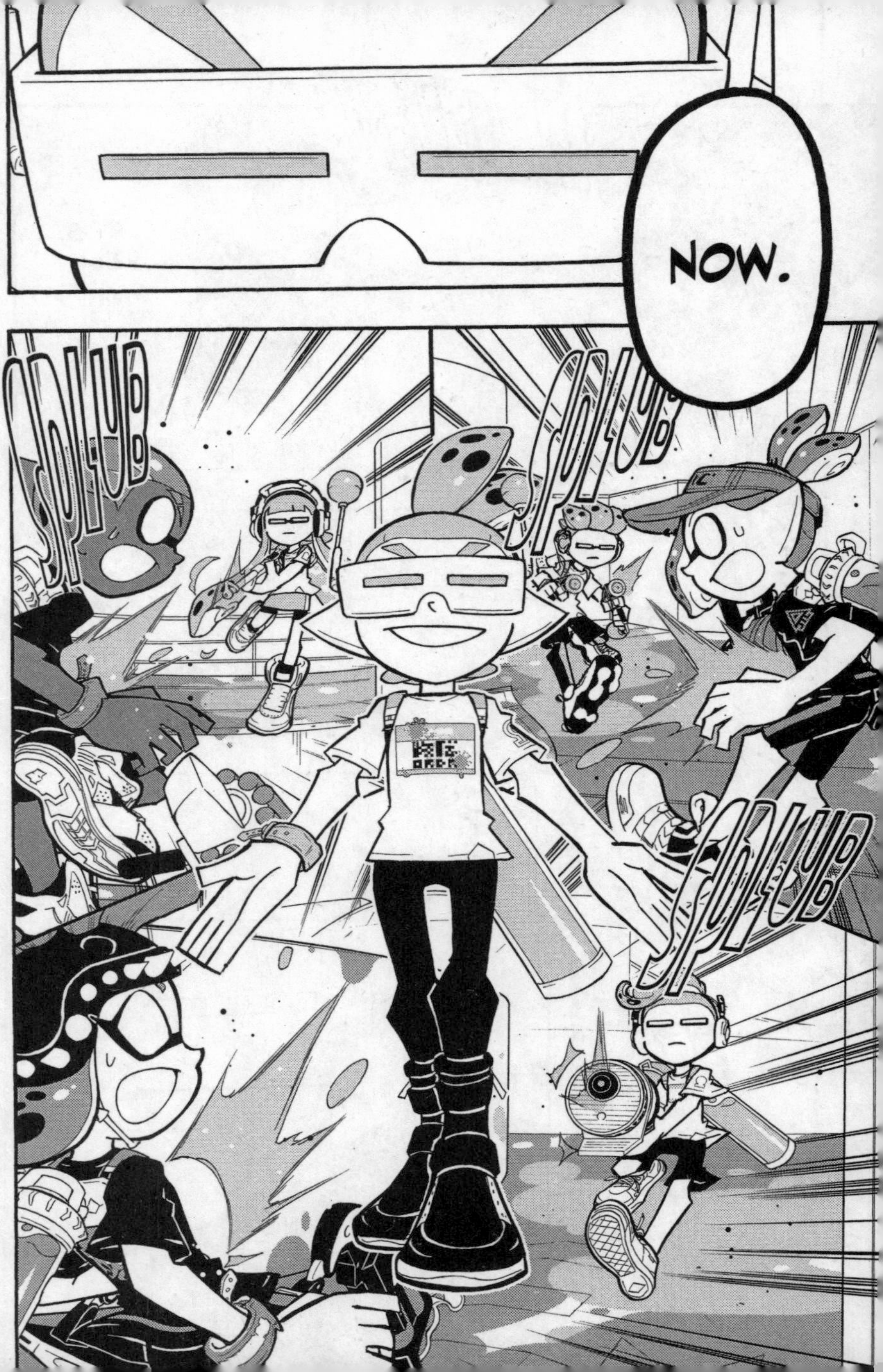
NOW.

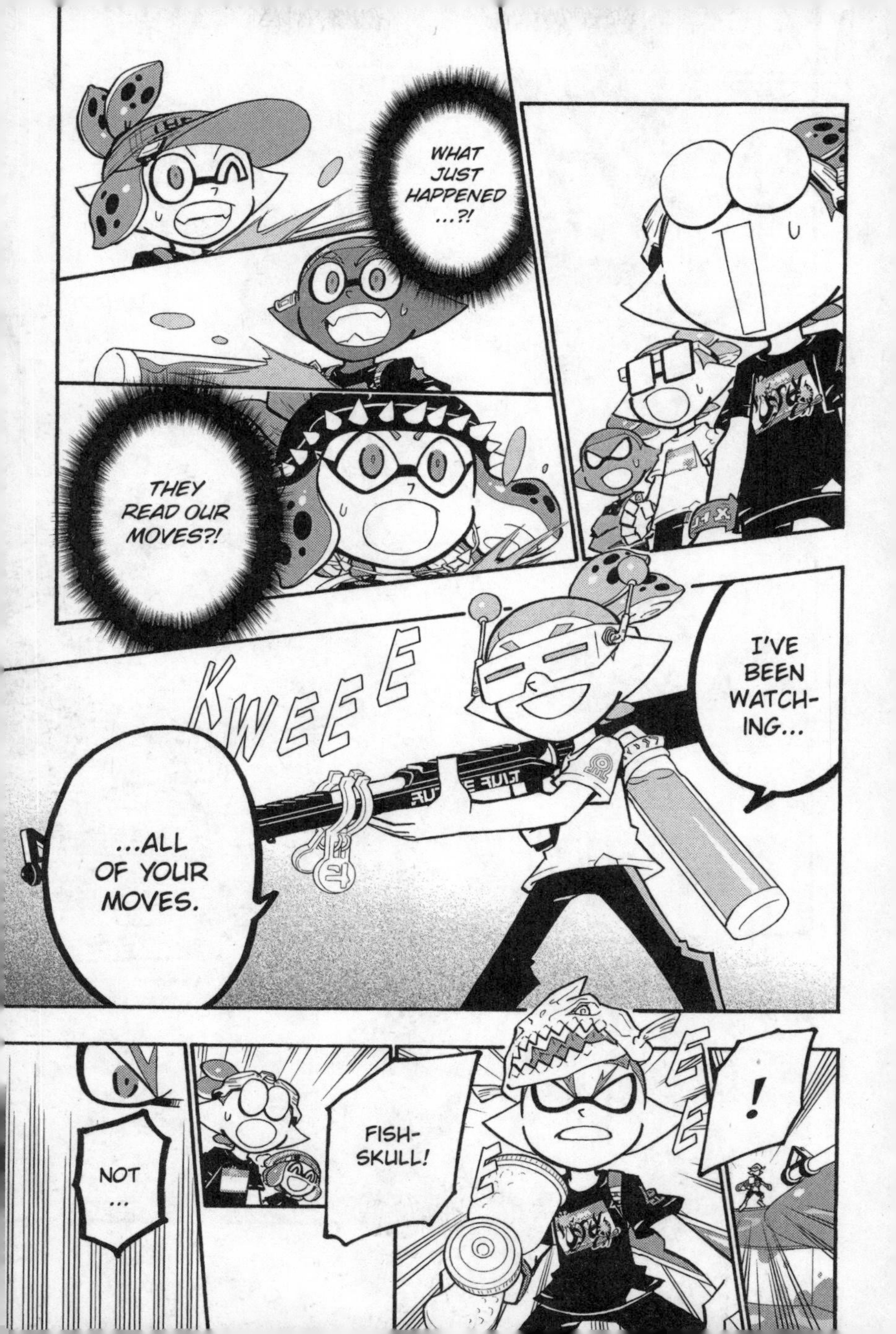
WHAT JUST HAPPENED ...?!
THEY READ OUR MOVES?!
I'VE BEEN WATCHING...
KWEEE
...ALL OF YOUR MOVES.
!
FISH-SKULL!
NOT ...

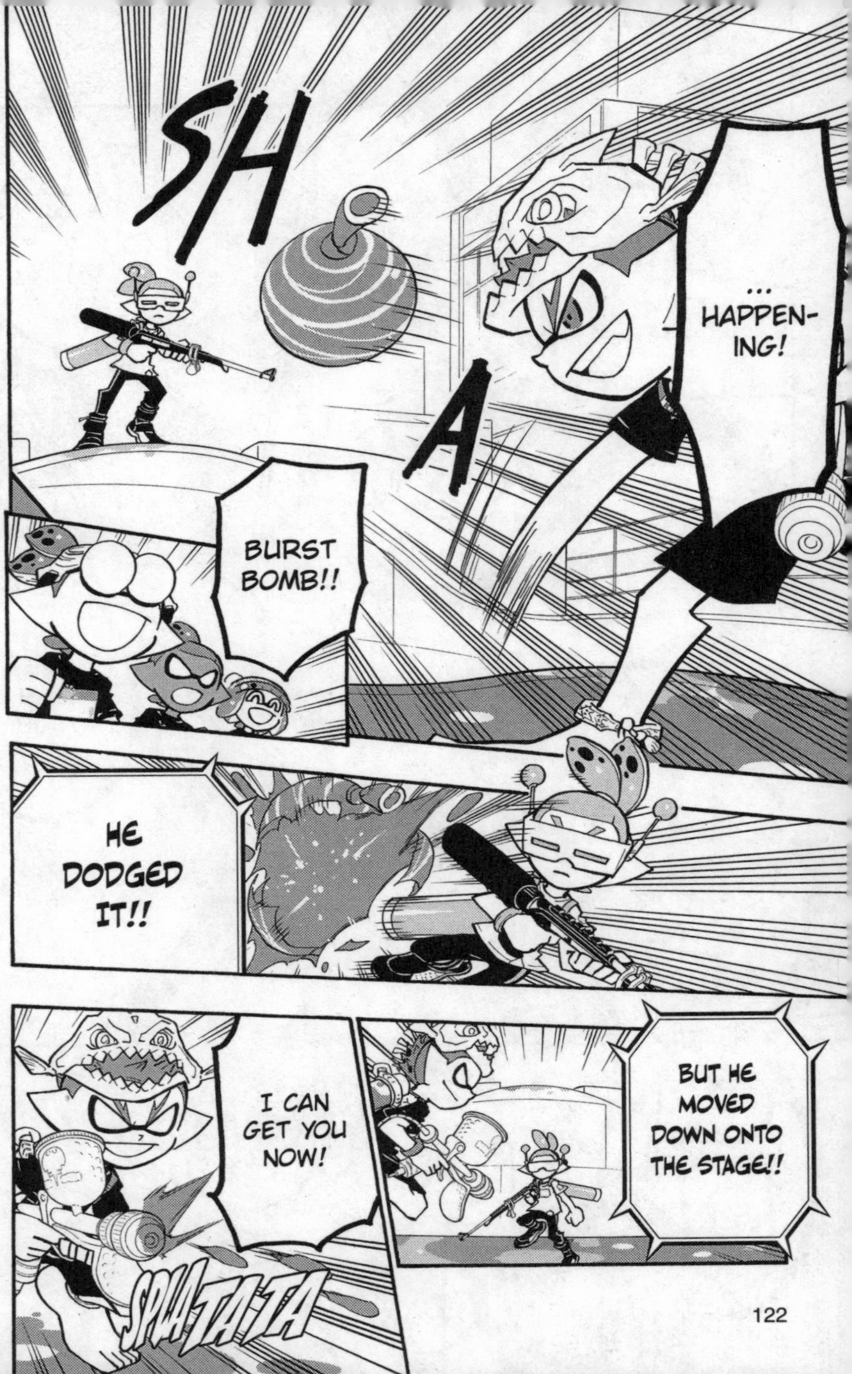
... HAPPEN-ING!
SH
A
BURST BOMB!!
HE DODGED IT!!
BUT HE MOVED DOWN ONTO THE STAGE!!
I CAN GET YOU NOW!
SPLATATATA

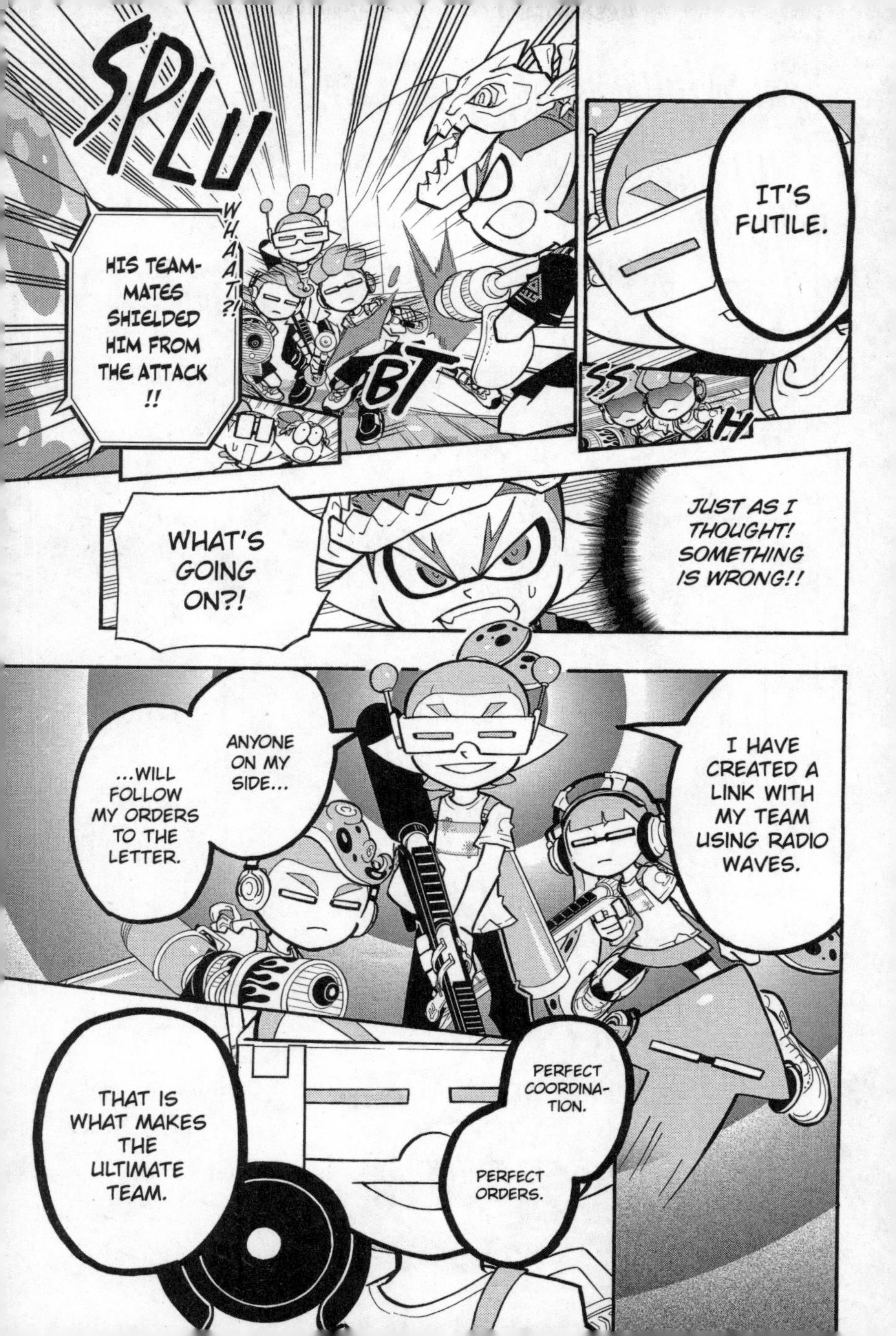
IT'S FUTILE.
SSH
SPLU
WHAAT?!
HIS TEAM-MATES SHIELDED HIM FROM THE ATTACK !!
BT
JUST AS I THOUGHT! SOMETHING IS WRONG!!
WHAT'S GOING ON?!
I HAVE CREATED A LINK WITH MY TEAM USING RADIO WAVES.
ANYONE ON MY SIDE...
...WILL FOLLOW MY ORDERS TO THE LETTER.
PERFECT COORDINATION.
PERFECT ORDERS.
THAT IS WHAT MAKES THE ULTIMATE TEAM.

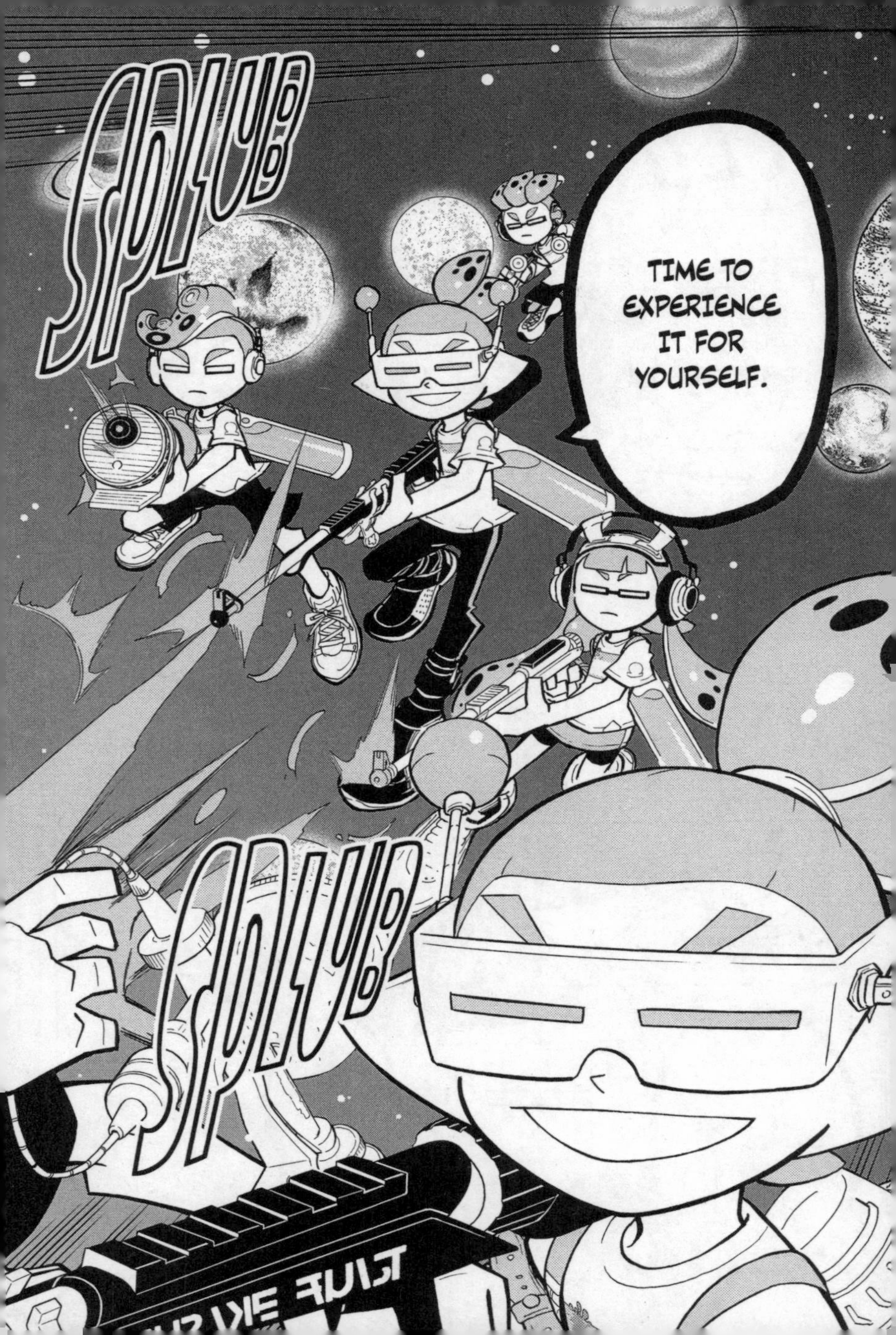
TIME TO EXPERIENCE IT FOR YOURSELF.

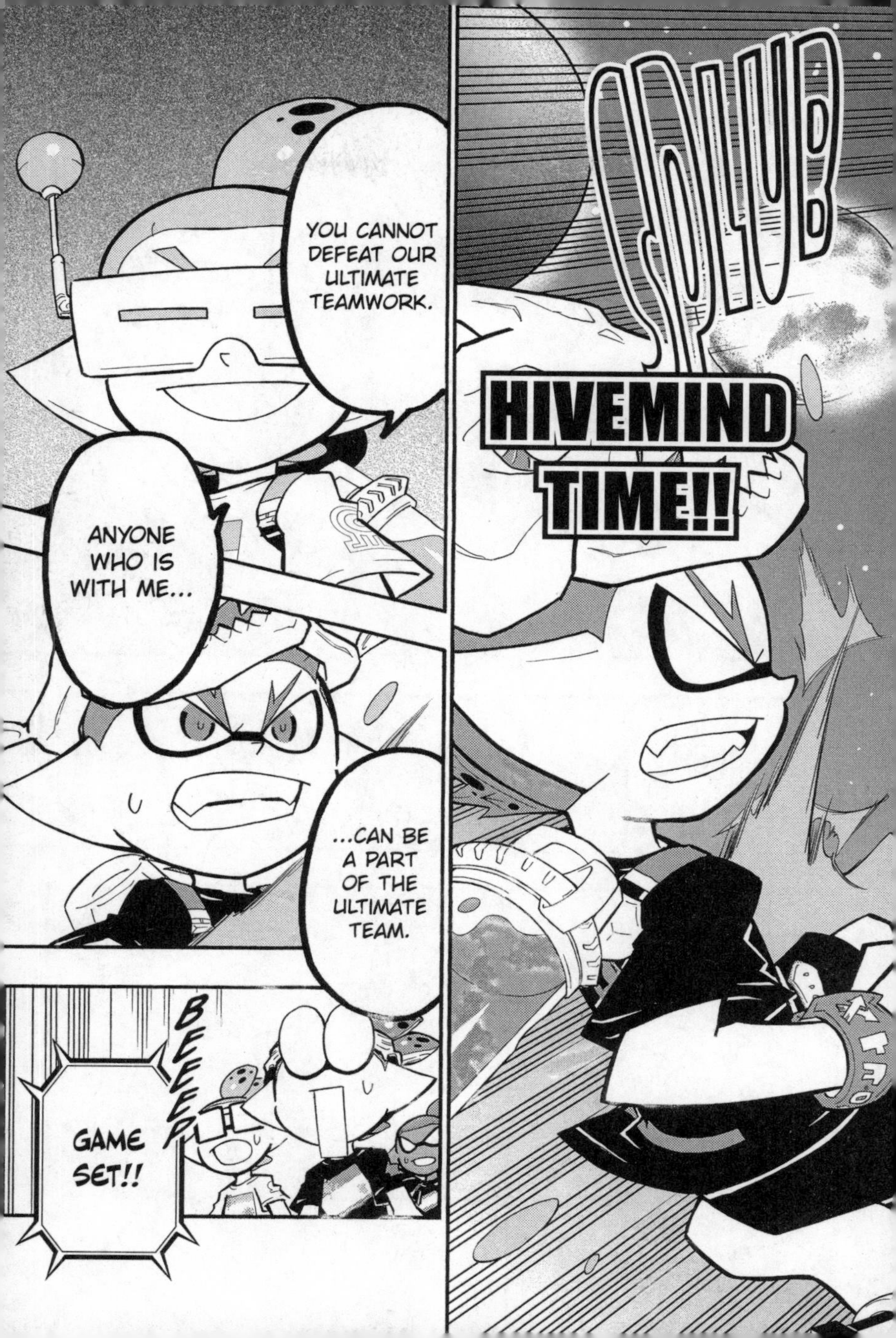
SPLUB
HIVEMIND TIME!!
YOU CANNOT DEFEAT OUR ULTIMATE TEAMWORK.
ANYONE WHO IS WITH ME...
...CAN BE A PART OF THE ULTIMATE TEAM.
BEEEEP
GAME SET!!

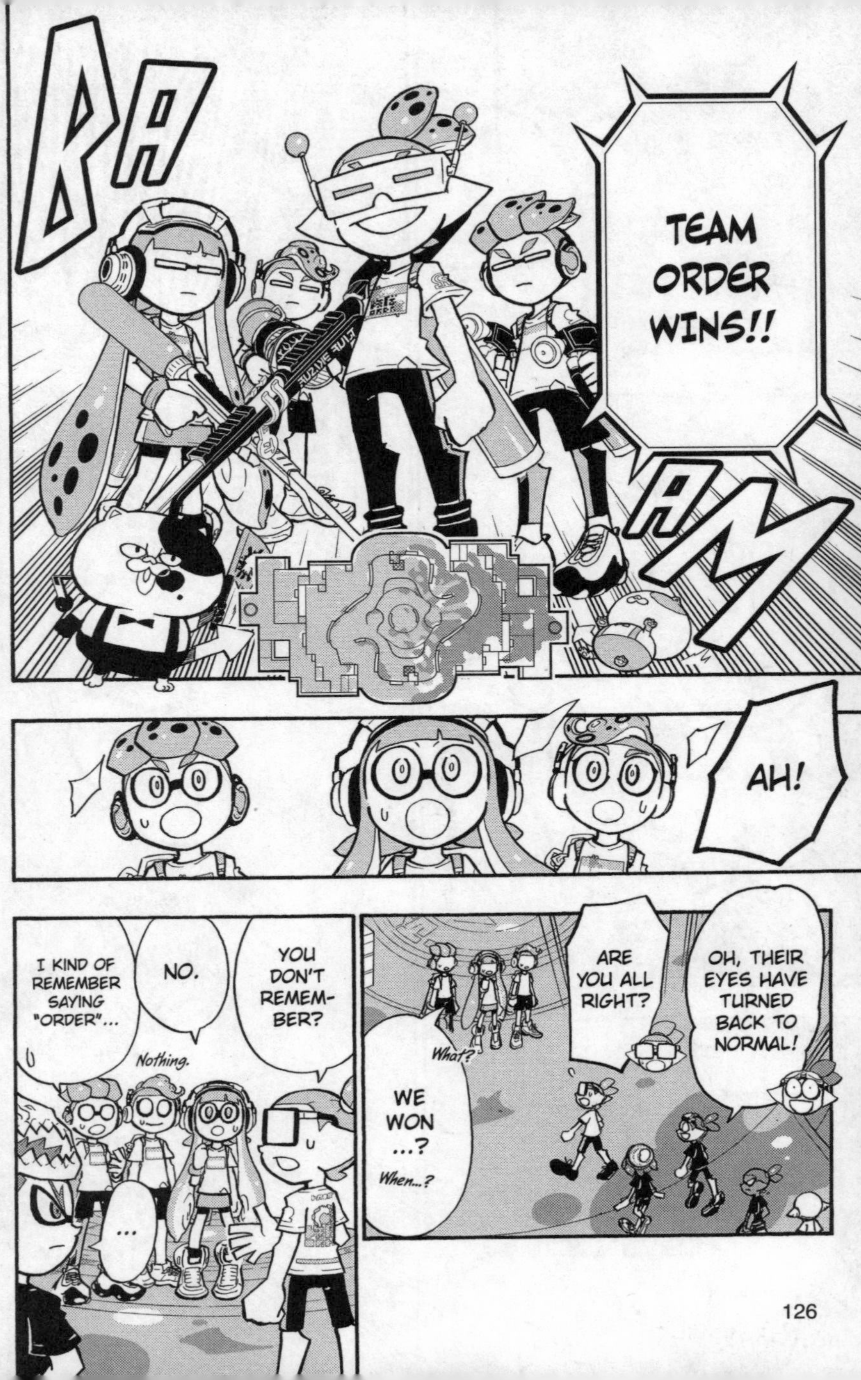
TEAM ORDER WINS!!
BA
AM
AH!
OH, THEIR EYES HAVE TURNED BACK TO NORMAL!
ARE YOU ALL RIGHT?
What?
WE WON ...?
When...?
YOU DON'T REMEM-BER?
NO.
I KIND OF REMEMBER SAYING "ORDER"...
Nothing.
...

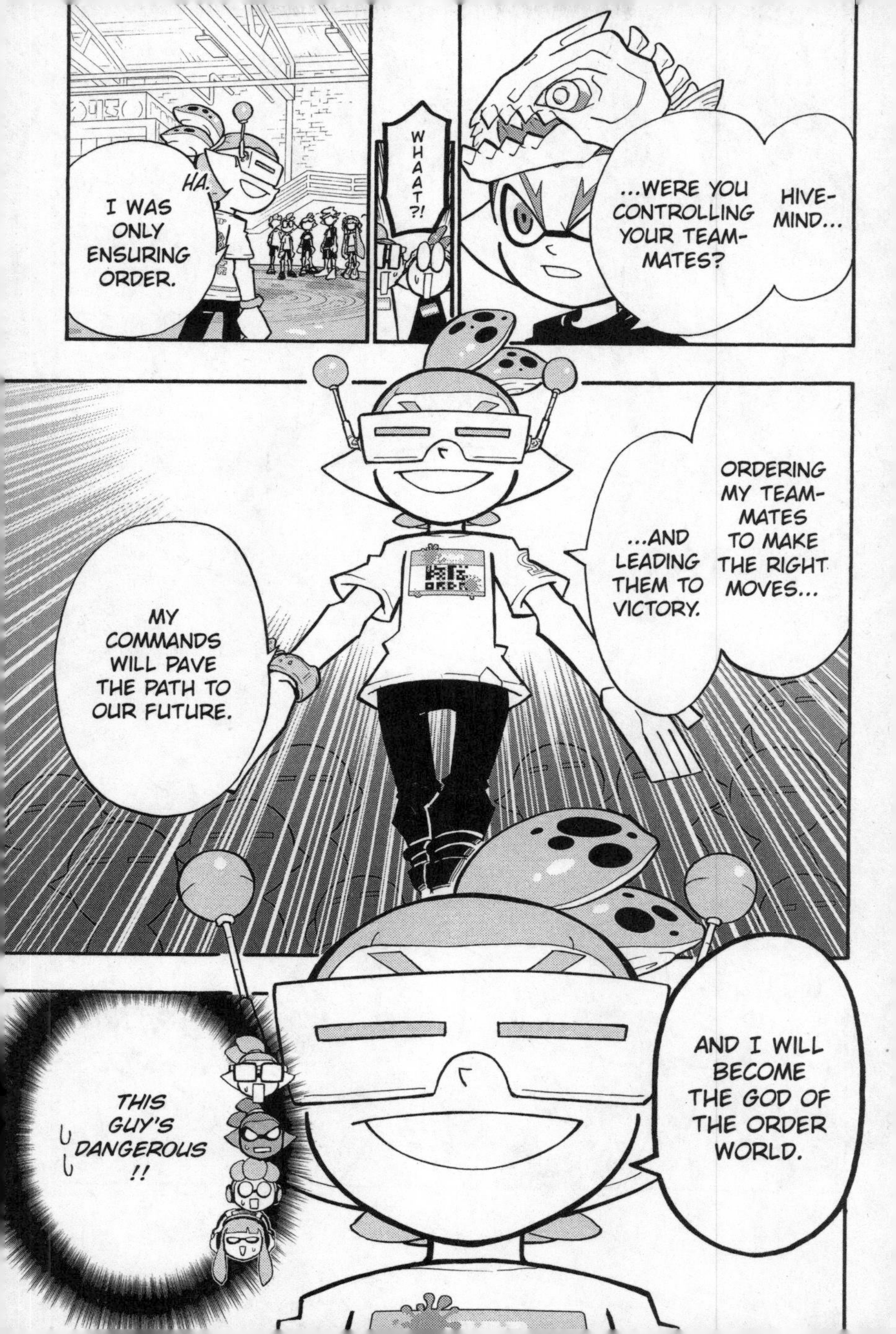
HIVE-MIND...
...WERE YOU CONTROLLING YOUR TEAM-MATES?
WHAAT?!
HA.
I WAS ONLY ENSURING ORDER.
ORDERING MY TEAM-MATES TO MAKE THE RIGHT MOVES...
...AND LEADING THEM TO VICTORY.
MY COMMANDS WILL PAVE THE PATH TO OUR FUTURE.
AND I WILL BECOME THE GOD OF THE ORDER WORLD.
THIS GUY'S DANGEROUS!!

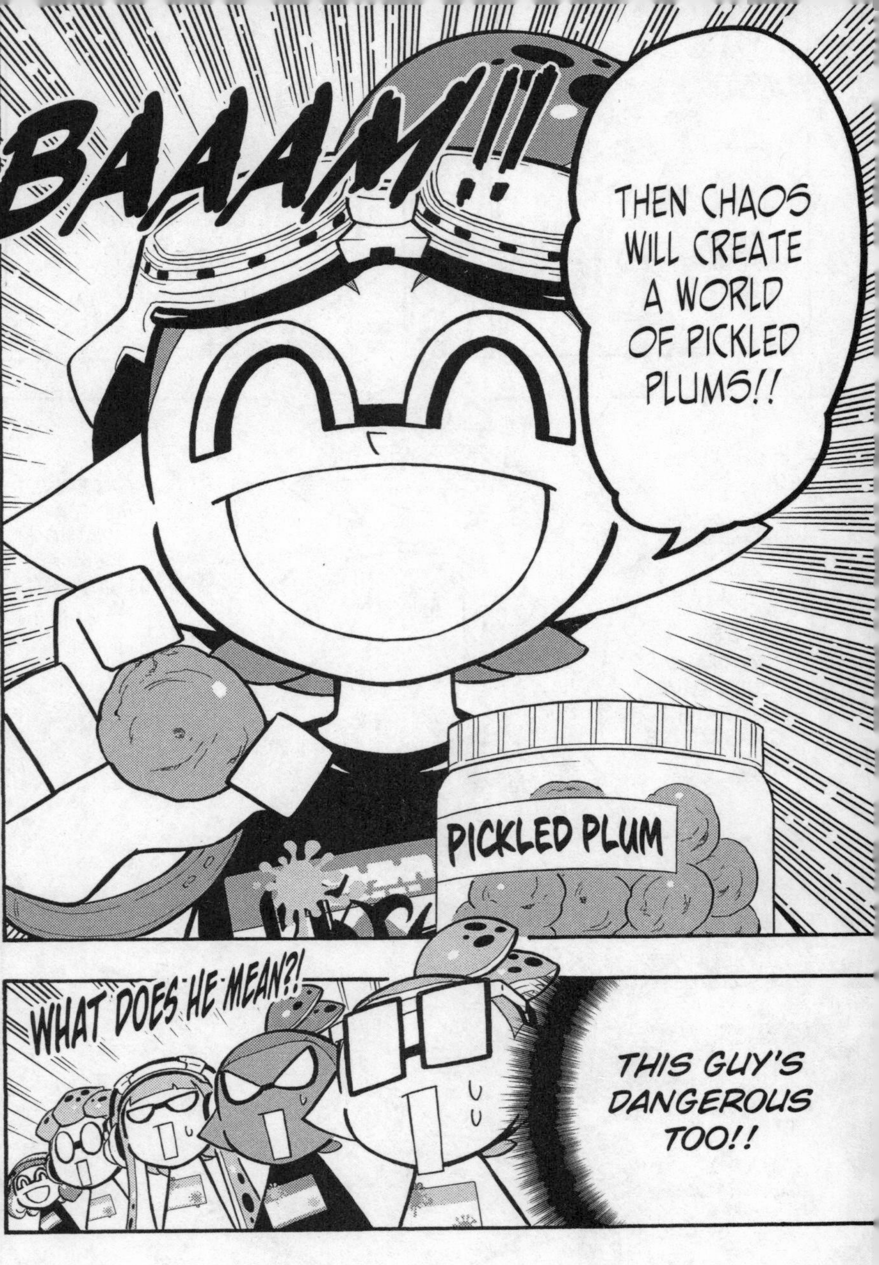
THEN CHAOS WILL CREATE A WORLD OF PICKLED PLUMS!!
BAAAM!!
PICKLED PLUM
THIS GUY'S DANGEROUS TOO!!
WHAT DOES HE MEAN?!

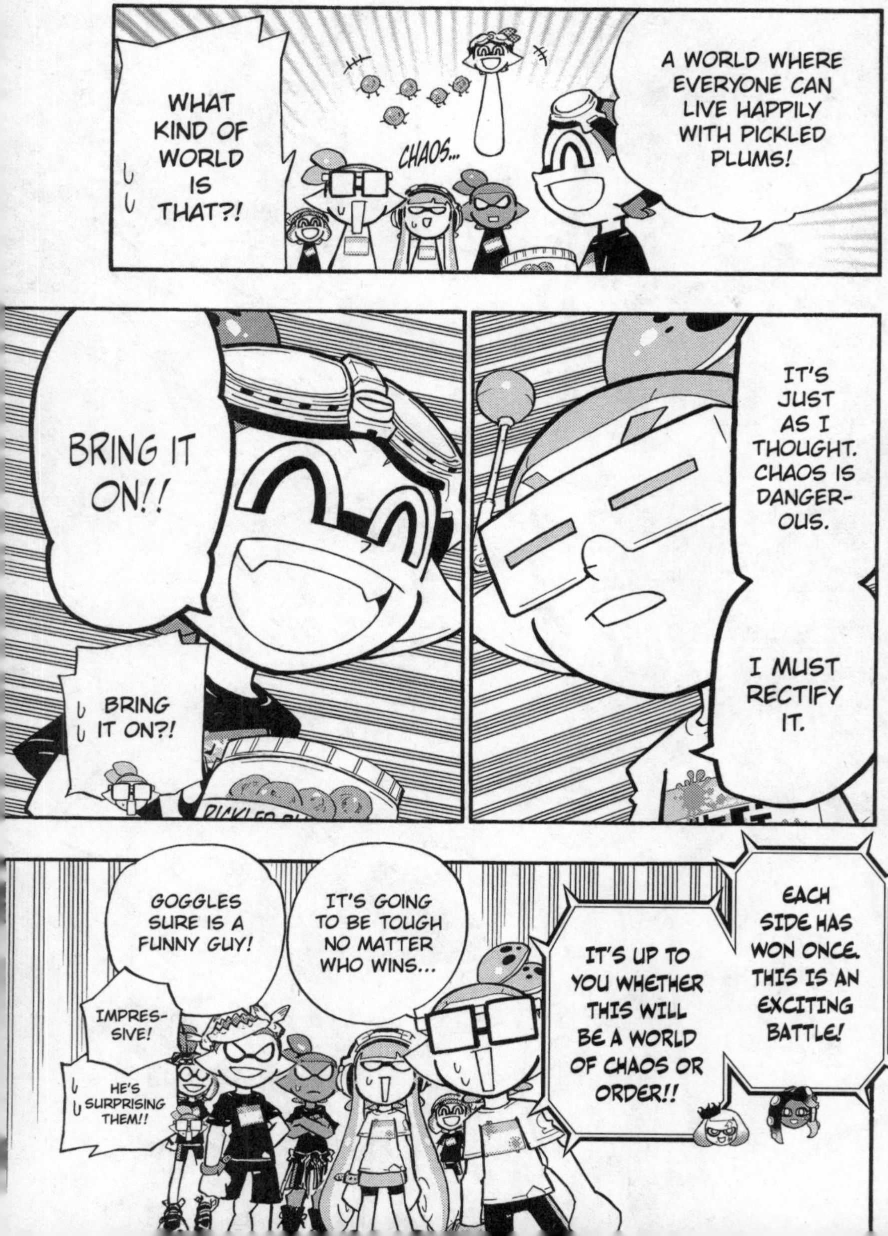
A WORLD WHERE EVERYONE CAN LIVE HAPPILY WITH PICKLED PLUMS!
CHAOS...
WHAT KIND OF WORLD IS THAT?!
IT'S JUST AS I THOUGHT. CHAOS IS DANGER-OUS.
I MUST RECTIFY IT.
BRING IT ON!!
BRING IT ON?!
EACH SIDE HAS WON ONCE. THIS IS AN EXCITING BATTLE!
IT'S UP TO YOU WHETHER THIS WILL BE A WORLD OF CHAOS OR ORDER!!
IT'S GOING TO BE TOUGH NO MATTER WHO WINS...
GOGGLES SURE IS A FUNNY GUY!
IMPRES-SIVE!
HE'S SURPRISING THEM!!

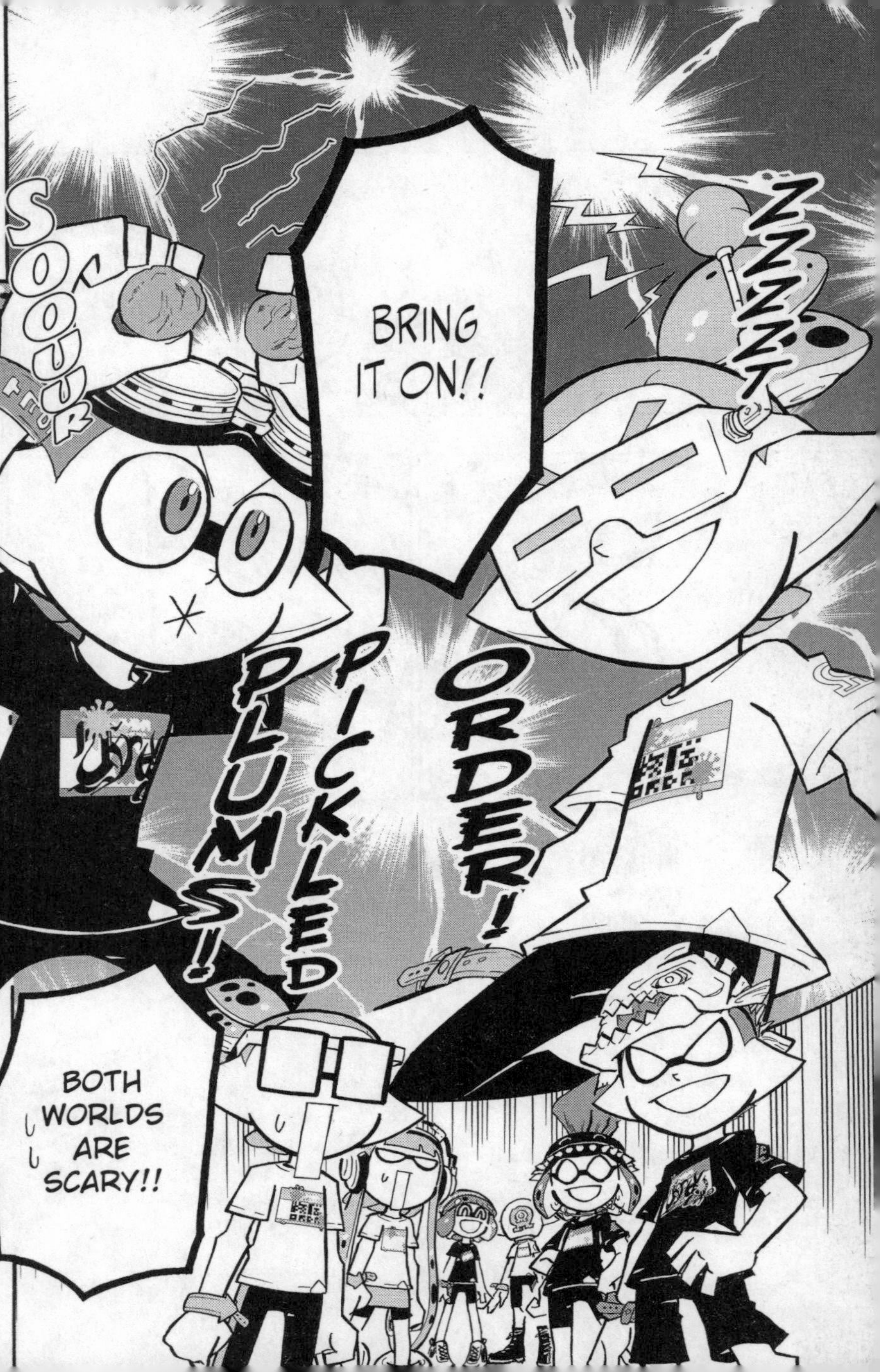
ZZZZZT
BRING IT ON!!
ORDER!
PICKLED PLUMS!
SOOOUR
BOTH WORLDS ARE SCARY!!

SPLATOON VOLUME 13 END / CONTINUED IN VOLUME 14

PICKLED PLUMS

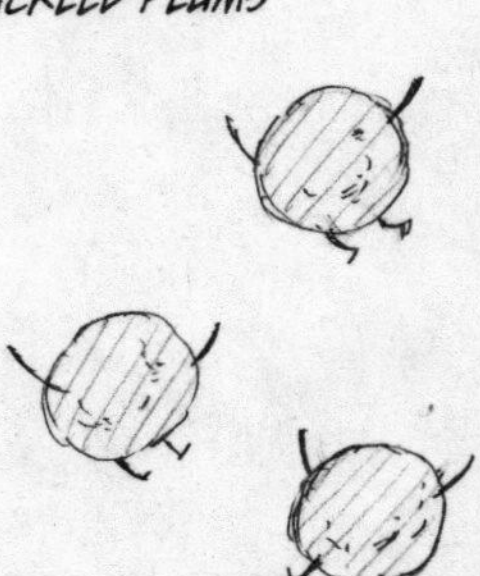

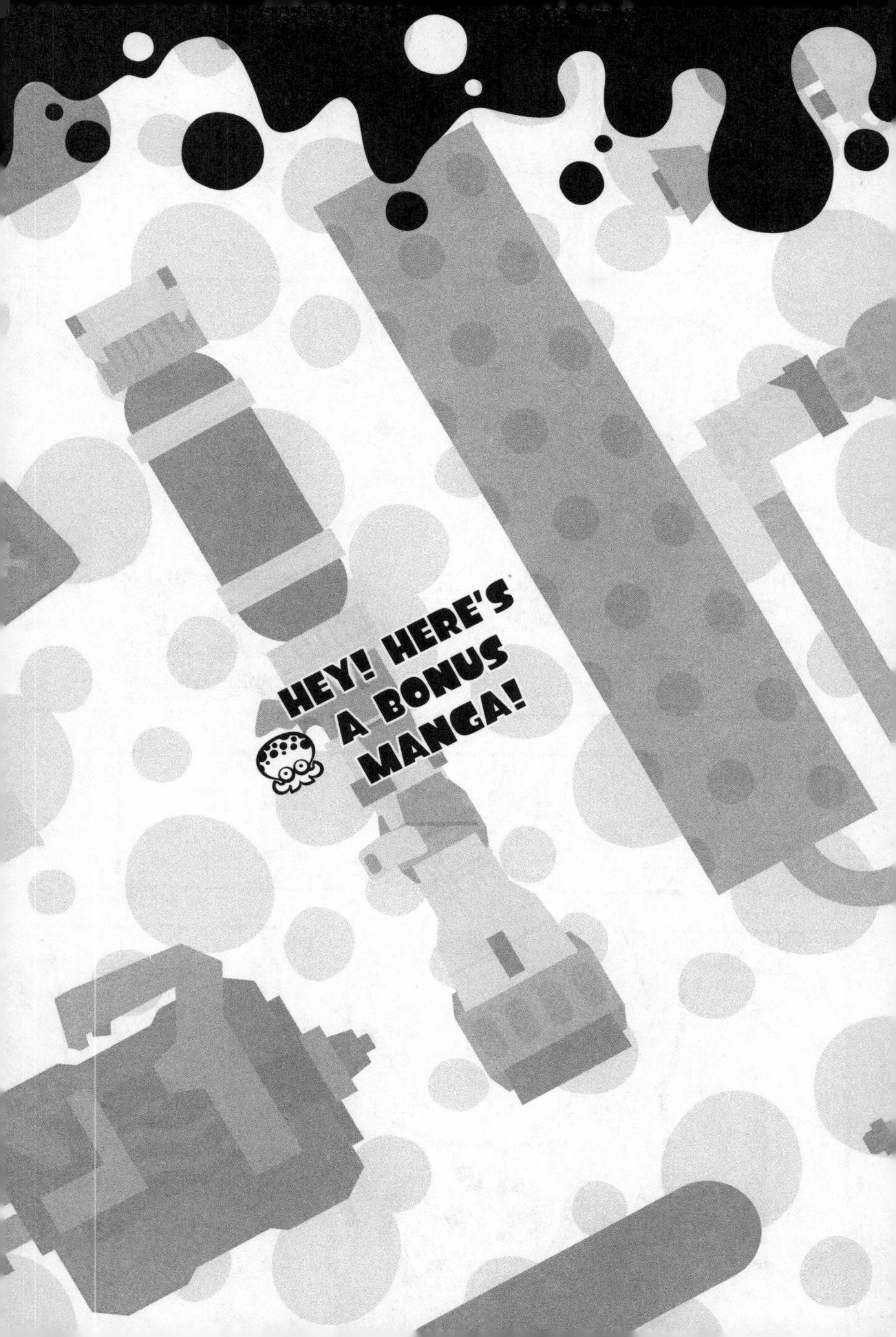
HEY! HERE'S
A BONUS
MANGA!

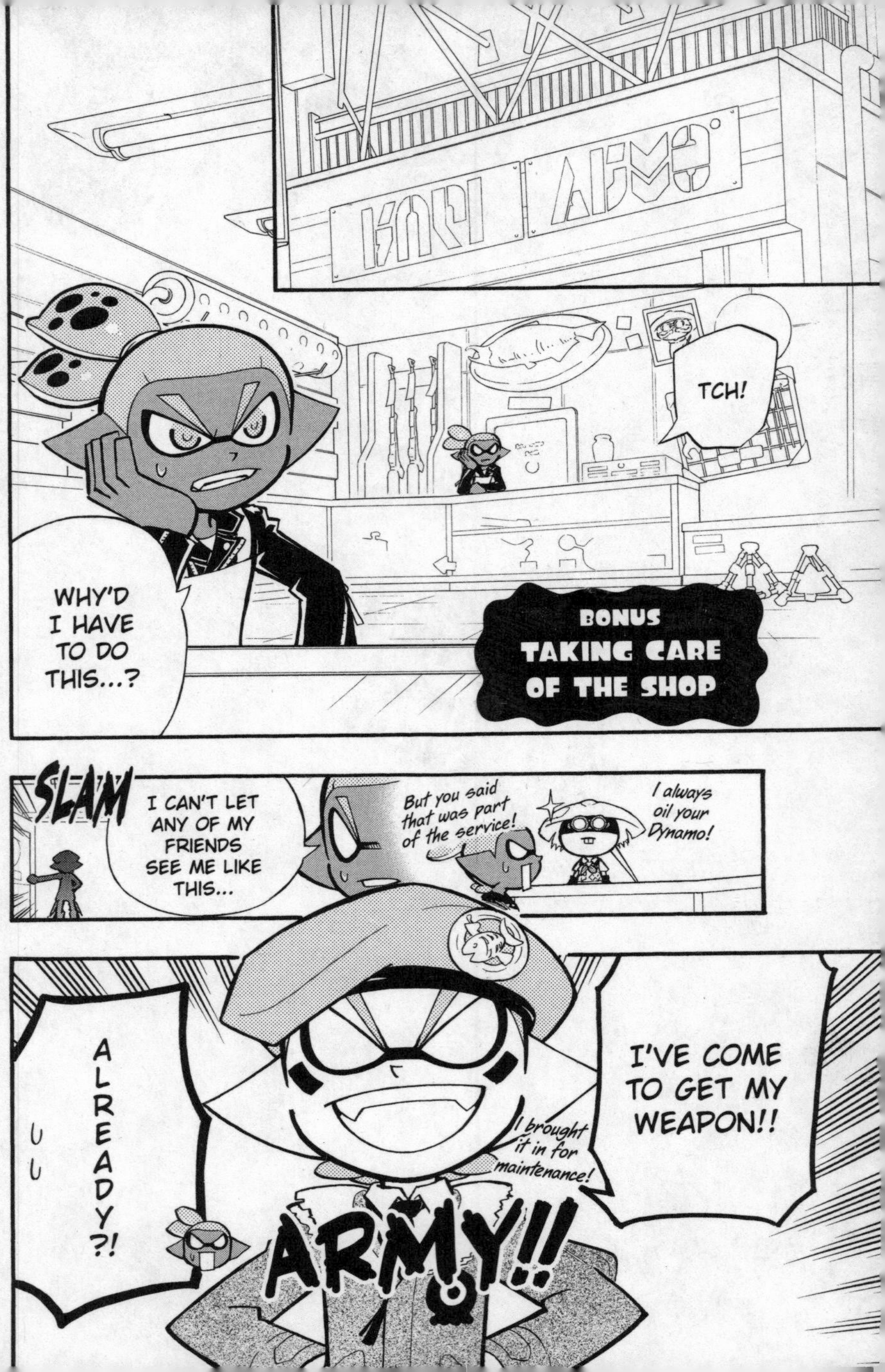
TCH!
BONUS
TAKING CARE OF THE SHOP
WHY'D I HAVE TO DO THIS...?
I always oil your Dynamo!
But you said that was part of the service!
I CAN'T LET ANY OF MY FRIENDS SEE ME LIKE THIS...
SLAM
I'VE COME TO GET MY WEAPON!!
I brought it in for maintenance!
ALREADY?!
ARMY!!

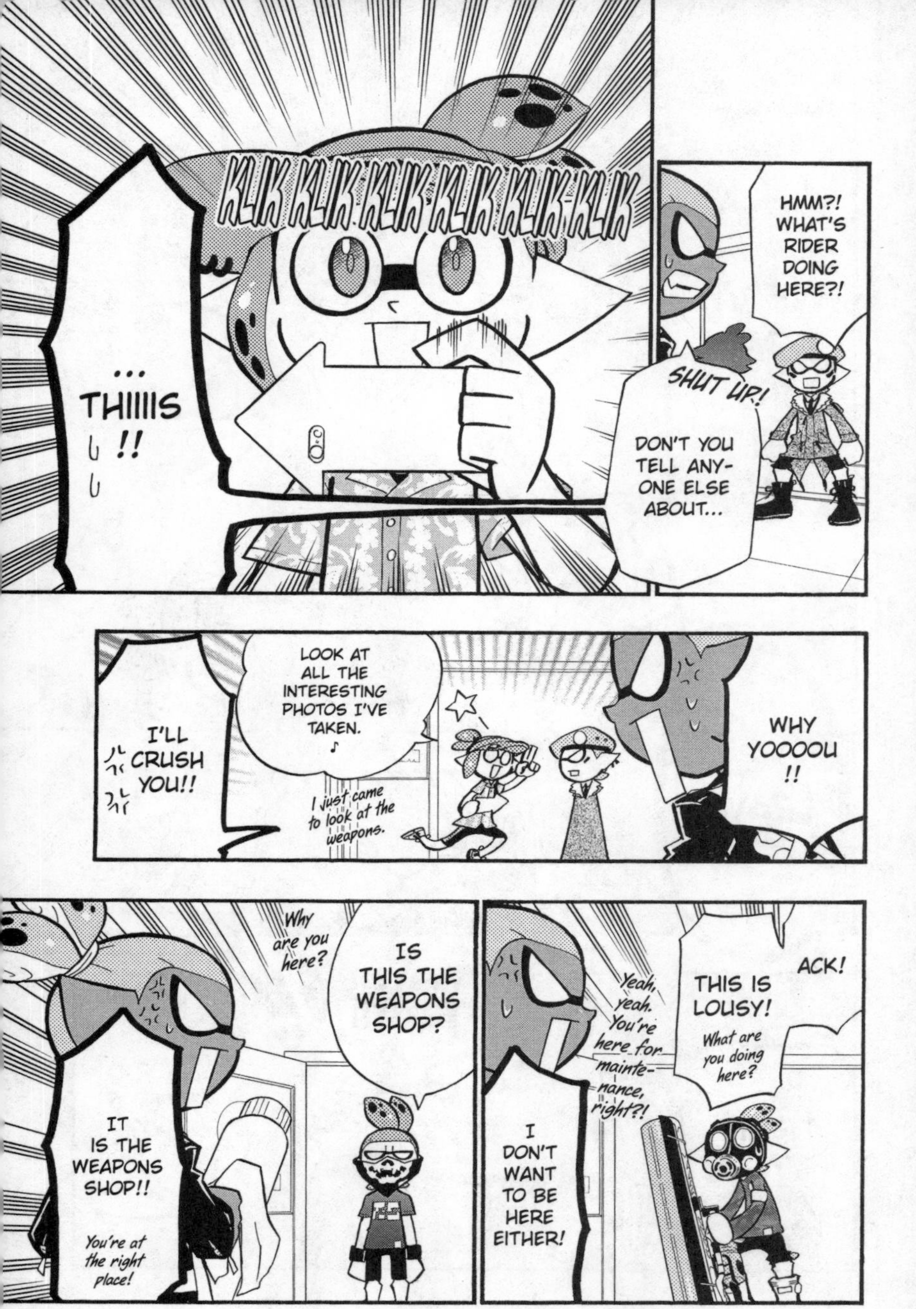
HMM?! WHAT'S RIDER DOING HERE?!
SHUT UP!
DON'T YOU TELL ANY-ONE ELSE ABOUT...
KLIK KLIK KLIK KLIK KLIK KLIK KLIK
... THIIIIS!!
WHY YOOOOU!!
LOOK AT ALL THE INTERESTING PHOTOS I'VE TAKEN. ♪
I just came to look at the weapons.
I'LL CRUSH YOU!!
ACK!
THIS IS LOUSY!
What are you doing here?
Yeah, yeah. You're here for mainte-nance, right?!
I DON'T WANT TO BE HERE EITHER!
Why are you here?
IS THIS THE WEAPONS SHOP?
IT IS THE WEAPONS SHOP!!
You're at the right place!

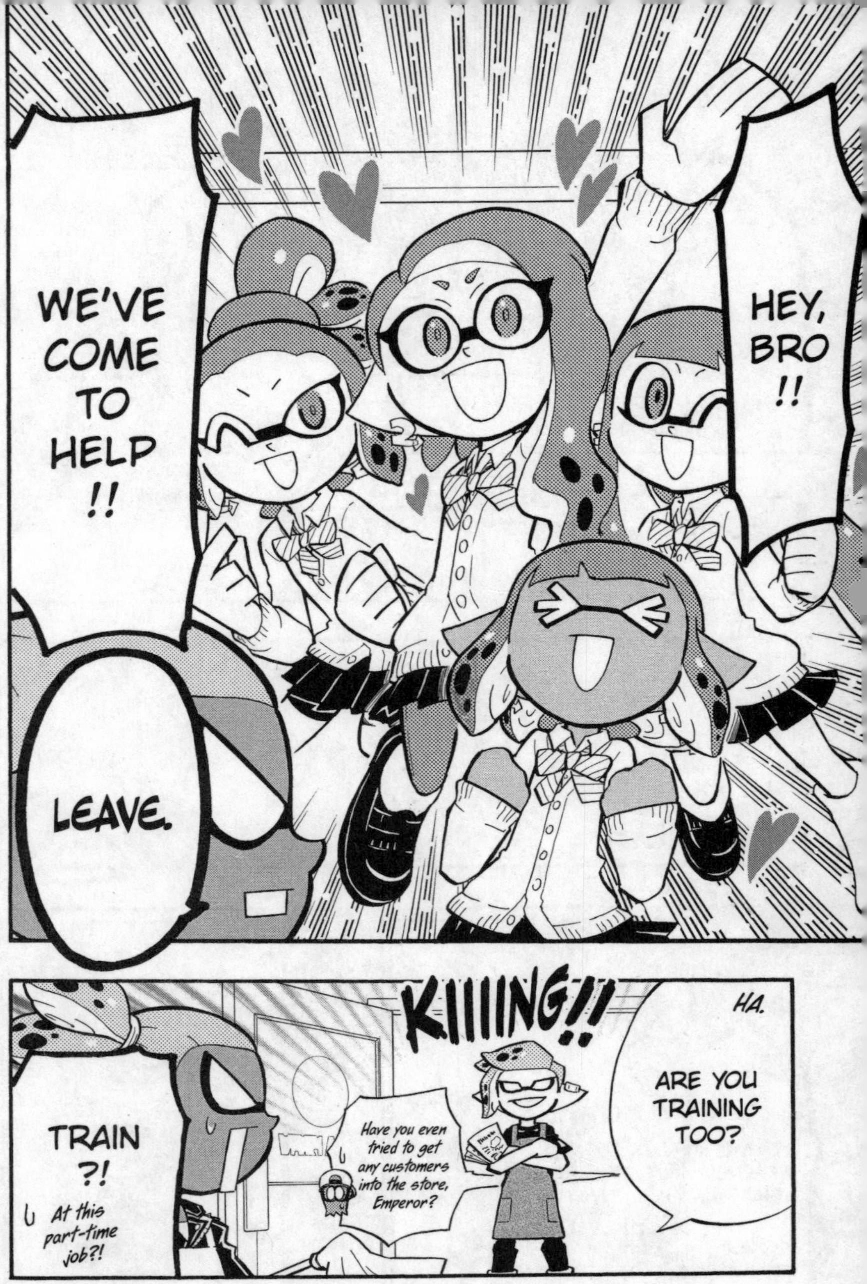
HEY, BRO!!
WE'VE COME TO HELP!!
LEAVE.
HA.
ARE YOU TRAINING TOO?
KIIIING!!
Have you even tried to get any customers into the store, Emperor?
TRAIN?!
At this part-time job?!

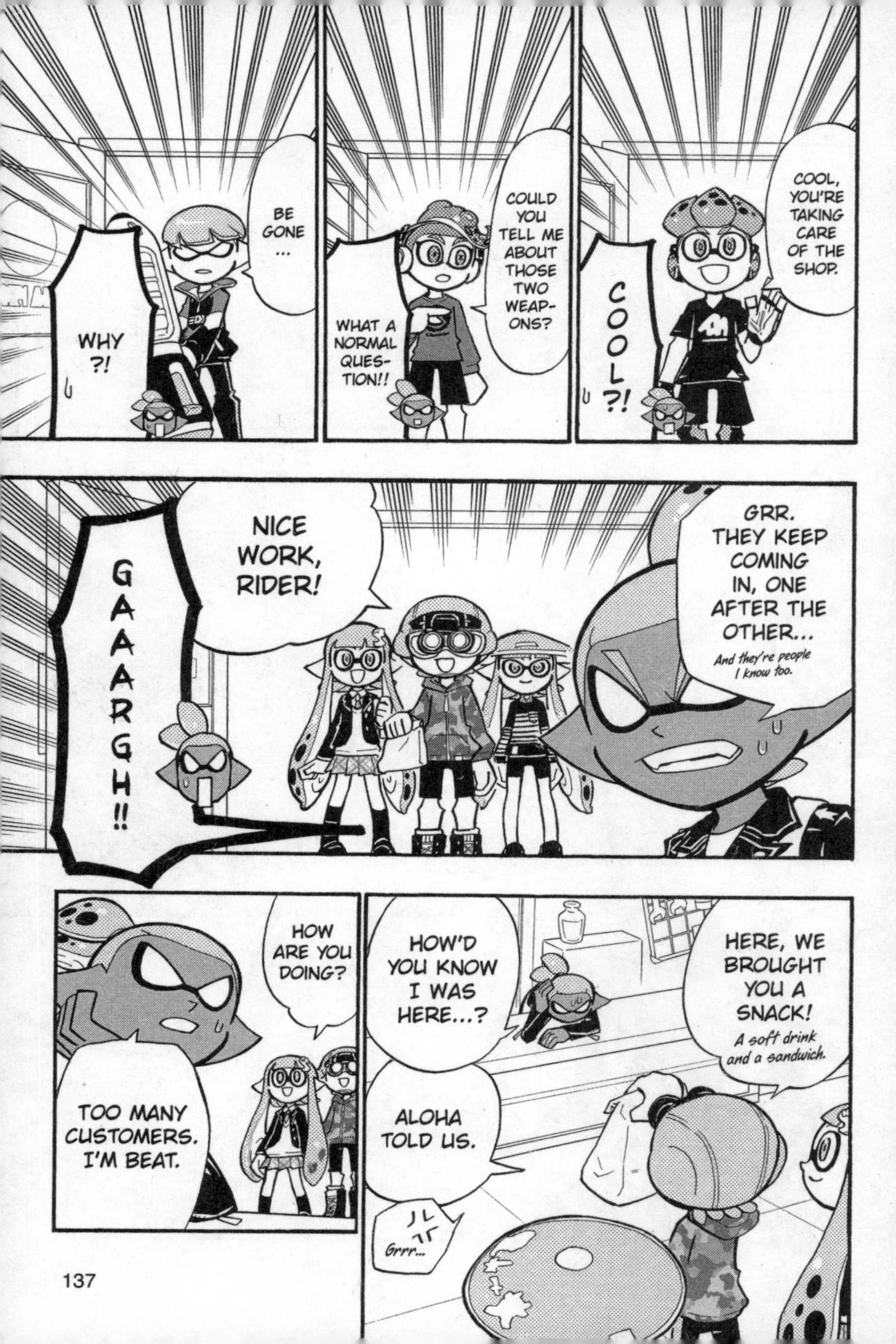

COOL, YOU'RE TAKING CARE OF THE SHOP.
COOL?!
COULD YOU TELL ME ABOUT THOSE TWO WEAPONS?
WHAT A NORMAL QUESTION!!
BE GONE...
WHY?!
GRR. THEY KEEP COMING IN, ONE AFTER THE OTHER...
And they're people I know too.
NICE WORK, RIDER!
GAAAARGH!!
HERE, WE BROUGHT YOU A SNACK!
A soft drink and a sandwich.
HOW'D YOU KNOW I WAS HERE...?
ALOHA TOLD US.
Grrr...
HOW ARE YOU DOING?
TOO MANY CUSTOMERS. I'M BEAT.

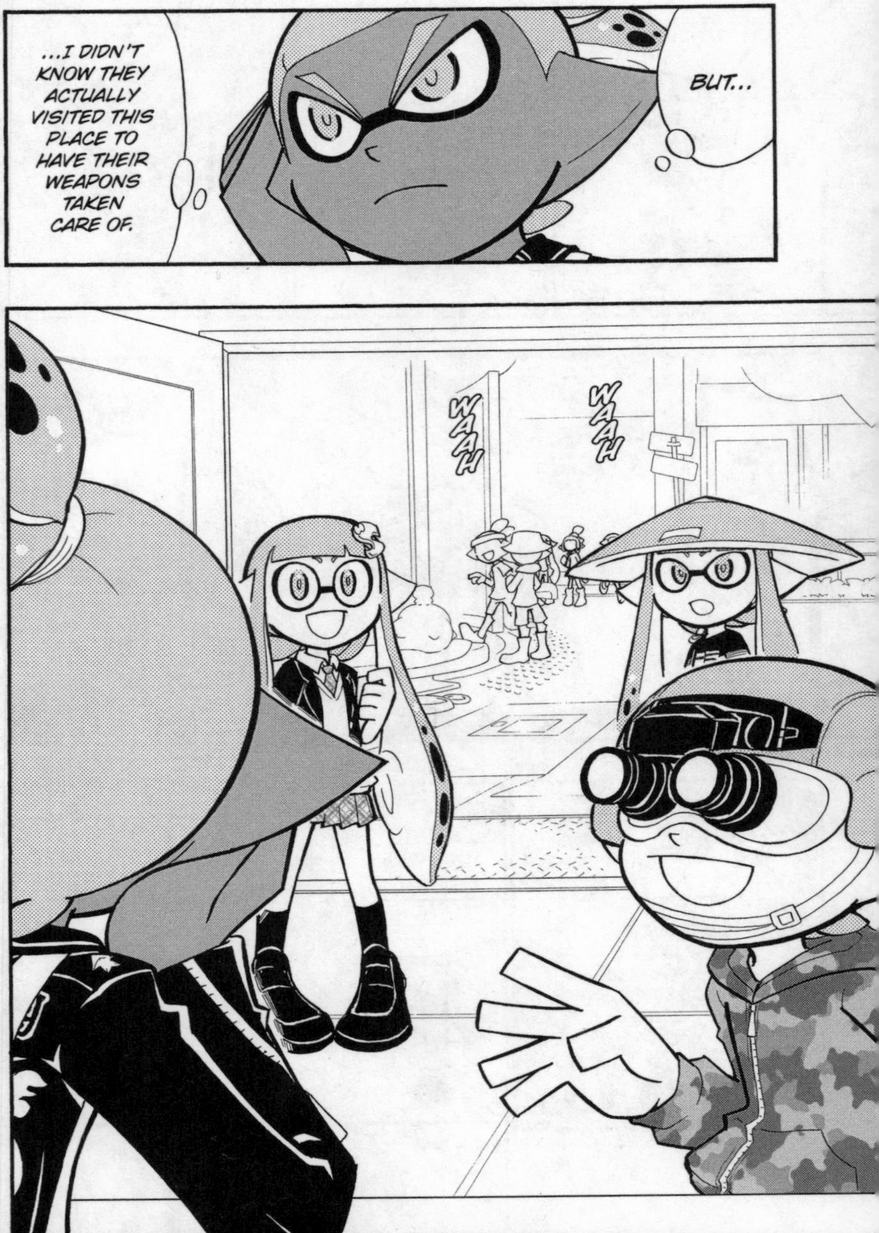
BUT...
...I DIDN'T KNOW THEY ACTUALLY VISITED THIS PLACE TO HAVE THEIR WEAPONS TAKEN CARE OF.
WAAH
WAAH

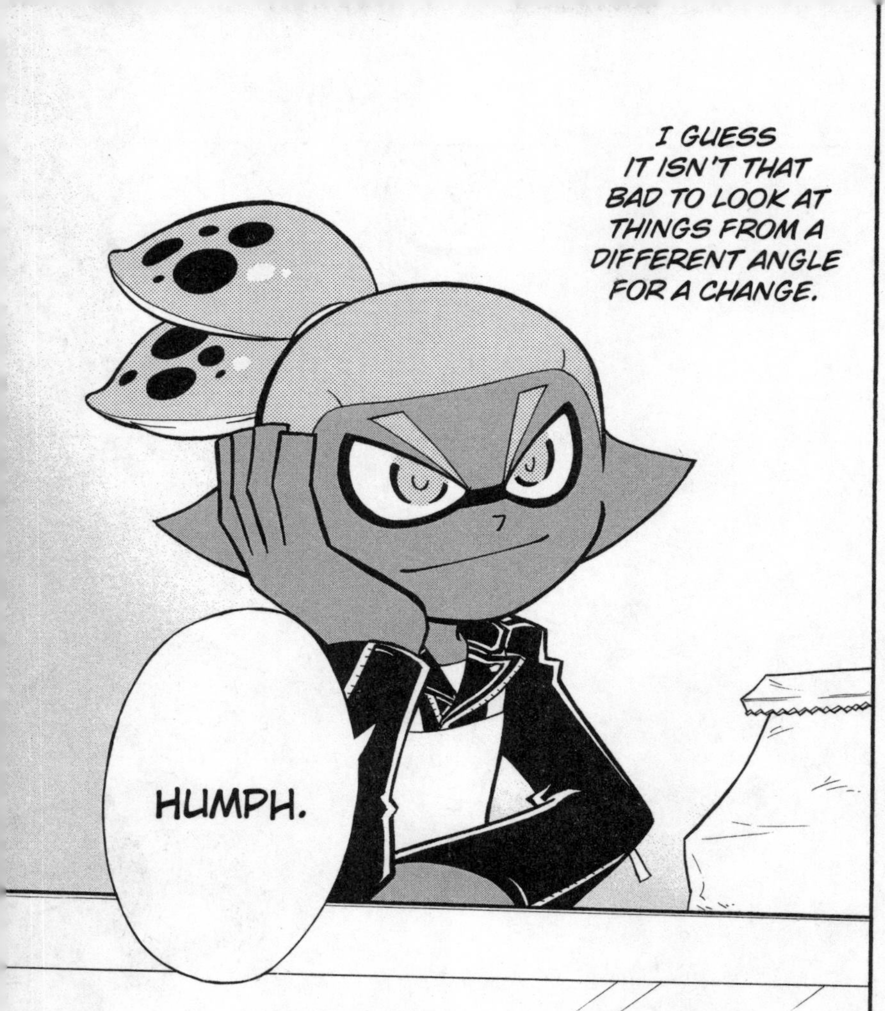
I GUESS IT ISN'T THAT BAD TO LOOK AT THINGS FROM A DIFFERENT ANGLE FOR A CHANGE.
HUMPH.

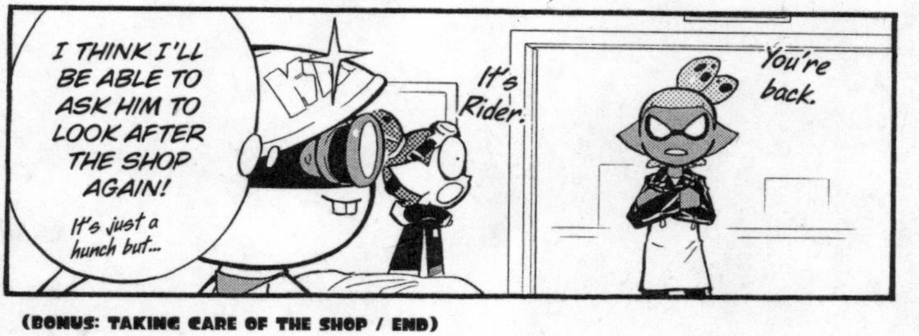
You're back.
It's Rider.
I THINK I'LL BE ABLE TO ASK HIM TO LOOK AFTER THE SHOP AGAIN!
It's just a hunch but...

(BONUS: TAKING CARE OF THE SHOP / END)

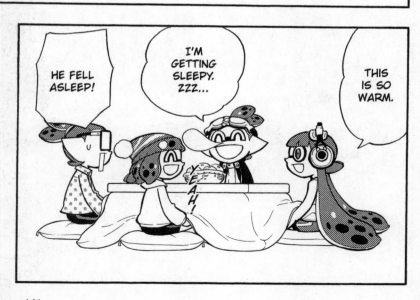

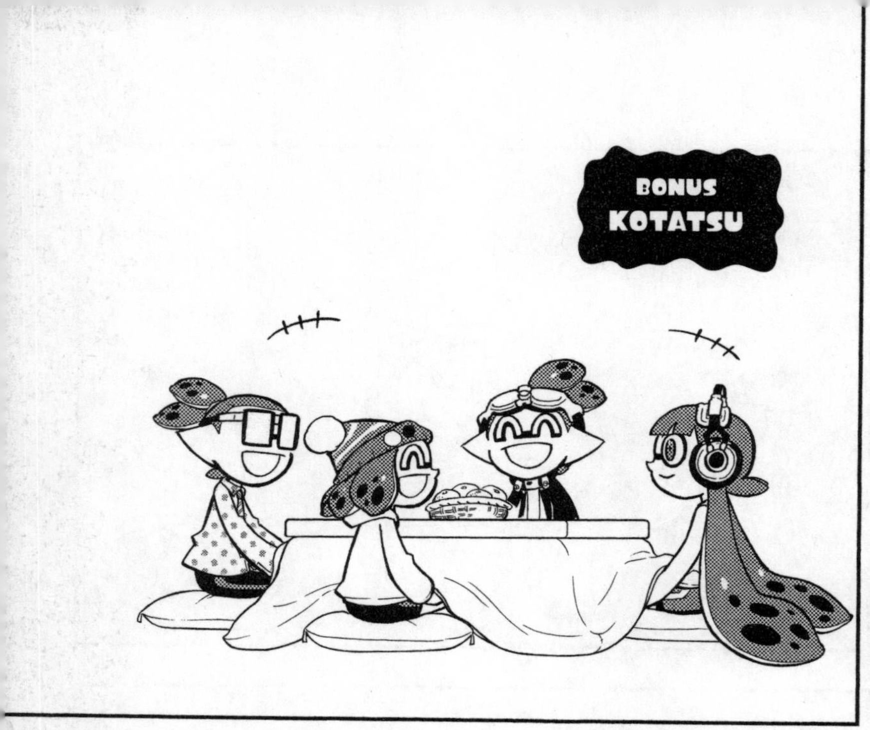
BONUS
KOTATSU

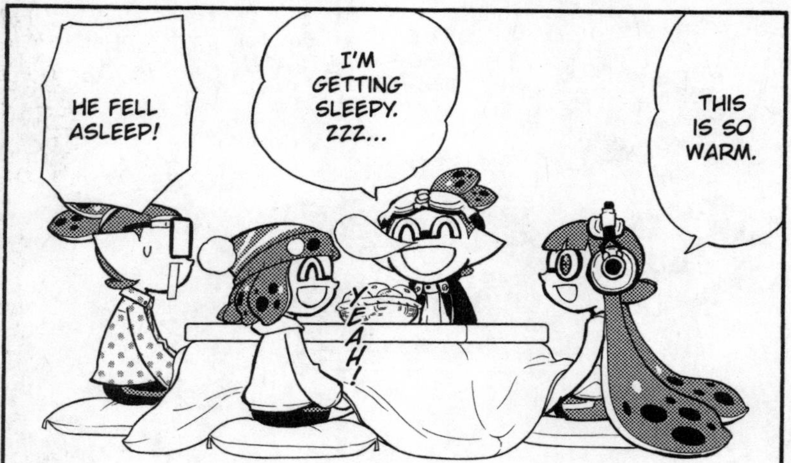
THIS IS SO WARM.
I'M GETTING SLEEPY. ZZZ...
HE FELL ASLEEP!
YEAH!

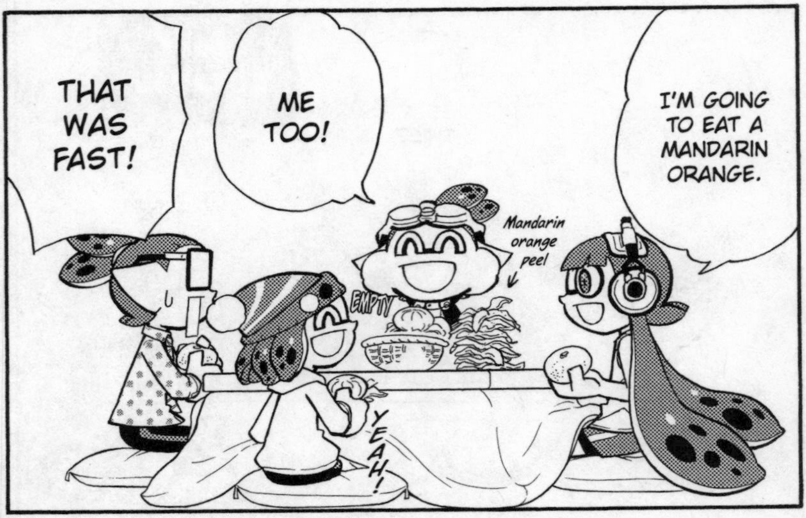
I'M GOING TO EAT A MANDARIN ORANGE.
Mandarin orange peel
ME TOO!
EMPTY
YEAH!
THAT WAS FAST!

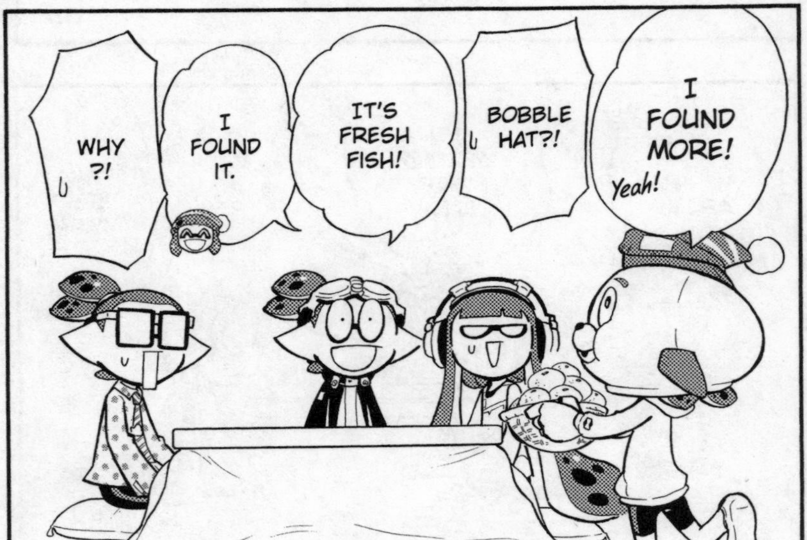
I FOUND MORE!
Yeah!
BOBBLE HAT?!
IT'S FRESH FISH!
I FOUND IT.
WHY?!

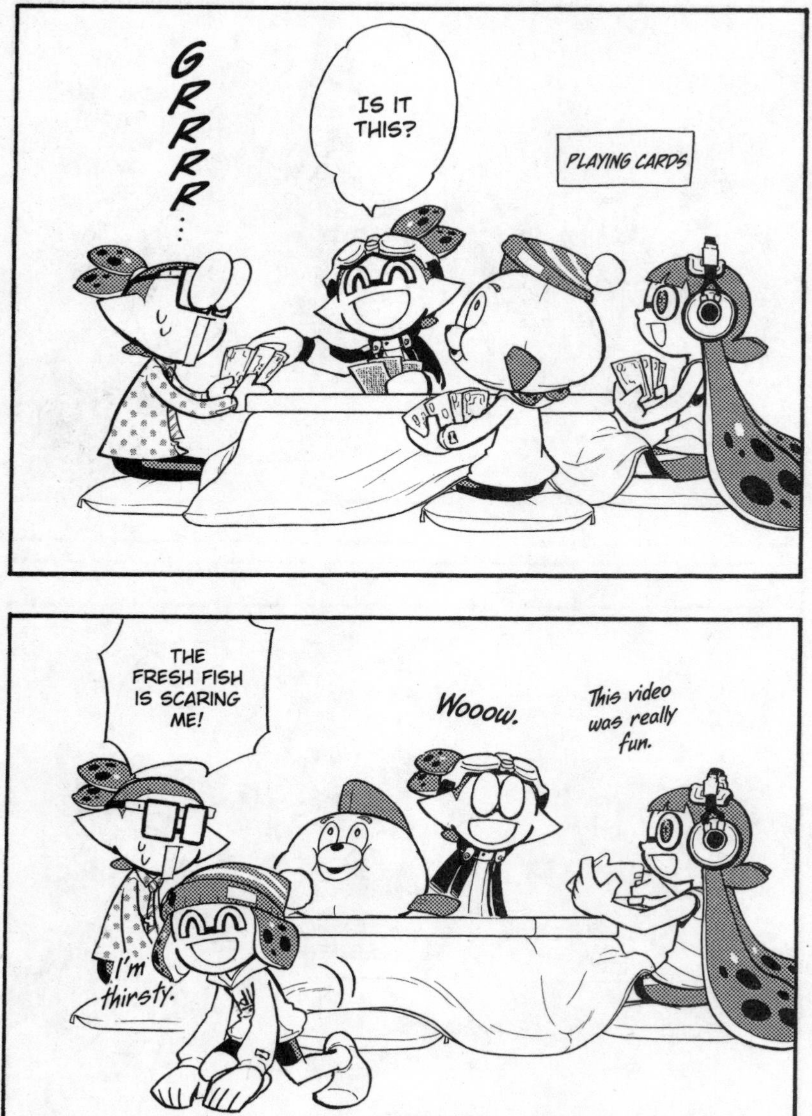
PLAYING CARDS
IS IT THIS?
GRRRR...
This video was really fun.
Wooow.
THE FRESH FISH IS SCARING ME!
I'm thirsty.

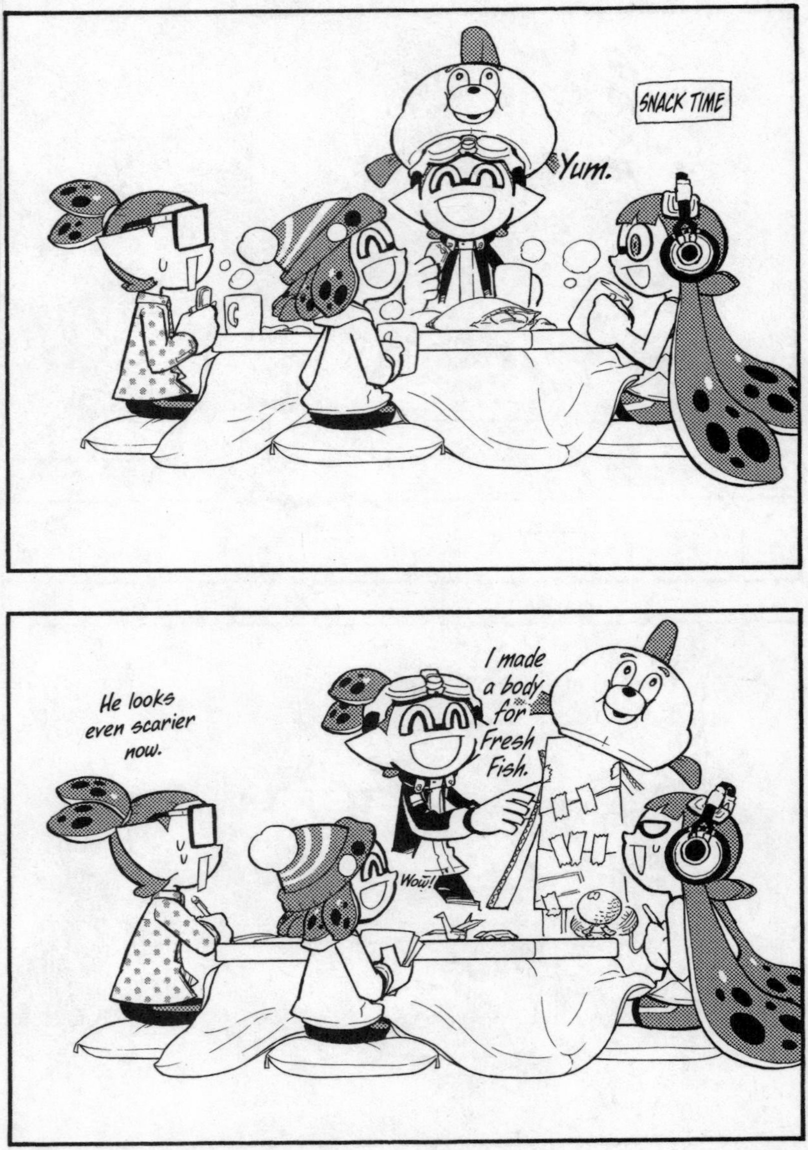
SNACK TIME
Yum.
I made a body for Fresh Fish.
Wow!
He looks even scarier now.

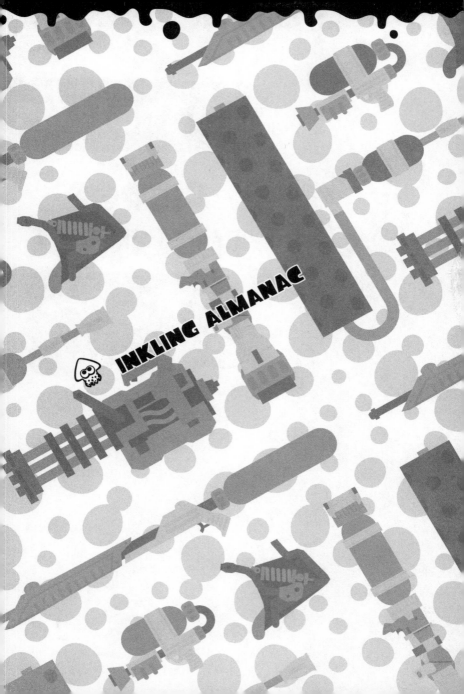

INKLING ALMANAC

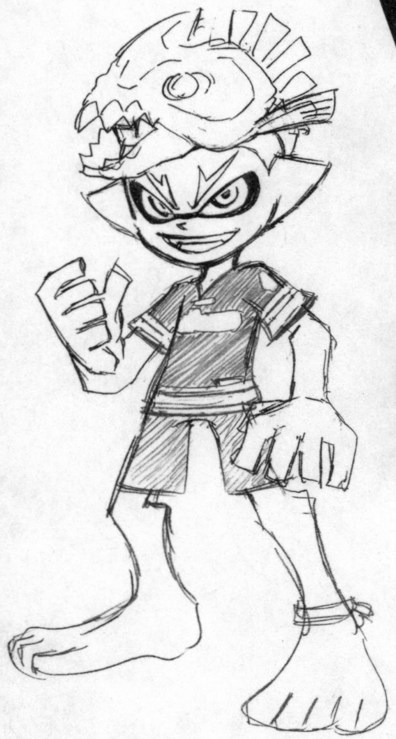

GUARDIANS

(Ink Color: Cobalt Yellow)

FIERCE FISHSKULL

Weapon: Aerospray PG
Headgear: Fierce Fishskull
Clothing: Octoking HK Jersey
Shoes: Friendship Bracelet

INFO

•When he goes to town, he buys sweets for Crest and Justice too.

Hairstyle: Spiky Haired

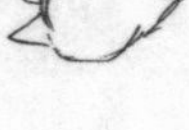

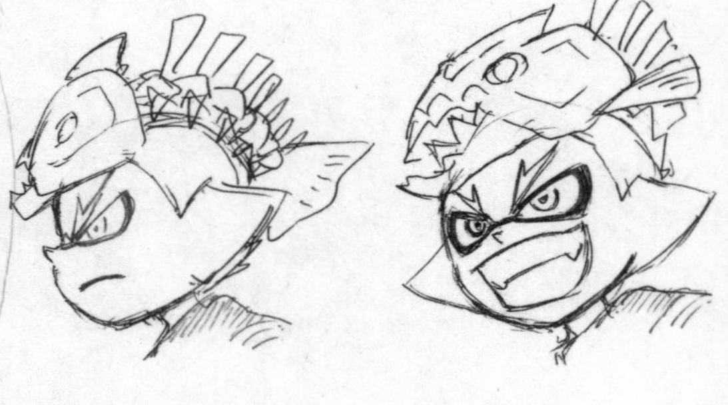

JETFLAME CREST

Weapon: Dark Tetra Dualies
Headgear: Jetflame Crest
Clothing: Annaki Evolution Tee
Shoes: Sunny Climbing Shoes

INFO

- She wakes up early every morning to train.
- She likes festivities and celebrations.

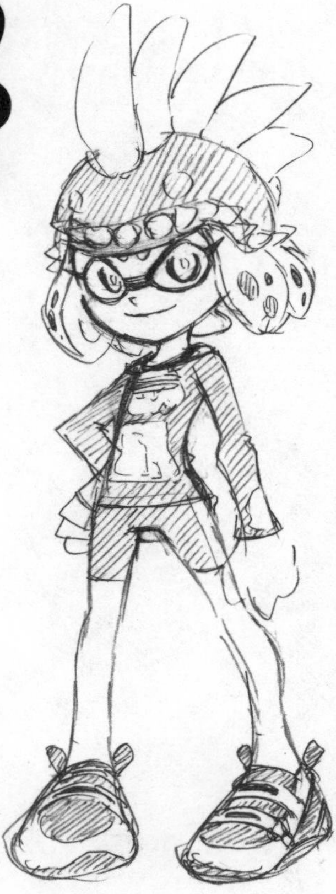

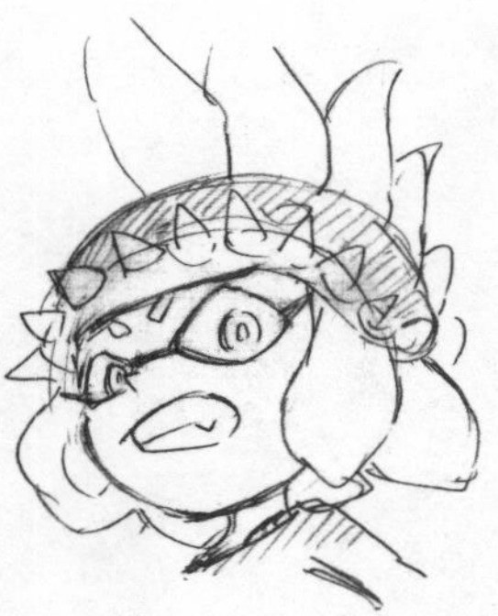

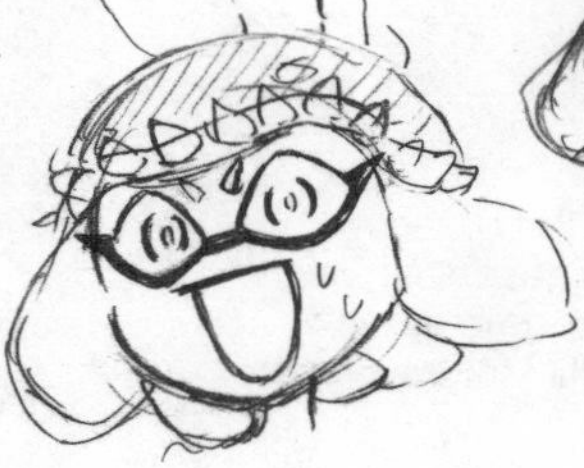

EYE OF JUSTICE

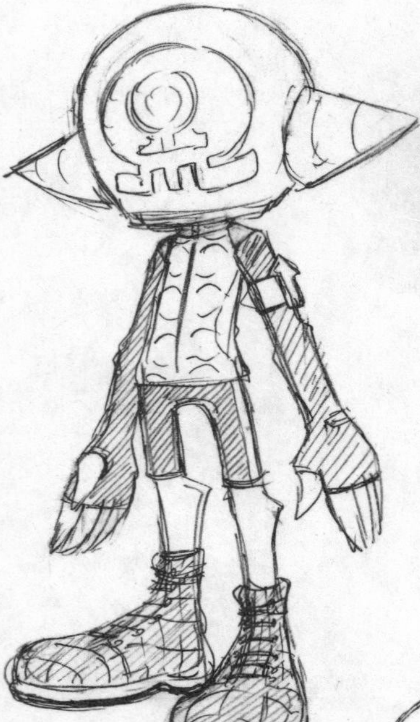

Weapon: Neo Sploosh-o-matic
Headgear: Eye of Justice
Clothing: Silver Tentatek Vest
Shoes: Annaki Arachno Boots

INFO

•He is capable of repairing Ink Cannons.

•He enjoys having Jetflame Crest place the Jetflame Crest on him every now and then.

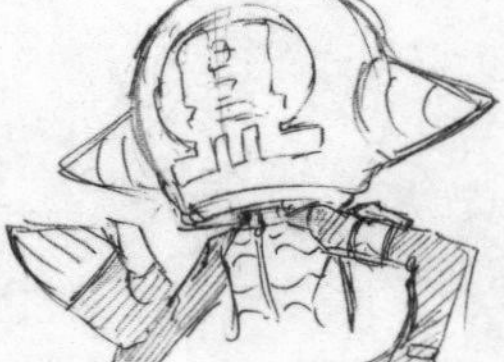

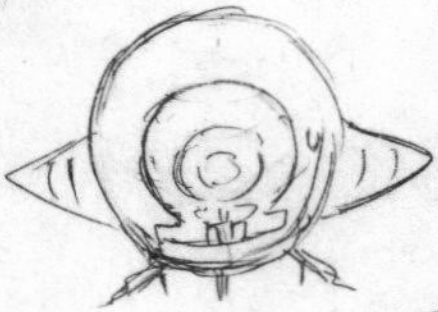

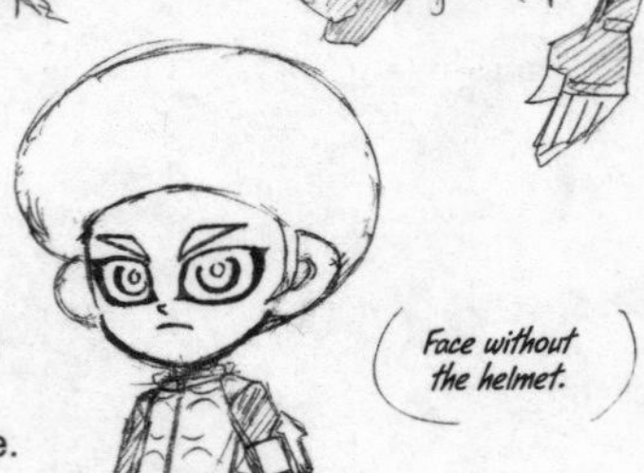

Face without the helmet.

INFO

•Fishskull and Crest had their duties passed down from their grandfather, and Justice took over this duty from a fellow Octoling with the same plan for the future.

SHELDON MOTORBIKE

(THE ADVENTURES OF SHELDON ARC)

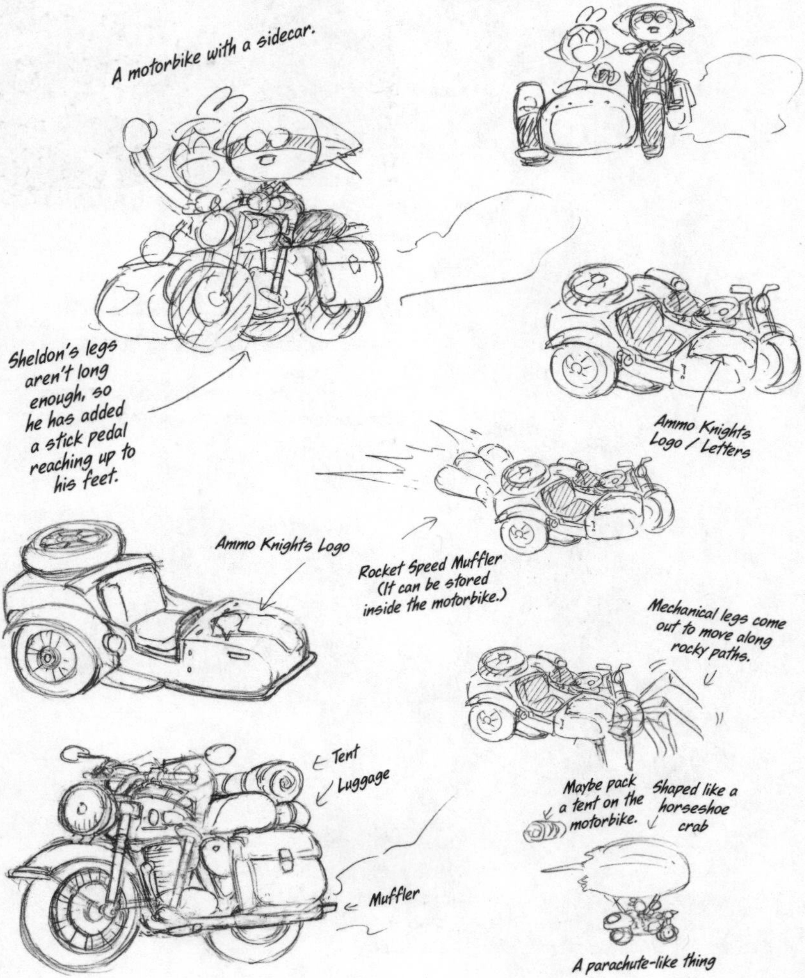
A motorbike with a sidecar.
Sheldon's legs aren't long enough, so he has added a stick pedal reaching up to his feet.
Ammo Knights Logo / Letters
Ammo Knights Logo
Rocket Speed Muffler (It can be stored inside the motorbike.)
Mechanical legs come out to move along rocky paths.
Tent
Luggage
Muffler
Maybe pack a tent on the motorbike.
Shaped like a horseshoe crab
A parachute-like thing

The Squid Research Lab drew this illustration for me using the character chart and settings of the motorbike!

The Squid Research Lab provided me with image material of Shellendorf.

↓

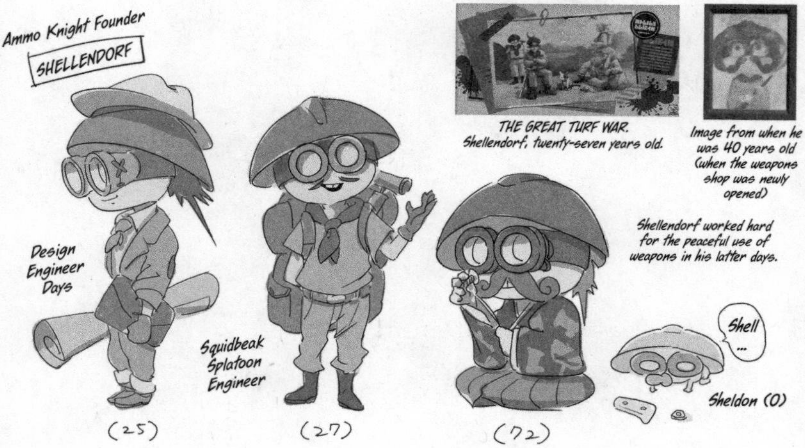

Ammo Knight Founder
SHELLENDORF
Design Engineer Days
(25)
Squidbeak Splatoon Engineer
(27)
THE GREAT TURF WAR.
Shellendorf, twenty-seven years old.
Image from when he was 40 years old (when the weapons shop was newly opened)
Shellendorf worked hard for the peaceful use of weapons in his latter days.
(72)
Shell ...
Sheldon (0)

They helped me with the design of the legendary weapon too!

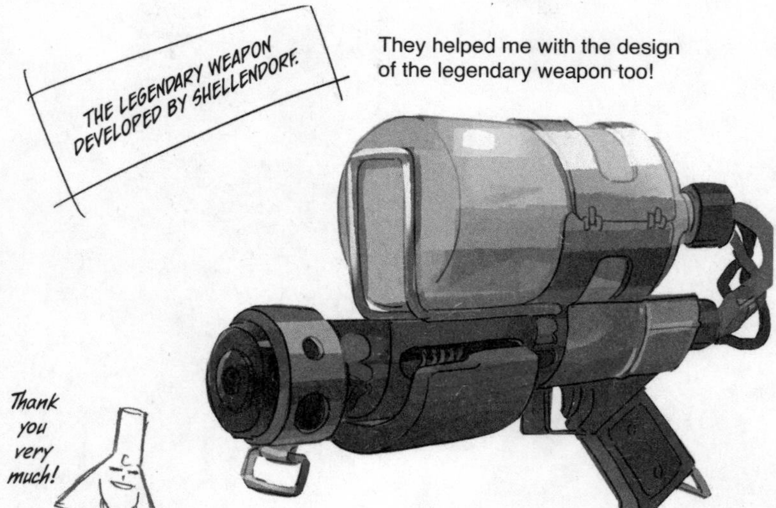

THE LEGENDARY WEAPON DEVELOPED BY SHELLENDORF.
Thank you very much!

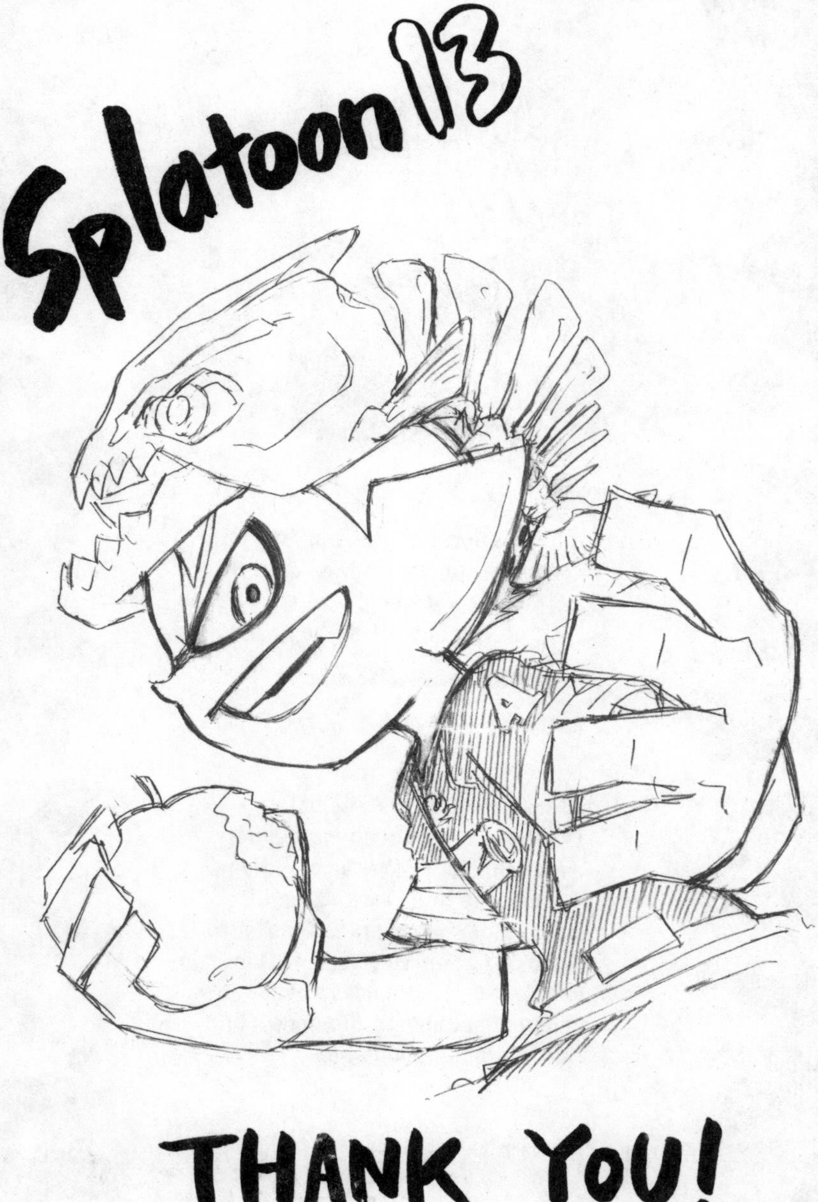
Splatoon 13
THANK YOU!

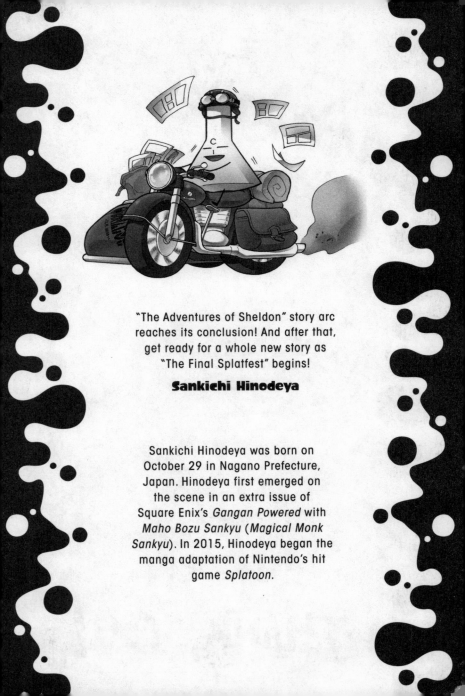

"The Adventures of Sheldon" story arc reaches its conclusion! And after that, get ready for a whole new story as "The Final Splatfest" begins!

Sankichi Hinodeya

Sankichi Hinodeya was born on October 29 in Nagano Prefecture, Japan. Hinodeya first emerged on the scene in an extra issue of Square Enix's *Gangan Powered* with *Maho Bozu Sankyu* (*Magical Monk Sankyu*). In 2015, Hinodeya began the manga adaptation of Nintendo's hit game *Splatoon*.

Volume 13
VIZ Media Edition

Story and Art by
Sankichi Hinodeya

Translation **Tetsuichiro Miyaki**
English Adaptation **Bryant Turnage**
Lettering **John Hunt**
Design **Kam Li**
Editor **Joel Enos**

SPLATOON Vol. 13 by Sankichi HINODEYA
© 2016 Sankichi HINODEYA
All rights reserved.
Original Japanese edition published by SHOGAKUKAN.
English translation rights in the United States of America,
Canada, the United Kingdom, Ireland, Australia and
New Zealand arranged with SHOGAKUKAN.

The stories, characters and incidents mentioned
in this publication are entirely fictional.

Original Design **100percent**

Printed in the U.S.A.

Published by VIZ Media, LLC
P.O. Box 77010
San Francisco, CA 94107

10 9 8 7 6 5 4 3 2 1
First Printing, September 2021

PARENTAL ADVISORY
SPLATOON is rated A and is
suitable for readers of all ages.

Splatoon

of this
graphic
novel.

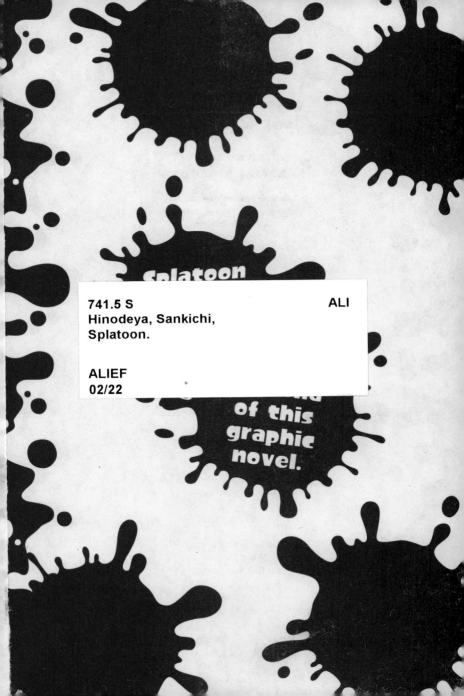